FAMILY WANTED

FAMILY WANTED

Adoption stories

Edited by Sara Holloway

Granta Books
London

Granta Publications, 2/3 Hanover Yard, Noel Road, London N1 8BE

First published in Great Britain by Granta Books 2005

Introduction and compilation copyright © 2005 Granta Books
For copyright in individual pieces see 'Acknowledgements and Copyright'
section at rear of the book

Lyrics on pp. 57 and 65 are reproduced from 'Common People'. Words
by Jarvis Cocker. Music by Jarvis Cocker, Nick Banks, Russell Senior,
Candida Doyle & Stephen Mackey © Copyright 1994 Island Music
Limited. Universal/Island Music Limited. Used by permission of Music
Sales Limited. All Rights Reserved. International Copyright Secured.

A CIP catalogue record for this book is available from the British Library.

1 3 5 7 9 10 8 6 4 2

ISBN 1 86207 753 3

Typeset by M Rules

Printed and bound in Great Britain by
William Clowes Ltd, Beccles, Suffolk

Contents

INTRODUCTION

Sara Holloway

Families have always been a fertile subject for writers. Families affected by adoption can be a more fertile subject still. To the usual familial themes, adoption adds its own potent elements: mysterious origins, the unfulfilled yearning for a child, the importance (or not) of blood ties to the nurturing impulse and to feelings of belonging, the quest for biological relations and the drama of the resulting reunions, and fundamental questions about what it is to become a parent, and a family.

When I first thought about adoption as the subject of a potential anthology, I jotted down a list of writers I knew had been adopted, which included Jeanette Winterson, Jackie Kay, A. M. Homes, Edward Albee, Bernard Cornwell, and a surprising number of others. I didn't feel there was necessarily any simplistic causal connection between writing and being adopted (though growing up with questions about your origins and a sense of being different might lead to the kind of temperament that would suit a writer), but I thought the conjunction could lead to some interesting and moving pieces. Equally, the other two sides of the adoption triangle, adopting a child – with its very different start, both more random and more deliberate, to the parent–child relationship – and the harrowing experience of giving up a child for adoption, struck me as subjects rich with potential. And so I decided to put together this three-part collection.

The process of assembling the anthology was unusually absorbing. I have not personally been involved with adoption (I have a biological daughter), but coming to a closer understanding of each viewpoint has been fascinating, and perhaps my neutrality allows me to sympathize equally with all three. I was often moved to tears while working on this book, more than on any other I have edited – over pieces that are confused and vulnerable or bitterly regretful, and over those expressing a ferocious love and joy which was equally moving. The pieces can also be very funny – they contain many ironies, and moments of hilarity or slapstick. And because the contributors have had to question ties and experiences the rest of us take for granted, they made me constantly reassess my own assumptions about being both a child and a parent.

Some of the pieces were previously published, taken from memoirs and anthologies and newspapers. I also commissioned new pieces. When these were delivered, I was excited to find that the results were more powerful than I had even hoped. There is great drama here, and also much deep thought, much hard-won and beautifully expressed insight into what it means to adopt and to be adopted and into how you might come to give up a child.

All but two of the pieces – an extract from Jeanette Winterson's *Oranges Are Not the Only Fruit*, and Lise Saffran's short story 'Men and Fish' – are non-fiction. One contributor has experienced two facets of adoption: Paula Fox was herself adopted, and she gave up a daughter for adoption. I have included extracts from her memoir *Borrowed Finery* about both these experiences.

No anthology is perfectly representative of its theme; all inevitably have their own repetitions and omissions. I wish I had been able to find more pieces by those whose adopted children are now adults, more pieces by parents who have adopted from their own country, and more by mothers who gave up their children – particularly those abroad. The voices of birth mothers from America and Britain, pre-Abortion Act, are starting to be heard, and I've included a few here. The voices of birth mothers in contemporary China, Latin America and Africa are harder to find. I have included just one, from Africa. But hopefully *Family Wanted* provides a fairly representative snapshot of adoption today: those adopted in the 1950s and 60s who are now coming to terms with their experience, and making decisions about whether or not to trace their birthparents; and those parents wrestling red tape to adopt children today, frequently from abroad.

Adoption is affected by economic factors and cultural mores, and as these change a snapshot of the next generation will no doubt be different. The closed system of adoption in Britain and the US led to much heartbreak. Now the belief that children should know where they originally came from is more prevalent. Although it won't remove all of the sources of trauma associated with adoption, the new openness will perhaps lead to a generation of adoptees less tortured by questions, though of course, for children adopted from orphanages abroad, the problem will often remain.

But whatever the changes in its legal status, or the psychological attitudes towards it, adoption will always exist. There will always be children born to parents who can't or won't look after them; and there will always be people who want to love and nurture those children and raise them as their own. And those involved in the process, particularly those as eloquent as the writers here, will always have something to teach the rest of us. As Daniel Menaker points out in the final piece, there is a wisdom in those who have experienced adoption – they have much to show the complacent majority about the essential contingency of our own origins.

For suggestions for contributors, thanks to: Fatema Ahmed, Phil Baker, Alex Butterworth, Rebecca Carter, Alex Clark, Rosemary

Davidson, Isobel Dixon, Natasha Fairweather, Victoria Hobbs, Carol Lefevre, Julia Lovell, Daniel Menaker, Robert Macfarlane, George Miller, Patrick Walsh, Sally Weale, Matt Weiland and Jessica Woollard. Thanks to Andy for encouragement and help on research. Thanks to Bella Shand for clearing permissions in already-published pieces and for being an essential sounding board, to Daphne Trotter for her copyediting, Colette Vella for steering the book through production and making useful editorial suggestions, and to the rest of my Granta colleagues for their patience while the project took up more time than I could afford. Thanks to my mother, Jean Holloway, for helping me to come up with the idea for the book, and for reading it in manuscript and making valuable comments. I'd like to dedicate this book to her. But most of all thanks to the contributors, for the honesty and generosity and skill with which they share their stories.

CHILDREN

CAKES AND ALE

Bernard Cornwell

My birth mother, Dorothy Cornwell, nursed me for two weeks. It was 1944, she was twenty-two years old, unmarried, and her father insisted she give me up, but she nevertheless kept me for that fortnight in the institution where she had been sent to have her baby. When I was ten days old a couple arrived and stood at the foot of the bed, from where they inspected the two of us. 'I could tell they weren't cuddly,' Dorothy has since told me. She was right.

'Do you know who the boy's father is?' uncuddly Marjorie asked.

'His name is Oughtred.'

'Oughtred!' Pause. 'He's not French, is he? Because if he's French we don't want the boy.'

Alas, William Oughtred was Canadian and, four days later, I was taken from Hackney to Benfleet in Essex. My name, which had been recorded as Bernard Cornwell on my birth certificate, was changed to Bernard Wiggins.

The Wiggins belonged to a sect called the Peculiar People. It was founded in the mid-nineteenth century, flourished in Essex for a hundred years and is now, happily, defunct. The name derived from the Bible where, in both the Old and the New Testaments, God describes his adherents as a 'peculiar people',

meaning, simply, separate from all others, and the Peculiars of
Essex believed that by keeping themselves separate from a sinful
world they might avoid temptation and so attain salvation.
Joseph Wiggins, my adoptive father, took me, I think, as a
Christian duty. He considered me, and the four other children he
adopted, as souls to be saved. Marjorie just wanted babies. She
liked babies.

The Peculiars were fundamentalists, by which I mean that
they took every word in the Authorized Version of the Bible to be
true. 'The prayer of faith shall save the sick,' says the Epistle of
James, and so the early Peculiars refused medical attention, rely-
ing instead on anointing with oil and the laying on of hands.
This, for a time, sufficed, but in 1908 the Children's Act declared
that to refuse medical attention to a child was tantamount to
criminal neglect, and so some Peculiars, preferring their children
to die in the Lord rather than be attended by a doctor, were
committed to prison. Others caved in, and the sect split into the
Old and the New Peculiars. By the time I joined the faithful the
split had healed, and my family, like most, had adopted a compromise solution by which the church elders were summoned to
a sick person's bedside and, if God failed to perform the requisite
miracle, then a doctor was called. One of my earliest memories
is of a group of men clustered about my bed, their hands press-
ing rhythmically onto my forehead, earnestly beseeching Almighty
God to heal me. God did not come through and so Dr Acres did
the business instead.

Medicine was not the only thing of which the Peculiars disap-
proved. Alcohol, tobacco, cosmetics, the cinema, military service,
comics, high heels, Roman Catholics, dancing, playing cards,
gambling, television, the list was endless and was endlessly
adaptable, for anything considered frivolous was also reckoned
sinful, and the immediate object of our lives was to avoid sin.
There was a mysterious 'sin against the Holy Ghost' that loomed
large in my young life, because this sin, I never did discover what
it was, was unforgivable and doomed the sinner to hell.

Repentance would not help. There was no salvation. For a time
I believed masturbation must be this sin, but I could not ask, for
sex was, of course, the sinister unacknowledged beast that lurked
behind the Peculiars' many fears. I also believed, for a time, that
I had single-handedly, or double-handedly perhaps, discovered
masturbation, and was quite happy to risk hell to enjoy it, but
sticky sheets were my undoing and the inevitable punishment
followed.

Stick and carrot. The carrot was the prospect of heaven and,
more immediately, the bliss that would follow conversion.
Conversion was important to the Peculiars. You gave your heart
to Jesus, were washed in the blood of the lamb, went to the
mercy seat, accepted Christ as your saviour and, miracle of mir-
acles, became Happy! 'I'm H-A-P-P-Y,' we chirruped in Sunday
School, 'I'm H-A-P-P-Y! I know I am, I'm sure I am, I'm H-A-P-
P-Y!' Except I was not and yearned to be, and for a long time I
believed my route to happiness lay in conversion. I tried. I tried
so hard. I became a serial heart donor for Jesus, but the happiness never arrived. Life did not suddenly become easier, I was not
filled with a gleeful certainty, I felt no different, the emotion
engendered by the threats of hell fire evaporated overnight and I
was still the same sinful beast. The carrot of heaven failed to
entice me onto the narrow path of righteousness and so the stick
was produced to beat me up it.

The stick was always a bamboo garden stake, about a yard
long, plucked from the fruit cage and wielded by my father, Joseph.
He was a tall man, strongly built. At school, where I was caned
often enough, the usual punishment was six swishes on the arse
which stung a bit, but I was immune to such feeble assaults for I
had experienced the Wrath of God administered by the garden
stake. There was a ritual to these punishments, which began with
me being locked into my bedroom and given time to reflect on my
sins. Then would come the footsteps on the stairs. My father
would unlock the door and order me to strip naked, after which he
beat me in a frenzy compounded of dislike, righteous fury and

despair for my soul. Afterwards, all passion spent, he would ask me to kneel and pray with him. I was thirteen or fourteen the last time it happened and Dr Acres had to be called. By the time he arrived the blood had been washed from the bedroom walls and the bedding had been changed, but there was no disguising the stigmata. I think the doctor offered my parents a warning because thereafter the bamboo stayed in its cage.

Was there no happiness? Of course there was. I remember playing Monopoly and I had an elaborate electric train layout and Arthur Mee's Children's Encyclopaedia, and there were Dinky toys as well as a big Meccano set which I liked and this pleased my father because he wanted me to take over the family's building firm when I grew up. St Paul had been a tentmaker, he told me often, and this was biblical authority for the truism that every Christian should have a useful trade. A practical trade. My father had left school at eleven, become a bricklayer and prospered until he employed over two hundred men. He preached to them in their lunch breaks and had the happy vision that I would follow in his footsteps. I see that in this paragraph my footsteps have wandered from the opening question; was there no happiness? Yes, there was, but it was forever threatened by the fear of God and by Joe and Marjorie's marriage, which was not happy.

The house was unhappy. Joseph was haunted by God while Marjorie was a bitter woman. I learned to fear the all too frequent sound of my parents' voices raised in argument for I had discovered that punishment inevitably followed such rows. I would lie in bed, hear the shouting downstairs and dread the dawn. The family prayers, in which, each morning, we read the Bible aloud around the table and then bowed our heads as Joseph prayed, would be sullen. Storm cones hoisted.

They adopted five children. The eldest, John, was a dozen years older than me and I knew very little of him. He vanished one day. Despairing of making him into a Christian my parents had somehow contrived, I think without the help of the courts, to place him in a Salvation Army reform home in South Wales. He would kill himself eventually. The youngest, Andrew, was much younger than me and by the time he was adopted I had left home. That left three of us, me sandwiched between two girls, Margaret and Ruth. Margaret, a couple of years older than me, was the favourite. She embraced the teaching of the Peculiar People and, though she was later to find refuge in the theologically suspect pastures of the Baptist church, remains a Christian. She is saved. Good for her, but she was no ally of mine. Ruth, a couple of years younger, was an ally, but we were easily divided and conquered. Survival was an individual thing, and my route was through hiding and lying. The first could delay punishment and the second could obviate it altogether and so I became a superb liar, able to separate a score or more of the tangled web's strands, and this facility, I think, has been of great use to me as a fiction writer. And when I was not telling lies I was fantasizing, another useful accomplishment for a novelist.

I knew I was adopted from the very start. At about seven years old I was told by Marjorie that she wished she had not adopted me, a position from which she did not budge, and this was a consolation. I knew I did not belong. To what I belonged I did not know, but I knew it was not the Peculiars, and I was thus freed to construct my own parentage. This freedom was constrained at the age of eleven when my father left his safe open for a few moments and I dived in, hoping no doubt to find some of those big, beautiful five-pound notes, and instead discovered a piece of paper on which my mother had written my natural parents' names and whatever other details she had learned of them. Dorothy Cornwell of East London and William Oughtred, Royal Canadian Air Force, of British Columbia. A cockney and an airman. In truth I rejected Dorothy and William from the fantasies, because they did not fit. I suppose I conjured up a duke and a showgirl? A princess? I cannot remember now. Today, of course, information like that written on the paper I discovered in Joseph's safe would be hidden behind a bureaucratic fence, but things had been different in wartime. Marjorie, when she married, was the assistant matron of an orphanage and had a professional relationship with the home where Dorothy gave birth, and so Marjorie was able to discover whence her babies came.

I hid the information. Years later I found the paper again and I briefly considered looking for Dorothy and William, but did nothing. I liked having no parents by then. Later still, as I approached my sixtieth birthday, I did find them, but by then I had no need of parents and it was safe to approach them. They are both living, both well. I met William first. I was fifty-eight, he was eighty, and he was the patriarch of a large, happy family. I met them all, father, two half-brothers, half-sister, nieces and nephews, in Victoria, British Columbia, and had the extraordinary shock of recognition. I was like them. I looked like them, snorted like them when I laughed, and was immediately comfortable with them. I remember standing on William's terrace above the Strait of Juan de Fuca and looking into his living room. It was late dusk, the lights were on and I could see them and they could not see me, and I just stared as they talked and laughed with my wife. This was family and I sensed Marjorie squirming in her grave because I had escaped. The same thing happened when, last year, I met Dorothy and one of my four half-brothers in England. My tribe. Like me.

Joseph was a good man, a very good man. He wanted heaven for us. He was honest, hard-working, earnest and wrong. He took me to Rayleigh once, a town not far from where we lived, and in the high street there was, perhaps still is, a small monument to some Protestant martyrs burned there by Queen Mary. 'One day, son,' he told me solemnly, 'I shall be burned here.' I was seven or eight years old and did not know what to say. 'The Pope and the Communists will kill me,' he claimed, and went on to explain that this unholy alliance was foretold in the Bible which prophesied that the legions of Rome would unite with the Red horde to extirpate the true faith from England. He believed that, just as he believed that God had cunningly placed the fossils in the geological record to test our faith. He was an unhappy man. At ten years old I stood outside his study, it was late dusk, the lights were on, and I could see him and he could not see me, and I watched him pray. He was in agony. He contorted himself. He raised his arms to God, beat them on his breast, he wept, he was pleading. Years after I recognized him in John Donne's lines: 'Batter my heart, three person'd God ... o'erthrow me, and bend Your force, to break, blow, burn and make me new.' He was in agony, yet he had done everything right. He had succeeded in business, given his soul to Jesus, rescued five other souls from sin, and he was unhappy, so angrily unhappy, and yet beneath the grim carapace of duty was a generous man capable of joy. But he had been born to and raised in the Peculiars and their puritanism was an inescapable part of his nature.

My nature derives from Dorothy and William. Theirs was an unlikely romance, ill-founded on lust and unrealistic hopes, but both are easygoing, humorous and tolerant. Life, they believe, is well lubricated by laughter. Neither, I think, want to delve too deeply into motives or philosophy, and both, I know, are unbelievers. Perhaps I merely ascribe to them my own nature, but I am certain we cannot escape nature and that nurture is, at best, a minor influence. The Wiggins family, in its unscientific way, was a small experiment in nature versus nurture. Five of us were plucked from adulterous parents and put in a home where a rigid code of behaviour was fiercely enforced, and the result? God, one: the devil, four. Joseph, Marjorie and their eldest son are all dead now, and those of us who remain are not family. We do not see each other, do not write, have no ties.

The adoption failed. A family failed to ignite. All of us were unhappy. I live now in the USA where I am friends of a couple who have adopted two children. One of those children, a daughter, was born to a love affair which failed. Her birth mother reluctantly gave her up for adoption and then, a year or so later, was reunited with her lover. The two married, had more children, thrived and, of course, felt remorseful about their eldest daughter whom they had given up. When Carrie, the daughter, was eighteen she met her real parents, who were overcome with joy. They introduced her to her siblings, her full siblings, and tried to draw her into their family's life. Carrie rejected them, resenting their overenthusiastic efforts to assimilate her. Her family, she told me, was her adoptive parents. They are Mom and Dad, not the birth parents.

There are no conclusions from any of this. Some families work, others don't. Carrie's adoption was a success, mine was a failure. The tragedy of mine was not my tragedy, but Joseph and Marjorie's. To adopt a child is an act of generosity, and they gave to me liberally, and in the end were bitterly disappointed in me. Yet my job was not to make them happy, but to survive, and survival meant rejecting them, their ways and even their name. After Joseph died I legally changed my name back to Cornwell, the last step of rejection and a symbol of conversion, because I am, at last, converted. I am H-A-P-P-Y, but my conversion was to atheism and frivolity. I recall a Peculiar People chapel, bare and cold, its sole decoration a scroll painted above the preacher's dais on which, in letters of red and gold, was written 'Be Sure Your Sin Will Find You Out'. In Cape Cod, on a beam above my desk, I have painted in letters of red and gold, 'Dost thou think, because thou art virtuous, there shall be no more cakes and ale?'

THAT AWFUL OCCASION

Jeanette Winterson

'There,' declared my mother, laying down the vacuum cleaner. 'You could keep a coffin in here without feeling guilty, not a speck of dust anywhere.'

Mrs White came out of the lobby waving a dishcloth. 'I've done all them skirting boards, but me back's not what it was.'

'No,' my mother answered, shaking her head, 'these things are sent to try us.'

'Well, at least we know they're holy,' said Mrs White.

The parlour was certainly very clean. I poked my head round the door and noticed that all the seat covers had been changed to our very best, my mother's wedding best, a present from her friends in France. The brasses gleamed, and Pastor Spratt's crocodile nutcracker took pride of place on the mantelpiece.

'What's all the fuss about,' I wondered. I went to check the calendar, but as far as I could see we weren't down for a house meeting, and there was no visiting preacher due on Sunday. I went into the kitchen where Mrs White was making a sad cake, a round flat pastry filled with currants and spread with butter.

For a moment she didn't notice me.

'Hello,' I said. 'What's going on?'

Mrs White turned round and gave a little screech. 'You're supposed to be at violin practice.'

'It's cancelled. Anybody else here?'

'Your mother's gone out.' She sounded a bit nervous, but then she often did.

'Well, I'll take the dog out then,' I decided.

'I'm just going to the toilet,' said Mrs White, disappearing out of the back door.

'There's no paper . . .' I began, but it was too late.

We set off up the hill, climbing and climbing until the town was beaten flat. The dog ran off down a trench and I tried to spot various landmarks, like the dentist and the Rechabite Hall. I thought I might go and see Melanie that night. I had told my mother as much as I could, but not everything. I had a feeling she wouldn't really understand. Besides, I wasn't quite certain what was happening myself, it was the second time in my life that I had experienced uncertainty.

Uncertainty to me was like Aardvark to other people. A curious thing I had no notion of, but recognized through second-hand illustration. The feeling I now had in my head and stomach was the same as on that Awful Occasion, and that time, as I stood by the tea urn in the vestry, I had heard Miss Jewsbury say, 'Of course, she must feel very uncertain.' I was very upset. Uncertainty was what the Heathen felt, and I was chosen by God.

That Awful Occasion was the time my natural mother had come to claim me back. I'd had an idea that there was something curious about the circumstance of my birth, and once found my adoption papers hidden under a stack of flannels in the holiday drawer. 'Formalities,' my mother had said, waving me away. 'You were always mine, I had you from the Lord.' I didn't think about it again until there was a knock on the door one Saturday. My mother got there before me because she was praying in the parlour. I followed her down the lobby.

'Who is it, Mum?'

She didn't answer.

'Who is it?'

'Go inside until I tell you.'

I slunk off, thinking it was either Jehovah's Witnesses or the man from the Labour Party. Before long I could hear voices, angry voices; my mother seemed to have let the person in, which was strange. She didn't like having the Heathen in the house. 'Leaves a bad atmosphere,' she always said.

I remembered something I'd seen Mrs White do on the fornication occasion. Reaching far back into the War Cupboard, behind the dried egg, I found a wine glass and put it against the wall. It worked. I could hear every word. After five minutes I put the glass away, picked up our dog, and cried and cried and cried.

Eventually my mother came in.

'She's gone.'

'I know who she was, why didn't you tell me?'

'It's nothing to do with you.'

'She's my mother.'

No sooner had I said that than I felt a blow that wrapped round my head like a bandage. I lay on the lino looking up into the face.

'I'm your mother,' she said very quietly. 'She was a carrying case.'

'I wanted to see her.'

'She's gone and she'll never come back.' My mother turned away and locked herself in the kitchen. I couldn't think and I couldn't breathe so I started to run. I ran up the long stretchy street with the town at the bottom and the hill at the top. It was Easter time and the cross on the hill loomed big and black. 'Why didn't you tell me,' I screamed at the painted wood, and I beat the wood with my hands until my hands dropped away by themselves. When I looked out over the town, nothing had changed. Tiny figures moved up and down and the mill chimneys puffed out their usual serene smoke signals. On Ellison's Tenement they had started to run the fair. How could it be? I had rather gaze on a new ice age than these familiar things.

When I finally went home that day, my mother was watching television. She never spoke of what had happened and neither did I.

WITNESS PROTECTION

A. M. Homes

Christmas 1992, I go home to Washington, D. C. to visit my family. The night I arrive, just after dinner, my mother says, 'Come into the living room, sit down, we have something to tell you.' Her tone makes me nervous. My parents are not formal people – no one sits in the living room. I am standing in the kitchen. The dog is looking up at me.

'Come into the living room. Sit down,' my mother says.

'Why?'

'There's something we need to talk to you about.'

'What?'

'Come,' she says, patting the cushion next to her.

'Who died?' I say terrified.

'No one died. Everyone's fine.'

'Then what is it?'

They are silent.

'Is it about me?'

'Yes, it's you. We've had a phone call. Someone is looking for you.'

Silence.

How does one not know what one already knows? After a lifetime spent in a virtual witness protection program, my cover is blown.

I am the mistress's daughter. I grew up with the information that my mother had been young and unmarried and that my father was older and married with a family of his own. In December of 1961, when I was born, the lawyer called my parents and said, 'Your package has arrived and it's wrapped in pink ribbons.'

My mother starts to cry. She says, 'You don't have to do anything about it, you can just let it go,' trying to relieve me of the burden.

'Tell me again, what happened' Details, minutia, as though the facts, the call and response of questions asked and answered, the art of getting the story straight, would make sense of it, would give it order, shape, form, and the thing it lacked most – logic.

'Where does she live?'

'New Jersey.'

The Lady from New Jersey. In my dreams, my mother is a goddess. She is the Queen of Queens, the Princess of Princesses, she is the CEO, the CFO and the COO. Movie star beautiful, incredibly competent, She can take care of anyone and anything. She has made a fabulous life for herself, as ruler of the world, she is totally together, except for one missing link – ME.

A letter. I decide that I want a letter. I need to go back and begin at the beginning. I call the lawyer who tells me the story of the woman contacting him. 'I'd like a letter,' I say, 'I want information – where she grew up, how educated she is, what she does for a living, what the family medical history is and what the circumstances of my adoption were – what really happened thirty-one years ago?'

I am asking for the story of my life. There is an urgency to my request; I feel I have to hurry and ask everything I want to know. As suddenly as she arrived, she could be gone again.

Ten days later, her letter arrives with no fanfare. It arrives in an envelope from the lawyer's office with a scrawly note from the lawyer apologizing for not getting it to me sooner. It is clear the letter had been opened, presumably read. Why? Is nothing private or personal? I am annoyed but don't say anything. I don't feel I have the right – that's one of the pathological complications of adoption, adoptees don't really have rights, their lives are about supporting the secrets, the needs and desires of others – and frankly because he was my one connection to her, I didn't want to piss him off.

It is typed on her stationery, simple small gray sheets of paper, her name embossed across the top. Helene's language is oddly formal and falters becoming less than artful, grammatically incorrect. I read it simultaneously fast and slow, wanting to take it in, unable to take it in. I read it and then read it again. Some of what she tells me is what I already know, what I have imagined. I wonder what it means to have imagined the truth, to have conjured what happened.

'At the time I was carrying this little girl it was not proper for a girl to have a child out of wedlock. This was probably the most difficult decision of my entire life. I was 22 years old and very naive. I was raised very sheltered and very strict by my mother.

I remember being in the hospital with her and dressing her the day we both left the hospital. I have never forgotten the beautiful black hair and the blue eyes and the little dimples in her face. As I left the hospital with the lady who was picking up the little girl, I can still see myself in the taxi and her asking me to give her the baby. I did not want to give her the child, however I did realize, I did not have the wear-with-all to take care of her myself. Yes, I have always loved this little girl and been tortured every December of my life from the day she was born that I did not have her with me.'

She tells the facts of where she was born, what street she lived on as a child and how she grew up. She tells the names of her parents and tells when they died. She tells how tall she is and how much she weighs. She writes of never forgetting.

Each bit of information invades me, swims through me, takes root, digging in. There are no filters, there are no screens. I have no protection from this.

She closes her letter by saying, '*I have never married, I have always felt guilty about giving this little girl away.*'

'This little girl . . .' is now thirty-one years old.

I am that girl.

A couple of letters later, I write to her and follow up with a call.

Hers is the most frightening voice I've ever heard; low, nasal, gravelly, vaguely animal and kind of witchy. I tell her who I am and she screams 'Oh my God! I got your letter. I've read it a thousand times. This is the most wonderful day of my life.' Her voice, her emotion, comes in bursts, like punctuation – I can never tell if she's laughing or crying. In the background there is a flick, a sharp suck of air – smoking.

The phone call is thrilling, flirty like a first date, like the beginning of something. There is a rush of curiosity, the desire to know everything all at once, there's no way to get the information fast enough, in depth enough, in any kind of order. What is your life like, how do your days begin and end? What do you do for fun? Why did you come and find me? What do you want?

Every nuance, every detail means something.

I am like an amnesiac being awakened – there are things I know about myself, things that exist without language, my hardware, my mental firing patterns, ways of being. Parts of me that are fundamentally, inexorably me are being echoed on the other end, confirmed as a DNA match, and it is not entirely a comfortable sensation – there are things about myself that I don't necessarily like.

'Tell me about you – who are you?' she asks.

I tell her that I live in New York, I am a writer, I have a dog. No more or less.

She tells me that she loves New York, that her father always used to go to the city and would always return with presents from FAO Schwarz. She tells me how much she loved her father who died of a heart attack when she was seven because 'he liked rich food.'

This causes an immediate pain in my chest – the idea that I might die of a heart attack early in life, the idea that I now know I need to be careful – the things I enjoy most are the most dangerous.

She goes on, 'I come from a very strange family, we're not quite right.'

'What do you mean strange?' I ask, fearing insanity.

She tells me about her mother dying of a stroke a couple of years ago, how she made the decision to pull the plug. She tells me about her own life falling apart, moving from Washington to Atlantic City. She tells me that after she gave birth to me, her mother wouldn't come to the hospital and get her, her mother made her take the bus home. Helene tells me it took all her strength and courage to come looking for me.

'If you told me to come up there right now, I would leave in five minutes.'

She wants everything all at once and it is too much.

'You can't see me yet.'

I am talking to the woman who has loomed in my head, larger than life, for the entirety of my life and I am terrified. I am decompensating, transgressing the boundaries and borders of reality as I know it. There is a deep fracture, a strange and nearly psychotic separation, a refrain constantly echoing; I am not who I thought I was and yet I have no idea who I am.

And not only am I not who I thought I was, but neither is she the Queen of Queens, the Princess of Princesses.

'Why can't I see you?'

I am tempted to tell her – you can't see me right now, because right now I am not visible to anyone, even myself. I have evaporated.

'When can we talk again?' she asks as we are hanging up. 'When? I hope you will forgive me for what I did thirty-one years ago. Will you call again soon? I love you. I love you so much.'

*

Our conversations are frequent – a couple of times a week; they are strange, seductive, addictive, punishing. Each one shakes me, each requires a period of recovery. Each time I tell her something, she takes the information, holds it too close, reinventing it as something else and delivering it back to me in a manner that leaves me wanting to tell her less, wanting her to know nothing.

'Do you think one day, we might have a portrait painted of the two of us?'

Her request seems to come from another world, another life. 'I have to get off the phone soon.'

'When can I see you?' she starts again.

'Helene, I need to take things slowly. This is all new for me. You might have thought about it for a long time before you contacted me, but for me it's a only a couple of weeks.'

As I try to explain, I know I'm in a losing battle. It is no longer a romance, it is no longer about providing me something I never had, it has become a burden, an unending series of demands.

'I have to go. I'm late for a dinner.'

'OK,' she says, 'but before you go out, put on your cashmere sweater so you don't get chilly.'

I don't have a cashmere sweater – Helene is expressing a fantasy, an image of an experience that is not my own, but has meaning, import elsewhere – in her past.

'We'll talk again soon.' I hang up.

I am losing myself, going out to sea.

On the street, I see people who look alike, couples, families, each face a nuanced version of the other. I watch how they stand, how they walk and talk – variations on a theme.

A few days later, I try Helene again.

There is the flick of a lighter, the suck of a cigarette.

'I'm angry with you, can you tell?'

'Yes.'

'Why won't you see me?' she whines.

I can't say because I'm afraid of you, because you seem a little crazy, because you will consume me. I can't say anything because it doesn't matter what I say.

'You're torturing me. You take better care of your dog than you take of me.'

Am I supposed to be taking care of her? Is that what she's come back for?

'You should adopt me – and take care of me,' she says.

'I can't adopt you,' I say.

'Why not?'

I don't know how to respond. I don't know if we're talking in fantasy or reality. I can't say I don't want a fifty-year-old child.

'You're scaring me,' is all I can manage.

'Don't be angry with me forever, if I'd known where you were I would have come and gotten you and taken you away.'

Imagine that, kidnapped by your own mother, the same mother who had given you away at birth – she lived not two miles from where I grew up and luckily didn't know who or where I was – I cannot imagine anything more terrifying.

'I'm not angry with you,' I tell her and it is entirely true. Of all the things I am, I am not angry. Horrified, seeing myself in her – the loose screw is not entirely unfamiliar – appalled that in the end I might end up rejecting the one person that I never had any intention of rejecting. But not angry. Not unforgiving. The more Helene and I talk, the happier I am that she gave me up. I can't imagine having grown up under her, I would not have survived.

There is a message on my machine – the voice raspy, accented, coarse. 'Your cover is blown. I know who you are and I know where you live. I'm reading your books.'

I dial her immediately. 'Helene, what are you doing?'

'I found out who you are A. M. Homes. I'm reading your books.'

It is the only time in my life I have regretted being a writer. She has something of mine and thinks she has me. She thinks she knows me, she believes she understands something, having interpreted me from my work.

'How did you get my number?'

'I'm very clever. I called all the bookstores in Washington and asked them, "Who is a writer from Washington whose first name is Amy?" At first I thought you were someone else, some other Amy who wrote a book about God, and then one of the stores helped me and gave me your number.'

She stalks me. I stop answering the phone. The sound of her voice is terrifying. Every time the phone rings, every time I call in for messages, I brace myself.

'Do you live with someone on Charles Street? Is he there? Does he not like it when I call?'

'How do you know I live on Charles Street?'

'I'm a good detective.'

'Helene, I find it very upsetting. How do you know where I live?'

'I don't have to tell you,' she says.

'Then I don't have to continue this conversation,' I say.

'Why won't you see me? Do I have to come up there and find you? Do I have to come up to Columbia University and hunt you down? Do I have to wait in line to get your autograph?'

'I need to be able to do my job. I need to teach my classes and go on my book tour and do all the things I'm supposed to do without worrying that you are going to hunt me down. You can't do that. I have to be able to lead my life.'

There are no limits; every drop I give is consumed instantaneously and then she is all the more famished, as though she is starving, nothing is enough.

'I need to see you.'

Blindness. The day my novel is published I accidently poke the *New York Times* into my eye and shred my cornea. The pain is searing. I fumble for the eye doctor's number and go rushing off to his office – returning hours later with what looks like a maxi-pad taped over my face.

The next day I read in Washington; the bookstore is crowded with old friends, neighbors, my mother and a friend, my grandmother and great-aunt, my fourth-grade teacher, friends from junior high, people from early writing workshops, etc. When I get up to read, they're shocked.

'It's fine,' I say. 'It'll be OK in a couple of weeks.' I crack open the book. My field of vision is a circle about two inches wide. I hold the pages directly in front of my face. My good eye is half closed in sympathy with the injured one. I perform as much from memory as possible. When the reading is finished, a long line forms, people wanting books signed, aspiring writers with questions of their own. In the soft distance, I see one of my best friends from junior high school and then a stranger, a woman, standing nervously, twisting an umbrella round and round in her hands. Instinctively, I know it is Helene. The friend notices that something is off and turns away. I continue signing books. The line begins to thin. Just as the last person is leaving, she steps up.

'What did you do to your eye?' Helene blurts in that strange rough voice.

'You're not behaving,' I say. The store is packed with people who don't know what ghost has risen up.

Despite what I told her, despite what I asked, despite that she didn't even live in Washington anymore, Helene needed to see me and that was more important than anything else.

'You're built just like your father,' she says.

Later, when I try and remember what she looked like, I have only the vague memory of green with white polka dots, brown hair piled high on her head. I remember seeing her arm and thinking her bones were small and that she was thin.

In the distance, a shadow emerges. My mother and her friend are coming towards me. I imagine the two mothers meeting, colliding. This is something that can't happen, it is entirely against the rules, no one person can have two mothers in the same room at the same time.

'There are people here whose privacy I have to protect, I have to go,' I say to Helene.

Helene turns and runs out of the store.

SHAPING UP

Robert Dessaix

John Brack's painting *The Car* (1955), a famous Australian painting, which hangs in the National Gallery of Victoria, Melbourne, shows a conventional family in a Triumph Mayflower.* There's a smugness about the family. Or, if not a smugness, then at least a self-contentment, a kind of thankful self-containment. They're sitting in a Triumph Mayflower, all skewed rectangles, two parents in the front and two children, a boy and a girl, in the back, and they're feeling rewarded by this outing for being what they are. They are a family. I find it hard to warm to them. I don't much like their shape.

I recognize the family's shape and mood, I recognize its resignation to the Rightness of what it is. Our family wasn't right at all. It wasn't just a matter of not being box-shaped like Brack's family (there were only three of us, for a start), of not sitting in two rows (all three of us, if we'd had a car, would have sat in the front seat), or of not leaving the driving to Dad (we took our outings in trams). No, something else about us was wrong. In fact, as I ponder Brack's angular foursome, I wonder if we were what's meant by a family at all.

*see http://www.nga.gov.au/federation/detail.cfm?WorkID=26247

Brack's Dad is grimfaced as a mummy staring sightless straight ahead, as if under orders – whose? He's the picture's dead centre. I can imagine his filling a useful niche somewhere in a network of other men, probably thinking he's at the hub of something. He has no curiosity, just a sense of answerability. He looks to me as if he'd be very keen indeed on answerability. My father, Tom, on the other hand, was a messenger boy at seventy, flying around the city in a taxi, filling his day with chatty chance encounters, responsible for almost nothing at all. Responsive – delighting in life's endless puzzles, often of his own devising – but not responsible, not even (maddeningly) for fixing the sagging fence or pruning the roses. I was in no sense his offshoot. He was going nowhere in me. I was his treasure.

And there's the matter of mothers. Brack's Mum looks kind-hearted and no-nonsense all at once, friendly with the neighbours, quick with the Dettol, tennis on Wednesdays if she's not too tired. It's Brack's Mum (I get the feeling) who breathes life into this family, nurturing the moister, human things. Not a lot of time for self-indulgence here, what with the children and her father's leg playing up and one thing and another, but she's a good mother. This is a woman who is confident of doing her best. My mother, Jean, on the other hand, was a fraught, griev-ing, triple-certificated nurse. Joy in things (the profusion of the garden, music, the radio, books, tea with friends, me – anything) just seemed to seep away. I have no idea where it went. She sought spiritual balm at the local library. Norman Vincent Peale was a favourite. She was a good woman. She was terrified she might drop and break me and, after all, I was only on loan.

And there's the matter of the young, too. The young Bracks are confrontingly Oedipal, as you'd expect. It's getting fuggy in the back seat already. Strictly speaking, on this particular after-noon in 1955 they may be pre-Oedipal, but when the time comes young Swollen-foot in the back seat there (pretty much of an age with me) will do Dad to death without much fuss. He'll do his duty. (Unlike Jocasta, though, I doubt Mum will ever dramatically remove herself. She will nurture, more and more ineffectually, until the day she drops. This will cause young Swollen-foot some problems and no one will help him with them.) I, on the other hand, did not do my duty. Tom and Jean, already middle-aged when I joined them, were not the sort of people to get Oedipal about. Who on earth would battle Tom, the plumpish bon viveur, for whom life was a sort of crossword puzzle you could play with for an hour or so and then cast aside, over the affections of Jean, who scrubbed her hands clean fifty times a day until they were rough and raw, in a war against impurity and defilement? In fact, I never, as it were, took the road to Thebes at all. Children like me will always avoid it if they can. (The boat to Mykonos, a day trip to Delphi . . . but nothing of which myths are made.) So I walked and sat and talked and dreamed differently (I'm sure) from Brack's children. I can tell from the way they're staring: 'We know who we are. Who are you?' I knew who I was not (I didn't belong to Jean and Tom, for instance), but not who I was, and so stared at other people differently from the young Bracks. And still do. And for the adopted child, it's worth remembering, everyone outside your head is Other People. It's I and they for children like me, not we and they, as it obviously is for the cocksure young Bracks. (In more solipsistic moments, of course, everyone outside your head is also dizzyingly you.)

So Brack could never have sat us in a car for our portrait. What you'd have got would not have been us. In the first place, we were more all over the place, the best we could have managed would be a straggly row. Brack's use of colour wouldn't have suited us, either. He coloured his family brown – a ruddy brown, it's true: there's blood there somewhere under those taut, earth-coloured skins – but it's still a restricted palette. It confirms my worst suspicions. We were many-hued as a family (if a family is what we were). I'd suggest reds and yellows for Tom, like his embarrassing Hawaiian shirts, shading into something mauver, something closer to lilac with streaks of white for Jean, and greens and blues for me, I think, a little to one side on the right, deepening to black around the eyes.

But over and above all those considerations of shape and colour, there was another crucial way in which we weren't right: we were not flesh and blood.

Flesh and blood! In that phrase I catch a whiff of eggs and sperm, the double helix (cunning corkscrew), things uterine and foetal, but also of something stiffer, something much more manly: inheritance, good standing, honour, pride . . . And death's there, too, of course. There's a glory in flesh and blood, perhaps even a kind of immortality (the sentimental kind), but there's also decay, decrepitude and messy dissolution. Flesh and blood, like the family in Brack's car, point in a single direction: deathwards. Indeed, they often hurtle towards it. Sometimes, like the interior of a railway carriage, a family may give the appearance of being static – there's certainly a caught-in-amber quality to the four-some in the Triumph Mayflower – but it's an illusion: the track has been laid and the train of families must move along it, carriage after carriage after carriage, with exquisitely purposeful pointlessness. Is it possible to get off? By comparison with Brack's, our family was splodge-shaped – there was nothing arrow-like about our family. We were shaped as if somebody had dropped something on the floor. We weren't going anywhere, at least as a family. Consequently, death meant something different to us, I think.

In a common-or-garden sense mortality hung over us every second of every day. Tom was sixty before I started going to school, while Jean, having observed death at work over many years in a children's hospital, kept reminding us we could all be wiped away without trace at any moment – funnel-web spiders, a bushfire in the gully down the back, child-stranglers, abrupt right-hand turns, heart failure – her friend Eunice upped and died of nothing at all one Christmas, beautiful, slender, blameless Eunice. This was the sort of thing that could happen. Jean was always clenched against it.

In fact, I can't remember not hearing Jean's voice warning me that 'we could die' at any time. It wasn't a voice cracking with tears, in case you're wondering, it was the voice of Jean the nurse, of Jean reading the chart at the end of the bed. If I were left alone (again), I was to go to a cousin (who had a real family – smelly children, abusive husband, carpets with cigarette burns, a piano with sticky rings on it). I'm not sure this threat of sudden abandonment was a good idea, however practical it might have been. I'd already had to deal with the notion, almost before I could talk, that however much my 'real' mother had loved me or wanted me, however lovable I had been, however blameless, a kind of abandonment had taken place. It had not been possible to ward it off. The reasons I was given changed over the years: my father dead in a plane crash, my mother's youth, her wish to marry another man . . . all true, it turned out, but only part of the truth, and in any case no comfort; love was clearly no guarantee of anything. Perhaps that's why in later life I felt spasmodically drawn to passion. At least you knew where you were with passion.

It's not that you don't feel wanted, by the way, as an adopted child. On the contrary, you feel almost dangerously wanted. Jean and Tom had wanted me from the moment they saw me in my bassinet at the hospital, cross-eyed, glowering and demanding to be heard. It was good in many ways to feel so singled out for love, to feel I was there for a reason. The photographs show Tom, already in his late fifties and early sixties, holding me up like a trophy, head back laughing with the unearned joy of it, or walking with me in the street, holding my hand, taking care of his treasure. There's no photograph of Jean holding me like this, as if her love was too fraught for film.

In another sense altogether, however, mortality was strangely absent from our sort of arrangement. We simply weren't geared to death the way Brackish flesh-and-blood families are. Birth, marriage, death, birth, marriage, death – they didn't loom up one after the other like stations on a line we were travelling along. As an adopted child I just landed plop one day. Not quite plop, to be scrupulously honest – it was a guided landing, but I did come plummeting down out of the blue. Reason and chance, you see – everything was a juggling of reason and chance. Blood is something quite different. Blood is not reasonable at all.

One element in our equation didn't seem reasonable, either: what had driven Jean and Tom to marry in the first place? Even a child barely higher than the kitchen table could see it was an unhappy concurrence. Why on earth had a happy-go-lucky merchant seaman (quite flash, actually, in his whites, snapped against a smoking funnel, mountains in the background) chosen to spend his life with a Calvinistic nurse from Perth? And why had this overwrought young nurse agreed to spend the rest of her life with a sloppy semi-theosophist who read nothing but the *Daily Telegraph* form guide and Marlborough's French Phrase Book. Clearly there had been some ghastly mistake. What should have been a momentary chance encounter, a swirl around some dance floor, an outing in some jolly group with lemonade and beer – a shandy, possibly, for the faster girls – had turned into a daily farce of lawn mowing, oven cleaning, wordless gatherings around the radio (me fiddling with my stamp collection) and yearnings – all three of us yearned, Jean in billows. Tom slept on the back veranda.

So we just were, you see, from my point of view; and that's what I mean by an absence of mortality from our sort of arrangement. Death might come bolting in from the wings, but it wasn't scripted in, at least not the way it is in families spawned from seed. Even when Jean stopped breathing in front of me one afternoon in the clanking madhouse she'd been locked in, and went chalky, instantly transformed into a story in my mind too painful to be recounted honestly, I didn't see her death as a step along a path (towards a chasm), I didn't see her snuffing-out as a few more inches of the rope I was a knot in, disappearing into the void. It was more a shapeless blot, a sudden ink stain spreading through the spotless weave I'd thought of as my life. When Tom

died while taking a breather from mowing the lawn one afternoon a few years later, it felt more linear, I must admit, more like
a push along the path to oblivion. But even then my sense of life
stayed fairly round – or, more exactly, spherical. And spheres
don't 'end', do they?

And so there you are: an awareness right from the cot that we
were shaped differently. In our 'family' there was a mixture of
the capricious and the reasonably willed that was barely an
option in blood-connected households. By comparison we were
oddly directionless, without momentum; we beetled and leaked
and stewed and spread like an ink blot, and then we shrank. The
families living in all the other houses in our street and our
suburb and our city were, we were led to believe, doing something quite different: they were branching downwards and
outwards and onwards. In fact, if I'd looked more closely, I'd
have found some very odd-shaped families a stone's throw from
our front door, but they rarely popped up on television or the
radio or in the magazines and the newspapers that piled up on
the back veranda. In fact a widow was bringing up two sons
next door, a childless couple lived in the mock-Spanish bunga-
low over the road, a spinster kept to herself three doors along
next to two more households lacking one spouse . . . And so it
went on, right up to the corner by the schoolyard where a sensitive schoolteacher lived in tasteful solitude and Mrs G. seemed
to have adult children but no husband or grandchildren to speak
of . . . In the schoolyard things looked rather different, for obvious reasons, replicating much more closely the way things ought
to be. Everyone at school seemed to have fathers and mothers in
their prime and a car and a block of land to live on. (At the
time, the idea of an apartment was still a wicked one: apartment
blocks were inhabited by failures of one kind or another –
people of soiled gentility, people from places like Budapest and
Vienna, people who were suspiciously single when they should
have been married and open to inspection, hanging out their

washing in a proper backyard.) Be that as it may, I felt we were differently shaped and that feeling was enough to change absolutely everything.

It changed, for a start, the way I loved (and love). Love in our family was not based on loyalty, you see, but on something I might call sympathy, a convergence of feelings, the slow elaboration of common ground. Love was a matter of a reasonable affinity. Loyalty, as a result, was always a puzzle to me. How odd, I'd think, that some school friend could so despise his brother or father, be so scornful of what he stood for (his friends, his taste in music, his driving, his crassness, his cowardice – of everything, really), yet clearly 'love' him, stand up for him, always come down on his side. Feelings such as these had a dimension I'd simply never explored. (It clearly wasn't Christian love, which I thought I understood, which seeks to love the image and likeness of God through all the messy imperfections of the fleshly being.) How odd that some friend's mother, for example, could feel such fury towards him, or sometimes nothing very clearly defined at all, perhaps even dislike him, yet still 'love' him, apparently, still hold his well-being dear, still want to keep him safely and warmly in his niche. This was loyalty, it seemed, but to what? Well, to the family, the line, the clan – to blood, not to put too fine a point on it. To flesh and blood. How animal it seemed to me then (as opposed to reasonably Christian). How excitingly Mediterranean, how tribal. Our family was based on reasonable affection. It was more contractual.

Perhaps that's why I've never been good at ties of loyalty since. At root I don't care a fig for the group, the organization, the church, the company, the corporation. I despise Big Brother, not because he's big but because he's a brother. He demands loyalty to . . . what? To his status as brother? What a child, with my background, values is reasonable fellow-feeling and heart-to-heart ties, not group dynamics. There's nothing deadlier for someone with my notion of ties than a promiscuously assembled office party or a warm-hearted family Christmas – to me they're as gruesome as a *danse macabre*. Mindless hierarchies celebrating being there, celebrating because they're there. In our family we celebrated things it was reasonable to celebrate – we rarely did things mindlessly. Christmas, as you'll have gathered, was regularly a disappointment: treeless and sensible, marked by socks and improving books I might spend the rest of the muggy day engrossed in, alone on the settee. In fact, Christmas still is a disappointment. Some years I hanker vaguely after a small tree (one I could replant, of course), a bit of bunting, a gaudy bauble or two, but what would be the point? If you want to sing praises to the Lord, sing, if you want to shop, shop, but revelling in commemoration of something, with people you have no special feelings for . . . no, it's never appealed. In our family we didn't revel. Brack's family almost certainly commemorates things, I can picture them at it. Christmases, birthdays, successiveness, the linearity of things, their own mortality. They're built for it.

Friends (and I wish we had a more nuanced word for what I mean by 'friend') become crucially important to people like me, much more important than family or tribe. In fact, words like 'cousin' or 'nephew' induce a kind of panic in me – when I hear them I want to shrivel up. In childhood they were enough to bring on an asthma attack.

Yet do friends constitute a family? Hardly. Nor should they, perhaps. Most friends have stronger loyalties than their ties to you, deeper loves than their love for you. Indeed, part of the excitement of friendship (in my sense) is its volatility, its unpredictability and impermanence. This is fortifying when you're feeling strong. Otherwise it can be debilitating. When my wife abruptly abandoned me years ago, for example, I felt not just weak but disabled. Then it was not comforting to cast a mental eye over my friends and realize that for not a single one of them was I in any way central.

Valued, appreciated, important, even loved in a few cases, but not bound by unquestioned ties. All my ties were open to question. No, I don't think friends really constitute a family.

In the very depths of my psyche, to be absolutely candid, a yen for irrational ties always stirred. When I was a small child, pottering along in the backyard after school, feeding the chooks, walking the dog and so on, one of my fantasies was of discovering I not only had blood-related siblings but a twin brother. Then, egged on by articles in the *Daily Telegraph* and *New Idea*, twins became triplets and even quadruplets. When reports started coming through of quintuplets and sextuplets, my excitement grew and my imagination expanded accordingly. Septuplets, for some reason, I skipped – I knew I could do better than that. Octuplets thrilled me unbearably – my twins were multiplying and refracting like images in funhouse mirrors. I was greedy for ever more identical twinnings. What on earth was going on?

A desire for blood relations, obviously, a desire to fit into a pattern of inheritance, and not always to be judged for what I was making of myself. But I now think it was also a desire to blur the burdensome sense of uniqueness an adopted child can have. Of course, your uniqueness is precious to you from the moment it's revealed, if it's explained to you in the right words. You were chosen, you were plucked out of a mystery to be nurtured and shaped into something matchlessly pleasing, something unlike anyone else in the world.

You are unrivalled (and hate rivals for the rest of your life). There would be no sharp-eyed aunts to tell you your musical gifts came from your grandfather or that you were quick-tempered just like all the boys in your mother's family. No, you were a unique configuration of qualities to be moulded with care and intelligence. In its way it was very spiritual. It was also a burden, as spiritual things can be. Moulding, moulding – I was forever moulding this grab bag of qualities. Would I make of myself a concert pianist? An athlete? A dancer? A French scholar?

A writer? An Egyptologist? A gigolo? I could blow on myself and take any shape I liked.

Much later in life, when I first saw photographs of my natural half-brothers – one in particular – I understood at last that my shape was not just a matter of blowing on myself as if I were a drop of molten glass. Part of my shape – even the way I stood, the way I smiled, the way I looked at others – had been handed down to me, down, in a line of descent. Descent was something I had no flesh-and-blood notion of at all. I grew still when I saw those photographs for the first time. And then I had to laugh. The joke they were playing was on desire.

I laughed (inwardly) at the same joke when I recently met my half-brother for the first time. Even as he walked towards me from the taxi with his overnight bag over his shoulder and an expectant smile on his face, even in my happiness to be seeing the first male blood relative I'd ever set eyes on, I was aware of the ebbing away of desire because desire was now comfortingly beside the point. And so it was soothing and gratifying to meet him, it was a gladdening thing to do, it was the right thing to do, but it quenched desire as contentment will.

And this is another way in which an awareness of being irregularly shaped changes the way you experience life. Brack's kids strike me as chips off the old block sitting in front of them. Society needs and values old blocks. It's built out of them. Bank managers, travel agents, insurance salesmen, estate agents, urban planners – they all like building with neatly fitting blocks. The squarer the blocks, the easier it is to slot them in and the more solid the construction. Odd-shaped blocks – hexagonal, hourglass, concave, daisy-shaped, spherical – are only safe at the very top of a structure or dangling from the sides, like bunting. Aristocracies thrive on this arrangement, lolling naturally at the top, while the freakish and bizarre at lower social levels cling on where they can. I didn't belong as a matter of course to either camp. This bred abundant fantasies of both: the palace and the bazaar.

The adopted child swells and ripens on fantasies. Sitting moodily where it landed on the square suburban block the adopted child can dream of fantastically shaped forebears – pharaohs, czars, divas, dancers from the Paris Opera, jumbo pilots, Zulu warriors, Hollywood stars, all those hexagons and spheres poised right at the top. I used to dream the Andorrans had decided to pension off the two bishops running the country and asked me to move into the castle above the capital and run it in their stead. A regal fantasy. (Oddly enough, when I eventually found myself on a train chugging past the real Andorra, locked up snugly in the Pyrenees a few miles to the west of the railway line, I felt not the slightest twinge of interest. That was the wrong Andorra.)

Square-shaped people dream (or so it seems to me) of accumulation, splodge-shaped people's dreams spread outwards like a stain. They dream more of experience. I see the square-shaped dreams in all their verticality on television nightly: to buy a bigger house, to Cape-Cod the house they've got, to get a second car, a more luxuriously appointed car, to get more friends (by dressing and drinking and dishing up food that feeds desire – for you), to get more security, admiration, pleasure, to set yourself up. Splodge-shaped dreams (I have the feeling) are more horizontal, more spreading: they're dreams of doing things, seeing further, tasting new tastes, experiencing states and sensations not encountered before, assuming new shapes, being something different. Being as opposed to having. They rarely feature on television. I shouldn't think Brack's family bothers with them overmuch.

And then there's virtue. One of the reasons someone like me is going to find Brack's family menacing is that it carries with it a sense of its own virtue. It's not just that these people think they make sense when actually they're just there, incurious about why, but they also conceive of themselves as virtuous. I mean 'Virtue' in its hoariest and most rambling sense of inherent value, of abiding goodness assigned to you by common assent because of your ancestry – your blood and your breeding. 'Of good family', people used to say, 'of good stock'. Good? To a child with little sense of forebears and descent, goodness and value come to mean something individually acquired, something you've learned to practise, like patience or generosity. They're not something you just inherit – it's absurd to live in the afterglow of dead relatives' achievements, you must colour yourself in.

There were rumours of inherited value when I was a child, vague references to French blood of a rarefied kind, French generals, a detached 'de' in the name, valour in the blood . . . and the temptation to grasp onto it, to see that as part of yourself is strong, I don't deny it. Yet when it became clear that this blue blood was a myth, I actually felt obscurely relieved, freed just to be myself. The Romantic in me was disappointed, naturally – all those rollicking tales and crumbling chateaux I no longer had any purchase on – but the realist was realistic and, taking stock, on the whole none the poorer.

A sense of virtue as something you must earn changes your attitude to a whole range of family-connected virtues, from having a nice home to sexual fidelity. These things, which appear to be not much more than conventions for procreating without too many hitches, are unlikely to appear virtuous in themselves to someone of my shape. A nice home with a guest room, a monogamous relationship with a loved spouse, a steady job with a respected firm – these things will only appear 'good' to the misshapen if they intensify and enrich your sense of being alive (without impoverishing other people's, I feel constrained to add).

And so, for people of this oddly hewn shape who are also attracted to their own sex, a homosexual arrangement clearly has many advantages, with its emphasis on choice, affinity, taste, marginality, affection, desire, fantasy, passion, contingency, risk and multiple intimacies. A core relationship is still possible, with all the satisfying depth that brings, but its borders are likely to be excitingly blurred, allowing passion, love and friendship more play. No longer need they be roped in a tight jumble to the central mooring.

Some homosexuals, it's true, find peace with themselves by modelling their lives on something closer to the arrangement in the Triumph Mayflower – with borrowed children or at least a Rottweiler or basset in the back, and a Dad driving and a Mum, less focused, peering amiably about. And why not? They want to be married – why shouldn't they be? Marriage vows, lifelong fidelity – they help some homosexuals feel less queer. Perhaps they come from more traditionally shaped families.

When I was first getting to know my natural mother, Yvonne, I remember feeling eager to assure her I was really terribly normal, despite my deviant behaviour in one or two respects. I wanted her to know I had a nice house, enjoyed gardening on Saturdays, went to bed early with a book as often as not, was deeply attached to my partner, who was very good with his hands, and went everywhere with him, got on well with my 'mother-in-law' – in other words, was shaped not so differently from one or other of the figures in Brack's car . . . well, to be brutally frank, from the wife. In the event I don't really think she deeply cares. What she wants to be assured of is that I'm happy. I still do it a bit, all the same – 'Yes, we watched that last night, too,' I tell her, or 'I was so dog-tired after cleaning out the gutterings and turning the compost all afternoon that I just fell into bed and was asleep by nine' – it's a habit that's hard to break. I want her to think I've got a family. One day I may tell her what I really did after turning the compost and be surprised to find she's completely unshaken. One day I'd like to explain to her, for instance, that I'd be much more devastated if my partner told me he no longer found my jokes amusing than if he told me he'd had a wild weekend with an Italian soccer star. That would be no threat to me – we both knew I wasn't an Italian soccer star when he took up with me.

Old age and death are a bit of a problem, all the same, or so it seems to me sometimes, staring at the ceiling in the early hours of the morning. (Perhaps my mother worries about that for me a little as well.) In the morning I suspect they look no bleaker than they do for anyone, but sometimes you can't help remembering that, if you're the one death robs of a loved partner, you won't be able to turn around and find succour in the succeeding generation, you'll have no socially acceptable role to play (bereft husband, grief-stricken wife – your colleagues at work will probably expect you to buck up and soldier on within days), there will be a few time-honoured rituals to obey to help you take ordered steps through the dark and make it safely to the other side. Your life may just explode on you, injuring you fatally . . . is that a time bomb in your nest?

Old age has been a taboo subject for most of us living as I live. Are we all doomed to wheeze our way deathwards in foul-smelling loneliness in a flat somewhere, dropping dead on the way out with the garbage one night? Or will we be propped up in a brightly polished Home for Aged Gays, sung to by the gay choir every second Sunday, dragooned into croaking out old Barbra Streisand songs around the piano of an evening with people we have nothing in common with at all, except something called 'gayness'? Will it be all right to be ugly? What will happen to us? Exactly what happens to everybody else, I imagine in my more sober moments: those of us who have money and loving friends will die with some scrapings of dignity, and those of us who don't won't. Family won't make much difference. The way we've loved during our lives will.

'Would you like to meet the family?' Yvonne asked me, once we'd got to know each other well.

'Oh, well, in time, perhaps,' I said, trying to hide my lack of enthusiasm with vagueness. 'I'm not so sure they'd want to meet me, as a matter of fact.' What I meant was that, while I was sure they'd like to meet me, I wasn't at all sure they'd like the person they met.

I've still met hardly any of them, apart from my mother – one half-brother, another half-brother's wife and a cousin. I don't need blood relations now, it's too late for them. It's too late for family. It's too late for reshaping. Sometimes I feel a bit like an untethered balloon with a hole in it, zigzagging crazily through the air, still half-inflated with desire but getting baggier by the minute and heading ultimately downwards. I doubt that's how my cousins and nieces or my half-brother think of themselves. I imagine in their case images of luxuriantly branching trees firmly rooted in the earth come to mind. Or buildings, perhaps, in these postmodern, self-constructing times, that reach upwards and outwards. I'll probably never find out. It doesn't much matter. At this point in my life a zigzagging balloon will have to do.

OEDIPUS DESCENDING

Jonathan Rendall

She did not really like to be called Elizabeth. She preferred Lizzie. We exchanged letters. She had pleasing handwriting. She confirmed that my father was Bryan Needham. He had been an undergraduate at Balliol College, Oxford. She was working as a secretary. He denied paternity. He said he could produce ten witnesses to say it wasn't him. He got a Third but was a good sportsman. Later they had another affair and he accepted it was him. He asked what had happened to the baby. When she told him it'd been adopted he was angry. That's what she said, anyway. 'He was the love of my life,' she wrote in a letter. 'But he was a bastard.'

I went down by train. The next day I had to go to America for an article. I would spend the day and evening with her and then get the night train to Gatwick. It was a bit ridiculous but somehow it couldn't wait.

At Reading I had to change trains. My head began to swirl. What the hell was I doing? I missed three trains. I went to the wrong platform. I couldn't think. Finally I got on the right one.

The hours passed in a flash. I tried not to think. I tried only to examine the landscape shooting past. After the stop before Totnes I was the only one in the carriage. I started to cry, uncontrollable weeping. I didn't know why. I wished it would bloody stop. It did, just as the train pulled in.

She was standing at the station gate. I recognized her imme-diately from the photos she'd sent. She wasn't crying either. She looked very attractive. The way she was looking at me – no one had ever looked at me like that. I could have done anything, turned around and got on the next train back, and she would have looked at me in the same way. That's what I thought. That was the difference. Only your Mum can look at you like that.

She drove to the intersection in her old Renault. It smelled of dogs. That was good. It was a while since I'd been around dogs. She said: 'I promised Martin I wouldn't, but sod it, do you fancy a drink?' We went to a hotel bar. The Royal Seven Stars. It wasn't difficult talking. It was easy. It was like a first date where there was no need for small talk.

At the cottage, Martin was huge. He must have been twenty stone. He was a crab processor, her third husband. He used to be a fisherman. He did the processing in a room by the kitchen. He'd given up drink. Now he just drank apple crush. He once bought thirty-eight bottles from Somerfield. He drank them from his old beer tankard. He kept the bottles behind the sofa.

The three of us sat in the kitchen. Martin talked for about twenty minutes, about his salvation through AA and the signifi-cance of our reunion. I wished he'd shut up. I didn't need explanations from him. I hated him. I thought, how did you end up with someone like him?

Lizzie was standing by the stove making soup. It was deli-cious. I like to stand like that while other people are sitting, as well. And I can cook. I must have got it from her. Why didn't he just leave us alone?

They took me to a pub in West Alvington. The Ring o' Bells. It was halfway down the hill. At the end I went to hug her, but she pulled away. She said, 'You're not going to make a scene, are you?' No, I'm not in the habit of it.

Martin drove us to the station in the dead of night. The wind got up and we took cover behind a hut on the platform while we waited for the train. Standing shivering there I felt a strange intimacy with these people, even Martin, yet at the same time could not quite believe that I was there at all. The train came and I was relieved. I sat in the carriage smelling strongly of dogs. That was not my normal smell. Lizzie was waving through the carriage window. The train began its long journey and sitting there I was no longer even sure that I was me.

The second time, in the autumn, I was to caddy for Lizzie in a golf tournament. She had taken it up a few years before, with immediate success. She'd told me in the letters. She was obviously a natural sportswoman. She'd played hockey for Devon once.

I had a car then – an old Citroën AX hatchback. I took it to Le Garagiste. That's what he called himself, this bloke. His twin obsessions were France and Citroëns. 'Will it get me to Devon?' I asked him. 'No problem,' Le Garagiste said. 'Get you any-where, the AX.'

I got there late. Lizzie had already teed off. The golf club was upmarket. The tournament secretary was faintly disapproving. She said if I waited by the Ninth, she'd come round soon enough.

I walked out across the course. It seemed almost cut from the steep hills. The sun lit the brown leaves. I breathed in the crisp air and remembered that, though I hadn't known it, I was a Devon lad.

I don't know golf-course etiquette, and had to duck a few times. The only golf course I'd frequented in the last twenty years was a pub nine-holer by Sandown racecourse. I'd played a friend there for a fiver a hole. Absolute carnage, that was.

I reached the Ninth. There was an old stone wall by the green. I sat on it, but after asking a couple of groups that went by, I realized Lizzie would still be a while. I began to feel a bit con-spicuous sitting up there. Who is he? Women's golf voyeur?

I jumped down and went behind the wall. From behind, I could still see the fairway, but they couldn't see me. In the tan-gled foliage, I noticed this patch had once been cultivated – the outer grounds of some big house. I began to feel silly hiding there among the roots, but also proud of her somehow – ridiculous, really.

Lizzie came into view. She looked very glamorous. She was wearing a blue sun visor and tight blue trousers. Her skin and hair were so clean. She looked different to the last time. I watched her lob a chip onto the green. Yes, a natural. She was by far the best player to have come past.

I walked out and grabbed her motorized golf bag. I must have flicked the wrong switch because it dragged me off towards a bunker. I just managed to stop it.

In the bag she had packed me a few things: cheese-and-pickle sandwiches and two cans of beer.

We ate and drank them on the way round, laughing and smoking.

That night there was a fancy-dress party. Martin dressed up as a clown. He looked, frankly, terrifying.

Lizzie was Marlene Dietrich, in a silver wig. I hadn't known about it, and just wore my green suit. She said that was fine. She said I looked handsome.

The people ebbed away. Martin was taking someone home. We were in the kitchen, just Lizzie and me. She asked me to open a bottle of cava. I don't know how many I opened. Then she went to the bedroom. I helped her. But we became entangled on the bed. To tell the truth, for a moment I wanted to fuck her, and I think she wanted to fuck me.

Christ, Oedipus descending. But at least Oedipus didn't know what the hell he was doing.

I pushed her away and she pushed me back. She was strong.

We went outside and she fell over. She refused to let me help her up. I looked at her in her silver wig. She was holding her glass of cava up.

She said: 'Now you know where you get it from.'

NEW YEAR'S EVE

Dan Chaon

Huck wants to know if I ever feel like calling him 'Dad,' and I have to admit that no, I really don't. I am thirty years old, and Huck is forty-seven. It's a little late for that sort of thing, I tell him, though he is, in fact, my biological father. It's hard to think of a guy who shows up at my place with a hiker's backpack, a guy who's sleeping on my couch, as a paternal figure.

But Huck reaches up and lets his fingertips run across my cheek and the bridge of my nose. 'Wow,' he whispers to himself, and then he takes his hand away.

'I'm not a fag or anything,' he says, defensively. 'I'm just sort of fascinated, you know? I always wondered what you'd look like.'

I have real parents: my mother and father, the people who adopted me when I was an infant. I have a life I am sort of pleased with: married, two sons, a big house in the suburbs of Cleveland. A teaching gig at Oberlin College. None of this registers exactly with Huck.

'What kind of sports did you play in high school?' he asks, after listing his own accomplishments: Quarterback, Pitcher, Hundred-Yard Dash Champion. 'I always imagined that you'd be athletic.'

'Well,' I say, and I don't know how to tell him that the only sport I excelled in was Dungeons and Dragons. 'Actually,' I say. 'I'm actually kind of uncoordinated.'

'I don't believe that for a minute,' he says. 'You look like a wrestler.'

For the record, I don't look like a wrestler. I look like a plump, sedentary English Professor, and in fact I have a horror of most types of organized physical exercise. When I was forced to run laps in junior high I used to hyperventilate and spend the latter part of gym breathing into a paper bag. I have the feeling that when he was in junior high, Huck was the sort of kid who had a name for people like me. And that name was 'Fag.'

Which is to say: we are not the fantasies that we had of one another.

When I was growing up in Nebraska, my dad was a construction worker who liked to go hunting and fishing on the weekends, and he was, I knew, more than a little mortified to be in possession of a son like me. A son who couldn't cast a line without managing to whip the hook into his own eyebrow, or tangle it terrifyingly into the blades of the boat motor; who couldn't be trusted with a gun, or even to wield a hammer without hitting his body more often than the nail.

Growing up, I used to sometimes imagine my biological father. I figured he lived in New York City. I thought he was probably a writer or an architect, maybe an actor. Once I saw a guy who played the best friend in a TV movie and I thought he looked a lot like me. *What if that's my father?* I thought. I followed the end credits very carefully, and secretly memorized the actor's name, which I remember to this day, though as far as I know he has never been in another film.

As it turns out, Huck is also a construction worker. Somewhere in an alternate universe, my imaginary father stands before a group of worshipful Ivy League kids in a tweed jacket with leather patches on his elbow and writes the word 'irony' on the blackboard. How is this possible?

My wife says that I am like my adopted father in a lot of ways. I have learned the modes of his moods – his dogged loyalty, his even temper, his sentimentality, his appreciation of loneliness.

I am also recognizably Huck's son. Our faces are versions of one another, even down to the same mole at the corner of our left eyes. Our hands match up; we have the same shoe size.

As for the rest of me, there's no accounting for it, and my wife shakes her head as I worry through the details.

'Maybe it's not nature or nurture, either one,' she says. 'Maybe you just invented yourself. Why is that so strange?'

We had chosen New Year's Eve as a kind of neutral territory. It is not a family holiday. Rather, New Year's Eve is a kind of blank space, the day when you throw away the old calendar and put up a fresh one, the day of resolution and remembrance. It was also, as my wife pointed out, the day when Huck and I had the most in common. We both liked to drink, and we both liked to stay up late, talking, smoking, telling stories.

You can probably guess the basics of his story – *our* story – which is like a sad Bruce Springsteen song. I was conceived in a small town in the Midwest. He was a football player and she was a cheerleader. She got sent away to a home for unwed mothers, and he finished up with high school, got out of town as fast as he could.

Eventually, Huck went on to a semester of college, and then dropped out and joined the navy, where, he admits, there were a lot of good drugs going around at the time. Speed, acid.

'I never stopped wondering about you,' he told me, the first time we spoke on the phone, and it felt a little like an accusation.

On the day of New Year's Eve, Huck and I walk down the aisles of the supermarket not far from my house, and it is kind of a bonding experience. We fill the cart with cashew halves and smokehouse almonds, chips and twelve-packs of beer. We don't talk very much but there is a kind of camaraderie. Grocery shopping is an oddly intimate activity, and it's good to know that we are both fans of beef jerky and hot sauce, that we both prefer beer in cans, that we can discourse on the relative desirability of various Little Debbie snacks. Every time it seems like we are in danger of running out of conversation, a new aisle of debatable products appears.

When we come at last to the checkout, Huck brings out a wad of folded bills from his front pocket, held together with a money clip.

'Oh . . .' I say. 'No, no . . . I can get this. Really.'

But Huck frowns fiercely. 'I haven't seen my son in thirty years,' he tells the woman at the cash register. 'I don't know what's wrong with him, but if he thinks I'm going to let him buy the beer, he's got another thing coming.'

The woman nods, slightly alarmed, and gazes at me. She watches as Huck puts his hand around the back of my neck.

'This is my son,' he tells her. 'I haven't seen him in thirty years.'

We sit in my study on the third floor of the house, the window open – despite the below-zero weather – to let out the smoke. The beer is packed in coolers of ice on the floor, and the space heater is on. I am trying to interest him in the music of Tom Waits, but he has a look on his face as if I have offered him a plate full of cold brains. He stands for a while staring at my CD rack, scoping it hopefully for something he will recognize before he sits down with a sigh.

We have almost run the gamut of approved male-bonding conversation threads: sports . . . music . . . cars . . . movies . . . and then we sit there for a while. Huck has his hands folded in his lap, and I look down, noticing the disturbing vein that is pulsing at my wrist. I take another sip of beer, and Huck clears his throat.

'So,' he says after a moment. 'Do you like to get high?' He puts his hand over the pocket of his flannel shirt, and raises his eyebrows.

It sounds like it would make a good situation for a movie, or at the very least a pithy and moving Raymond Carver short story, but the truth is that neither one of us knows how to proceed.

Nine months and thirty-something years have passed since I was conceived in the back of a car, high-school Huck and his high-school girlfriend, their first time, he says.

Twenty-five years have passed since my mother sat me down to explain the secrets. 'Do you know what it means to be adopted?' my mother said. 'It means that you are very special, because we chose you to be our baby.'

She told me that my birth parents were very young. 'Too young to raise a baby,' my mother said earnestly. She didn't know much about them – only the vague non-identifying information that she got from the adoption agency, a neat little package that told their hair and eye color and ethnicity, a short narrative of their activities and interests. My mother remembered going to the adoption agency to pick me up, the infant me. I was sitting in a crib amongst a group of babies in cribs, and she was struck by the little plastic framed mirror that had been affixed to the bars. She watched as I stared at it, as I touched my reflected face with my sticky infant paws. 'That was the only toy you were interested in, that mirror,' she told me, and later, when she was very unhappy, when she became a mentally ill drug addict, she would retell this same story over and over, bitterly, pointedly – the cribs, the mirror. As if perhaps her life might have been different if she'd chosen a different baby.

But I can't tell stories on my mom to Huck. It seems sort of unpatriotic – like complaining about life in the U.S. to British people.

Similarly, he can't really talk honestly about my birth mother.

'She was a really sweet person,' he says diplomatically. 'And incredibly beautiful. I was really crazy about her.'

He hesitates. 'We talked about getting married,' he says, earnestly. 'But our families were against it.' He looks at me for a moment and then away, and I know that of course there was no serious discussion of marriage. She was fifteen and he was sixteen. High-school kids, I think. Children. And it occurs to me, as he talks to me about his plans for marrying this girl, that he had felt relieved when she was sent away. And I can tell by the look in his eyes that he spent the rest of his life being ashamed that he had been relieved.

He has been in touch with my birth mother a few times over the years since my birth. Sometimes he has called late at night and they have talked for hours, he claims; other times, she asks him never to contact her again.

'She goes back and forth,' he says, wistfully, and takes a sip of his beer. 'She's married, but she never told her husband about it. So it's tough for her.'

'I'm sure it is,' I say.

'When I get back home, I'm going to talk to her,' he says. 'She'll want to know about you. What you're like. It may take her a while to come around, but eventually . . . I think she'll be as excited as I am to get to meet you. This is, like, the most magical moment in my life. That's what I'm going to tell her.'

'Well,' I say. I try to imagine my birth mother, the former cheerleader, the 'suburban housewife,' as Huck says now, joining us on the magical third floor of my house with the magical coolers of beer and the magical joint that Huck keeps passing to me. 'You don't have to do that,' I say. 'I mean, if she wants to contact me, I'd certainly be glad to hear from her, but it sounds like it's complicated.'

'You don't think it's complicated for me?' Huck says grimly. 'It's complicated for me. It's complicated for you. You've got a wife, you've got kids. You've got to explain all this to them. It's complicated for everybody. Why should she get all the sympathy?'

'I don't know,' I say. 'I guess . . . I think it would be traumatic to have to relinquish a baby for adoption. I mean, you go through all that pain to give birth and then your hormones are going crazy and . . . well, it seems like it would be traumatic.'

Huck looks at me balefully for a second. 'Traumatic!' he says. 'That's what people think when they're teenagers, right? They're like, "Oh, I've had a trauma, I'll never get over it." And then you get to be my age and you realize that your whole frickin' life is a trauma. You survive, man. You know? I swear to God. I spent every single day of my life since you were born thinking about you, and shedding real tears about it. I'm not lying. And am I bitching about being traumatized? No. I dealt with it. And I think she should get a spine and deal with it too. Don't you? "Get your butt in gear and be happy, woman, because I found our son!" That's what I'm going to tell her.'

'Hmmm,' I say, and I take a long drink from my beer. 'I don't know.'

It's a little bit before midnight now, and the radio is getting more and more earnestly hysterical. They are getting ready for the final countdown.

Being born, I didn't have any particular plans to make other people unhappy. But it occurs to me, sitting across from Huck, that adoption as it was practiced thirty years ago was a machine for misery. I am glad to be alive, of course, but I'm also aware that I exist as a strange fluke of the legal system, a relic of a repressive period in American history. These days, the solutions are so much simpler than they were then, and I have to wonder if my birth parents would have had an easier time of it if Roe v. Wade had been in place when I was conceived. Those poor, dumb, horny Midwestern kids: I would have definitely recommended the abortion, if I weren't the fetus in question.

But of course there's no turning back, there's no remaking our lives. Huck and I listen to the cheers of the crowd as the ball drops in Times Square, and we clink our beer cans together: Cheers! Happy New Year!

I am thinking about the end of *The Great Gatsby*, that beautiful sentence. *So we beat on, boats against the current, borne back ceaselessly into the past.*

I don't say this aloud, though. Not now. Huck presses his lips against my forehead, and pulls my face into his neck. 'Happy New Year, my son,' he whispers, and what can I say? Despite everything, there is a future between us. Despite everything, we are, right now, pretty happy.

CONFESSIONS OF AN UNCONTROL FREAK

Dominic Collier

You will never understand
how it feels to live your life
with no meaning or control . . .
                                    Jarvis Cocker

According to my adoption counsellor, Control is the key to understanding the condition of the adoptee. It works like this. When a child is adopted there are three participating entities: the natural parents, the adopting parents and the adoptee. Of these three, two get to exercise some control over the situation by making decisions; and one doesn't. This leaves the adoptee with unresolved control issues.

As an adoptee, this infuriates me.

It also infuriates me that just over thirty-seven years ago, at St Thomas' Hospital on the banks of the River Thames, opposite the Mother of all Parliaments, in Swinging London in the middle of the first Summer of Love, the woman who had recently given birth to me abandoned me. I was what was still politely known as a love child, more colloquially, a bastard. I was three days old.

I'll probably never be sure, but it's overwhelmingly likely that I was conceived by accident. Accidents are events that take place unexpectedly, unfortunate occurrences, happenings not essential to the nature of things. Accidents are unintended: they are not

meant to happen. In my infuriated, Humpty-Dumpty world, if
something is not *meant*, it follows that it lacks *meaning*. And a
thing that lacks meaning cannot be understood, and that which
cannot be understood cannot be controlled, the accident of my
birth thus providing further dubious validation for a lifelong
failure to control myself.

This is how it is with me anyway, as an adoptee. And this tenuous association of intention and control is experienced as a
paralysing sense of insignificance.

I have always known that I was adopted. My first tangible
memory of this knowledge was at Christmas 1970 or 1971,
making me three or four. I got a book for Christmas, *Mr
Merryweather's Family* I think it was called, about adopting
children. I remember enjoying it and pointing out that these
Merryweather children, like me, and my brother and sisters,
were adopted. This was normal, and also special. We, the
adopted ones, were special because we were chosen, not just
made. My mummy and daddy told me this often when I was
little, before they kissed me goodnight, after prayers to Gentle
Jesus Meek and Mild. God was in his heaven in those days – a
Methodist heaven, lots of golden light, Jesus with a well-cut
beard, birds, flowers, children – and all was well with
the world.

I was proud of the fact that I was adopted, happy about it. I
still am. I always have been. Along with rage and sorrow, happiness and pride are the two emotions I associate most strongly
with adoption.

As a child, being adopted meant only good things. It was
when I was twelve or thirteen, when adolescence fell like night,
that the anger and the sense of loss began to trouble me.
Confused and alone, I withdrew from the workings and agreed
standards of mainstream society and crept away into the darkness beyond the edge of town. And like my man Jarvis losing
his brain somewhere in a field in Hampshire, I left important

parts of the Meaning and Control construct behind me.

I became an outsider. I was lonely, I was alienated, I was feeling insecure. I was seeking my own unique identity and I was looking for excuses. What do you expect? I was an adolescent.

And I was adopted. Bingo. That'll do. In my unknown origins lay all the individuality and all the difference I could ever need.

Of course, when it suited me, it was very convenient to align myself with my mother's strong creative bent, my father's bookishness, both qualities taught and acquired through persistent, patient, generous nurture. The older I get the more I see how like my parents I am. But when I was alone and fourteen and no blood tied me to the world at all, I came swiftly to the conclusion that I didn't know who I was.

I don't know who I am! It was true and the possibilities were endless. I've narrowed them down a bit now – not much – but back then I was thinking of spaceships, treasure troves, tropical mangroves and tribal drums. I was thinking of graveyards on dark and stormy nights, riders bearing sealed messages, the tattered flag flying over the deserted fort and the baby wailing in the ruined tower, the doctor galloping out in the flood as the bridge was washed away. I was thinking of a mysterious, powerful, wronged father whose identity must remain secret, and an utterly pure, unimpeachable, virgin mother . . .

So far so Freud: this wish for a new and superior set of parents is the Family Romance of every child's imagination.

But I was also thinking of a stupid slut and a cock-swinging shyster too dumb between them to use a condom and too selfish to deal with the consequences.

And I was thinking, 'I'm not meant to be here.' I felt like a visitor from another galaxy who had crash-landed on the wrong planet. On bad days, I still do.

In the lurid world of my teenage mind I was imagining that I was this bastard changeling prince–pauper kid from outer space; but back in mundane reality I was actually a screwed-up smart-arse fourteen-year-old getting heavily into drugs and studying for my O levels on the siege island of Hong Kong in the early 1980s. I ran wild, completely amuck. I got very good at being very bad very quickly. I was surly, rude and, for a while, as downright criminally antisocial as a white middle-class teenager can be. I accelerated like a getaway car through family rules, educational rules, social rules and then the laws of the land, moving effortlessly from cigarettes, to booze, to soft drugs, to hard drugs, to dealing all kinds of drugs, to car theft, to housebreaking . . . By sixteen I'd lost it entirely and I was very lucky indeed to be arrested and convicted on some relatively minor charges at that point.

Hong Kong 1983. I look back at that humid era and I shake my head and I sweat. I cast out remorse a long time ago and I don't regret anything but I wouldn't do that again in a hurry.

Throughout this live-fast-die-young phase I maintained, when questioned, as I often was, that I behaved like this because 'society' (I meant 'authority') was a fucking joke and I couldn't take it seriously. Because I wanted to. Because I needed the buzz. Because why not? Because the world was insane and we were all to blame anyway. Because I was bored, because I was angry, because I could. Because there seemed as much point in behaving this way as in any other way, and it was a lot more fun breaking the rules than playing by them, and because it appeared that nobody could stop me.

I don't recall ever claiming that it was because I was adopted. But I certainly thought it and at a distance of nearly twenty years it's hard for me to separate what I did from what I thought, or to view these things objectively.

It was an extreme period. The deadly lustre of my mysterious origins has never been quite as bright or burnished again since. I'd deliberately avoided asking my parents about my genetic origins up until this point. I preferred the mystery to the reality, and I was also very wary of showing any kind of churlishness or lack of gratitude to my parents. It wasn't them I was rebelling against. But when I was sixteen, soon after and, I can see now, as a direct result of a short but frightening series of appearances in the criminal courts in Kowloon, I finally, reluctantly, asked my mother what the story was: who was I and where did I come from before I was picked up out of the reject bin at the age of six weeks?

When you are adopted you don't have any blood relatives. You have role models and you have books and TV and friends to show and tell you what blood ties might be like, how they might be different to mere proximity and shared experience in a family, but you don't ultimately know anyone who's like you are.

If you are lucky you feel as though you belong, are meant to be where you are, with the people you are with. And if you don't? Too bad: better find some other way of being yourself. For a long time I used drugs to do this. I love getting high, catching a buzz, changing my brain state. It's a mixture of enjoying the physical and mental effects and refusing to conform: knowing and enjoying the fact that I'm in a different place to almost everyone else, a place where meaning is, at best, relative and ambiguous, and control is a choice that's not always available. It is, perhaps, for someone who has never been comfortable with it, a way of enjoying being adopted.

I'm in my late thirties now. After what might be half a lifetime or more of trying to come to terms with my adopted status, what have I learned? Who am I? I still don't know.

Awww. Shit man, that's a bummer, ain't it?

That's the voice of my natural father, my blood father, the man whose face, perhaps, I share; whose careless genes, maybe, gave me these dark, suspicious eyes, this lurching, shambling, loping gait, this temper, this humour, this verbosity, half of this entire existence. This anger!

I hear him often, like an invisible rogue parrot perched upon the shoulder of my mind: chirpy, laconic, observant, apparently sympathetic: but ultimately disinterested. I'm *my* problem – not his.

An American airman is all I know of him. Embellished by my

own arbitrary desires and designs, he comes from the south, Tennessee, and a long line of farmers. They are lanky, amiable, hardworking but fundamentally amoral people, superficially kind and generous but disrespectful of property – their own and others' – and ultimately of life itself: a bestial tribe who breed like rats and kill like coyotes, fond of music and dancing and laughing and talking and drinking and fighting and fucking . . . A lot of Celtic in their roots, I reckon, with a good sprinkling of Mediterranean. Sun-loving spaced-out good-timers who don't take it all too seriously. There are many worse ways of living life and using it up than simply having a good time, and oftentimes, in their own accent and dialect, I envy them. I want to be with them.

And I can dream up shit like that all day long but I still don't know what the guy was like. It's still a mystery.

I don't know anything about my mother either. She was the other half of the brief, unglamorous, not unfamiliar story. By her own account she was an Irish nurse who was swept off her feet by an American airman, who knocked her up and then disappeared, leaving her deeply disillusioned, one imagines, and unable and/or unwilling to deal with Irish family values – this was 1967 in England but, owing to a rupture in the Irish Protestant time/space continuum, still only about 1850 in deepest Ulster, whence she claimed to hail – and the hard life that surely faced her and her unborn child.

I think about her often, this woman within whose womb I was conceived and nurtured for nine months, whose DNA in an egg the size of a pinhead provided and provides half of my own basic physical material, who expelled me from her body, and who departed the post-parturition ward, and me, her – only? first-born? – son, seventy-two hours after this expulsion – with a final kiss? with one last longing look at me? with never a glance back, but tears of sorrow in her own shadowed eyes? – never to return.

And man, I wonder what she was thinking then.

When she checked into the hospital, before she walked out,

she provided written details about where she was to be found, how she was to be contacted, who the father was and so on. These turned out to be a fiction, a meaningless pack of lies. The name she gave was false, her National Insurance number was fake, the hospital she claimed to work at had never heard of her and the forwarding addresses – in South London, Manchester and Ulster – simply didn't exist. Three constabularies put men on the case to find her – so that she could legally sign away any claim to me, thus enabling my legal adoption – but they all failed to locate her, my scarlet mother. She had vanished.

And so it was left to the NCH to look after me while the court made me its ward, in order for my parents legally to be able to adopt me: one child, male, forty-five days old, three previous owners, some more careful than others.

If I needed any more disincentive to trace my natural mother than the life-altering disappointment I have witnessed in other adoptees who have reunited with less than ideal natural parents, the knowledge that three different, specially trained police forces couldn't find her thirty-seven years ago when the trail was warm is wonderfully off-putting: the trail is stone cold now, gravestone cold; and I'm no policeman. She's gone for good.

So I know nothing about her and I'll probably never know. She probably wasn't even a nurse. Or Irish. And he probably wasn't an American airman.

All the same, it's what I was told about myself when I asked as an adolescent and I needed to know something, when my personality was still in flux, still up for grabs, and I've wrapped my character around this Atlantic hybrid like yarn around a bobbin. Basing myself on this supposed Fenian–Yankee heritage, working mainly from characters in novels, I became a loud-mouthed arrogant drunken violent boor, a loquacious, sociable dreamer with an unlimited sense of the possible and the power and freedom of the individual. I *feel* Irish/American, a mixture of helpless victim and rebel upstart. It fits my meaningless and uncontrolled adoptee profile. This much is true.

And like my mother, the imaginary Irish nurse, I do prefer the endless potential of fiction's falsehood to the crushing finality of fact.

When I'm most alone I comfort myself with the fact that my mother was unable or unwilling to abort me, to kill me or have me killed, as she might have done. My life in her hands she respected, when I had no control and she had all, and she saved it and gave it to me.

And however old I get, and however disillusioned I am, and however the skies darken and the Hakken-Kraks howl and I cite Aristotle and claim that it's better to be dead than alive and best of all never to have been born – despite all that, I know that I was given the chance to be, to control my own existence and do with it what I will, and to create meaning even when I find none.

It's never easy to answer the 'Why did you have me?' question. What do you say? 'We were drunk' is often the true answer, but not a kind response to an existentially troubled child. Similarly, 'The condom split' and 'Your dad said he was going to pull out' are honest, but not necessarily things you'd want to lay on your offspring as reasons for their existence.

'We were young and in love and so very happy that it seemed entirely normal to want to recreate ourselves through the miracle of reproductive biology, that there might be more of such happiness' is a very good answer indeed but not one that necessarily makes any sense to someone who wasn't there at the time, particularly if that someone was the result and is not enjoying the life you've unilaterally provided them with.

One thing that no one wants to hear is that he or she was an accident. But whether they are told it or not, most adoptees work out that the biological parents didn't necessarily have that 'more happy, happy love' thing going on. We work it out, and we have to face the fact that we are, most likely, accidental, the random product of unchecked sexual desire, maybe not even necessarily mutual; and not a lot else. Unplanned, unwanted, at best an annoying by-product, at worst an active irritant . . . These aren't great origins. They don't describe an orderly and predictable universe. That's been my experience anyway. The sense of dispossession and inconsequence has, at times, been unbearably frightening and painful.

Then again, I'm not unique in my chaotic beginnings, and there's great comfort in an everyday life whose rhythm is indistinguishable from millions of others; just as there is in the lyrics of a three-minute pop song: *sing along with the common people, sing along and it might just get you through*. And I have children of my own now. My first and only blood relatives. Sons and daughters, two of each. Half of me! Like almost any parent, I love them completely, easily, happily. In addition to the welcome responsibility I have for their lives and their upbringing, they have brought me new answers to the question of who I am. I watch a son who looks like me instinctively kicking a ball exactly the way I did it at his age and I know a little more about myself. I share a favourite song or poem with a daughter and hear the echo of my own laughter in hers as she catches the rhythm and the rhyme that made me chuckle thirty years ago. These are my people and I am made more whole by being among them.

In a mild way they don't know half of their blood either. They share my mystery. They don't seem to be too bothered about it – maybe because they do know the people who made them, their natural parents. The insecurity over lack of identity clearly doesn't stretch beyond one generation.

'Does it matter?' asks my eldest child, seriously, when I ask him if he wonders who my natural parents were.

'Not to you,' I tell him, strangely comforted by both his concern for me, and his lack of concern for his genetic roots.

As an adoptee I'm made more real by my own children. They are apparently secure in the knowledge of who they are. They will not seek to answer the unanswerable questions that tortured me in my teenage years. Their circumstances are different to mine and they have not inherited the identity crisis that has plagued me for most of my life. But whether this will enable them to find more meaning, to exercise more control over themselves and the world they live in, than I have done; or whether my rogue tendencies are coded in that blood I so wanted to share with someone, and will out, and my children are destined to wreck and get wrecked at every opportunity in adolescence, and beyond, before they find something at least approximating to peace of mind – if not meaning and control – I don't know.

THE FORTUNATE ONES

Sandra Newman

They are poorly understood. Accounts of them differ. They are the gods of a previous civilization, leftover gods, half-forgotten gods. Their laws are out of kilter with contemporary morals, their justice barbaric, their ways archaic. They are invoked, correspondingly, as takers of vengeance for crimes resented elementally, in the blood: primarily the murder of a parent. Most commonly called the Furies, they also have the name of Eumenides, or Fortunate Ones.

In the version of the *Oresteia* I saw, at the Cottesloe Theatre, in London, the Furies were portrayed as a black-suited chorus of men and women whose faces were veiled – blotted out – in black. They wore vaguely Eastern European hats, *bürgerlich*. And they looked, to my Ashkenazi eye, like ancestors. They were those forces you cannot know, yet which pursue you.

And to me, they represent the truth that family is a reckoning. The family is nemesis, as we unhappily realize at Christmas, going home stripped of our potency and dignity for one more round with our personal Furies.

I met my parents when I was twenty-five. They had given me up for adoption at birth, and I knew nothing about them. As long as I remember, though, I'd known I was adopted. I never speculated much about my origins. Deep down, I assumed I really had no parents.

When I was twenty-five, then, my birth father hired a private detective and found me where I was then living, in London. He found my birth mother, too: she was still living near him under her maiden name. We began to correspond, and some months later my first husband Amos and I traveled to California to meet them.

People are usually surprised to hear that it was my father who took the initiative, not my mother, and not – as in the lion's share of cases – me, the child. The reason is simple. My father loves family. He is a dogmatic, fervent advocate of family. He comes from a large, close-knit and affluent Jewish family; the kind where there's always some bar mitzvah with a cast of thousands. In Minneapolis, they are *important* – a dynasty which owns a slew of car dealerships, part-owned the football team, sponsors the symphony so amply the conductor dines with them; they are Mayor-grade rich. Once involved with such a family, one is regularly called upon to jet off to some godforsaken Hilton and attend some (birthday, wedding, bar mitzvah) banquet at which there will be dishonest toasts.

As a young man, my father rebelled against that world. It was the sixties; he spent a year in Marrakech, espoused leftish causes, dropped acid. Less sympathetically, he got my mother pregnant and deserted her. At the time I was born, he was living on a kibbutz. He was expelled from that kibbutz, in the middle of the night and violently, for stealing food.

The following year he got another girl pregnant. This time he was in love; he married her. He went back to Minneapolis and took a job in his father's firm.

Soon there were three children. He was a businessman. He created the leasing business for the family's Ford dealerships. Clandestinely, in business meetings, he wrote poems. He published a book of scathing verse about corporate life. Finally he quit and took his family off to California, where he became a dealer in contemporary art.

Since those days, he has divorced and remarried, published one more book of poetry and two novels, and changed profession once more. He now deals in high-end real estate in LA. He buys a whopping great mansion, moves into it, re-models it, and finally sells it for a threefold profit, usually to film industry royalty. In this business and through trading on the stock market, he's become a multimillionaire in his own right.

When I drove out to meet him, he was living in a castle. It was a mock-castle, admittedly, built in the twenties by the gangster Bugsy Siegel. It has ten-story towers and guest wings – it is mammoth. From the top floor, the gardeners on the far lawn appear as ants. There are statues by the pool, there are phones in the lifts – it's a Jack-and-the-Beanstalk house that makes you feel puny and afraid.

It took us some time, driving up and down Mulholland Drive, to find the private road to Dad's Castillo del Lago. It was a neighborhood where Bridget Fonda, Tarantino, Cher-type people lived, and the lawns were marked with signs that threatened 'Armed Response'. The only humans visible were hosts of gardeners – uniformly Hispanic, staring when the car slowed. They labored among palms, blooms, and flashing, pastel sprinkler rainbows. Everything trembled in the sun's downpour.

My husband and I were then living in a squat. We were impoverished students in the style of the day. We knew the quick fixes for shoes; money was for food. We were anarchists, too – as a knee-jerk, eighties, London pretension which boiled down to scorning Mammon and his favorites and his works. Like most such people, we came from the middle class, and the money for this trip was from the recent sale of my husband's small flat in Dalston – an inheritance he intentionally squandered during our brief marriage.

At last we found the drive and keyed in the security code to part the automatic gates. By then, there was a panicked haste, as if we were fleeing some malign gaze. We were bathed in sweat, short-tempered, tired. I remember the door of carved dark oak, the decision not to use the massive knocker. I was the one who pressed the bell – we were laughing about something, in the accord we then had, that of naughty children sneaking to the woods past bedtime. Then my father opened up, a short, dark, baby-faced man, who was the first person I ever saw who looked like me.

In the months after our visit to California, Amos wrote the libretto of an opera. It was called *Cigala* and it took place in my father's castle.

The cigala of the title refers to a fable. The ant is labouring away dutifully through the summer while the cigala sings and plays, laughing at the toils of the ant. Then winter comes along and the cigala is hungry. She goes to the ant's door and begs for food, but the ant rejects her, citing the cigala's carelessness through the fertile months. In Amos's opera, I was Cigala. My father appeared in it as an ego-crazed tycoon paterfamilias, married to someone based not on his real wife but on Amos's mother.

The action was solidly scurrilous, including sex scenes between myself and my father, and between the mother and her chihuahua. Amos appeared as my brother, who bore an incestuous love for me. He and I were continually being spied on by a stooge of my father's named Snitch. The house itself was bugged and filled with surveillance cameras which my father used in order to control the activities of the inhabitants, and especially to make sure that Amos and I could not have sex. What spoke through the play was idealistic, heartfelt detestation – not of my father or Amos's mother, but of family in general. In *Cigala*, family was grotesque, a parody, a lie.

My birth mother and I have never cared for family. She has no other children. I have none myself. If she has been to visit her sisters, she might comment, 'I got through it.'

I met my mother, Sally, for the first time in a coach station. I had never seen a photo of her, and I realized as I entered the waiting room that I had no way of recognizing my own mother. Still we walked up to each other unerringly and started talking. We talked through the night and through the following days. She was right away my favourite person.

Sally traveled through Europe pregnant with me: she was wild then. In Israel she ran out of money and was taken in by kindly strangers. Her hatred of her middle-class Lutheran upbringing was such that she tried to give me up for adoption in Jerusalem, but was foiled by the Israeli insistence that both parents be proven Jewish.

After I was born, she became a sixties radical. Because she used to practice shooting as a young girl, at Berkeley she ran workshops teaching women how to use guns, preparing them to fight in the coming revolution. Nowadays she works for NASA as a crew trainer, coaching astronauts to perform experiments in microgravity. She lives in a shack-style house in the redwood forest. By chance or telepathy or odd genetic leaning, Mom and I both studied Russian at university. Once she took me on a business trip to Moscow: I met the cosmonauts. Like me, she always has some boyfriend. Like me, she is sloppy; she'll let some toothless homeless guy room in her shed; she solves her money troubles, which are legion, by the ostrich method.

This essay will not be about her. Since she's not a problem for me, there's no conflict, a staple of narrative. We've always had an equal, loving friendship. My father, on the other hand, has always been a problem, a Kafkaesque Papa, a Fortunate One. My relationship with him has been adversarial, a battle over what it means to be his child.

Once, in the early days of our knowing each other, we were passionately arguing on the balcony of his mansion, when I realized that I was late for my flight. We jumped into his Mustang convertible and sped away. We drove in silence, both disturbed by the fight before. As we approached some train tracks, the barriers began to come down, and the lights flashed, signaling an oncoming train. My father floored it, and the car made it under the barrier just in time, flying into the air as it cleared the tracks.

In that argument, he said for the first time that he loved me just the same as his other children. I will say right now that I do not love him as his other children love him. I may love him as much. But the scene I have outlined is not a father–daughter scene. It is pure Hollywood and plain romantic.

I don't know to what degree it's appropriate for a father–daughter relationship to be a romance. I know on two occasions, my father has introduced me to strangers as his wife, and has had to correct himself hastily. It's not a sexual attraction – not on my side, and I am certain not on his. But a long-lost father is not just a father but a mythical character, halfway to a *prince*. We met when I was twenty-six, and no goodwill can alter that. Despite our best efforts, the words 'father' and 'daughter' with us wear inverted commas. We've grown close, but it's a matter of *how* and *how much*.

Of course, we are both writers. We talk about our writing projects and about books. My father is an egghead avant-garde writer whose most recent work is 1,500 pages long. It is supplemented by large public projects – including the construction of a pyramid outside LA. A geologist is working for him, finding a point deep in the earth which will come to the surface in roughly 100,000 years: when this is found, my father plans to bury there a super-durable, ball-shaped copy of the Ten Commandments, to be a puzzle to future generations. He is the liberal arts equivalent of a mad scientist. He does the things that my bored friends and I in college once imagined we would do, if we just had a million dollars.

On the other hand, socially, he is conservative. Much of the 1,500 pages of his opus is concerned with the modern decline in manners. He complains that people no longer dress to go out; young people don't defer to elders; crass ignorance is normal. In all these respects but the last, I have offended him. Time and again, I am, by his lights, rude. He sees me as a roughneck, his lost child raised by wolves.

We also clash over traits I share with my mother. My father gives impatient advice about my money problems, hints that my current shiftless boyfriend ought to go – counsels me, in short, that I should be a different person. Every single time, he reduces me to tears.

These are the problems people typically have with parents. But one complaint my father has with me is unusual. His opinion is that I do not know how to be intimate. He places the blame for this on my adoptive parents.

If I don't like family, there is naturally a reason. My adopted family was – as the euphemism goes – dysfunctional. My mother first attempted suicide when I was nine. Our family thereafter centered on her migraines, her depression – our group project was keeping mother alive. At dinner, Dad, my brother, Jeff, and I sat in anxious silence while Mom gave updates on her mood, chronicled the side effects of her medication, weighed the pros and cons of another hospitalization.

There were nine suicide attempts in four years. Coming home, I'd open the front door and listen. My heart would race until I heard her footsteps. She killed herself once and for all when I was thirteen.

Then my family turned into pure aftermath. My father did nothing but eat snacks and watch television. He had no friends, the phone was never for him. His hobby was his pornographic video collection. Jeff and I stopped talking to each other altogether; we didn't speak for twenty years. We had a three-story house, and after Mom's death, Dad, Jeff, and I each took a floor. My status in the family meant that I got the basement.

I left America at eighteen, and stayed away for eighteen years. As a student in London, I took the hypocritical course of accepting money from my adopted father while thinking of him as an old friend I had outgrown. He was good for what he was, but he was not my father, and that wasn't a family, and I had no home.

He died young, like my adopted mother – leaving all his money to his second wife, a drug addict and gold digger thirty years his junior. And there was nothing to salvage from my parents' wreckage, no redemption. All they had to give their children was mourning. As far as intimacy goes, they taught us how to live without.

When Joe, a Massachusetts acquaintance of mine, was sixteen, one day he started rowing with his father in the street. It was a hackneyed father–son spat; the theme, 'You can't control me.' But Joe is an adopted child: he is black and his father white. Police spotted big Joe shouting at a white man and tackled him from behind.

Already angry, Joe responded to the sudden attack by fighting wildly. He broke one policeman's finger and another's ribs. They beat him to a pulp, it was, he says 'full-on Rodney King.' They emptied two cans of mace in his eyes. Once it had started, his desperate father could do nothing. Joe was arrested and faced charges of assault on a police officer and resisting arrest.

As almost never happens with the Massachusetts State Police, the story has a happy ending. The police agreed to drop all charges if Joe's father did not sue them. And a few months later, at some local fair, Joe spotted one of the cops who maced him, in a boxing ring, offering to take on all comers for a donation to some police fund. Joe was in the ring in a second. There was some controversy over whether to allow the boy to fight: he was so young, he might be injured, it was unfair. The cop made comic remarks to the crowd about the kid's slim chances. Then the fight went forward. Joe knocked him out flat.

On the face of it, this is a simple tale of wrongs righted. But it also speaks to me, in a more literary strain, of the relationship between adopted children and parents. The parent in the story *cannot protect* the child. And in some way, this is because the child is not his. The child must redress his own wrongs, take on the cops alone. At the end of the story he has beaten the adversary, has defended his right to act as if he has a father. But his father has faded from the story. He triumphs alone.

An adopted child is really a wolf raised by humans. We are love children, bastards, unrespectable by blood. The world has *chosen* to raise us, from the goodness of its heart. The world is under no obligation. We are not its kin.

Letting this cut both ways, though, the injunction to *honour thy father and mother* applies to us only if we choose those terms. We can create our own code, born with no boss. Our parents never gave us life. Our lives are like something found lying in the street. And in our old age, we will not turn into our parents – we are truly, defiantly, one of a kind. We may become monsters, angels, something new under the sun. And ours is the world of magic, fairy tales and legend; from Thumbelina to Dorothy of Oz down to Jesus, mythical figures don't have parents.

In the *Superman* comics, the adopted child Superman loses his powers when confronted with kryptonite, the rock from his planet. His home soil makes him average – on Krypton, Superman is nobody. Family is a kryptonite that robs us all of strength. It may be because your family disapproves of your profession, politics, or spouse. It may be because they have a fixed idea of you; you are lazy, hysterical, your brother is the smart one. When I see my family, I shrink and suffer, paradoxically, because I am an orphan.

It was always my father's hope that I would become a real member of his family. 'I love you just the same as my other children' – the statement's naked untruth makes it no less intoxicating, impossible to happily dismiss. My siblings also try to include me. I was maid of honour at my sister's wedding though we've only met on a handful of occasions. Blood relatives at random (grandfather, uncle, half brother) will sometimes state in no uncertain terms that they love me. This generally has a boy scout ring to it; the self-regarding tone of someone's good deed for the day.

Because my brothers and sister were raised together by my father, they share a history and culture that are strange to me. They are, above all and unmentionably, rich kids. When the family comes together, the talk is *their* old times, *their* childhood home, *their* dead pets. I am welcome to observe, most of the time.

At my father's last birthday, my half siblings asked me if I wanted to go in on a present for Dad: they were buying him a grove of trees in Israel. When I was a child, they used to hawk these Israeli trees in synagogue; you'd buy one to be planted there to green the desert. The symbolic value, of course, was paramount. It was a pledge of faith in the state of Israel. In this case, I worried that abstaining from the present would seem like a pledge of faith in Palestine – it was an issue on which my Dad and I had clashed. Still, as I'd already bought a present, I declined.

When my father opened the card telling him that my brothers and sister had bought him that grove of trees, he burst into genuine sobs of emotion. Immediately I felt like a baffled visitor from Mars. I felt sympathy for the people but I was not of them. And I felt painfully exposed; they knew I was not of them. At that private moment, I thought, how they must have wished I'd leave them alone.

That was not a moment to indulge my feelings. But at my own birthday dinner it was the same. My family lounged around the table discussing their past, their old family home, the good times they'd had. There is no blame involved, and they are doing just what anyone would do, and they mean well, I think. (Sometimes, of course, I think the lot of them are monsters. Because my new family do not ask about my old adopted family ever. And I suspect if my adopted family were not so *dysfunctional* (tragic),

I might mention them. If they were rich. If they were, like my real family, each gifted in his way, charismatic, knowledgeable about architects, artists, poets of the T'ang. If we'd had those Chuck Close paintings, Robert Frank photographs, et al, hanging in our family home, and if that were a castle.

My old, adopted family were working-class-made-good. They were average till they turned tragic (squalid). And I do myself no favors (I believe I read sometimes on my new, monster family's faces) by alluding to these low connections. But this is just in my (squalid, low-class) head. I think.

Still, growing close to them was a long, painful process of discovering what I was missing and could never have.

And sometimes they seem like so many paper dolls, hands joined eternally, meaningless. Standing in a circle, smiling only at each other, they will use their wealth to make a world where my kind can be silenced. Sometimes I believe all these same things I painfully believed when I was twenty, when I read Foucault and hated all establishments. But now it is my father, literally, who excludes me. My sister and brothers, all these people who have my face and thus no face.

The Fortunate Ones, in the final play of the *Oresteia* trilogy, are made to relinquish their claim on Orestes, a matricide and therefore rightfully their prey. The concluding act consists of a legal mediation in which a new role is defined for the Furies. They are to be sidelined, made toothless, shoved into the background in a fuzzy role as guardians of the city. The Athenians will honor them on certain occasions: when celebrating a marriage or the birth of a child. 'Our powers are overthrown,' the Furies lament, but go finally into the cave Athena chooses for their new abode.

Orestes goes free.

In the end, of course, we just grow up. We walk out of the theater and a whole world is going on outside. Although your family may be as tragic, squalid and grotesque as Agamemnon's, no one cares. In many ways, I've just joined the family of man in being in thrall to a disappointing family. Like all the rest, I go 'home' with a sinking heart and come away obsessive, boring people by repeating conversations with my Dad. I am angry for days. I nurse trivial grudges. I am needlessly hurt. I go for *certain occasions*: a marriage, the birth of a child, a bar mitzvah. And sometimes I, too, become a Fortunate One, my face blanked by a smile of doped, blood-intoxicated love.

MERELY INFORMATION

Martin Rowson

I was meeting my brother for a drink. He was early, and by the time I arrived he was already getting drunk. I was annoyed at first, but decided to stick with it. This was, after all, the first time we'd ever met.

He had travelled to London specially to see me, after his aircraft carrier, the USS *Enterprise*, had anchored off Portsmouth that morning. A year earlier I had not even known of his existence. His name, like mine, is Martin and, in a strange way, I felt that I had met him before.

In 1997, after years of doing nothing about the fact that I was adopted, I finally applied to see my original birth certificate. I discovered that my mother's name was Kathleen Ann Gould, and that she had named me Martin. Martin Gould. I came away from that meeting with the social worker who gave me my birth certificate feeling very strange, conscious of an almost physical presence beside me in the car. That was Martin Gould – the other Martin, my spectral doppelgänger, another me with an entirely alternative thirty-eight years of life behind him. His presence dogged me for another day, then began to fade.

My brother Martin tells me that that was him (despite my strong sense that it was, in fact, an alternative me). He is two-and-a-half years younger than me, and now bears his father's surname, but on his original birth certificate he was Martin Gould, too, and had believed he was the only Martin Gould until very recently.

Apart, however, from a few persistent gobbets of self-generated ectoplasm, for another three years I knew nothing about Martin Gould aside from his (and my) mother's name and that he (and I) had been adopted through the Church Adoption Society. I had made a few attempts to find out about Kathleen or the Church Adoption Society, but in both cases I drew a blank. So, with some regret, I let things lie. Then, early in 2001, I contacted the Children's Society, which told me that the Church Adoption Society had changed its name too, to Childlink. I called them, but was told that their offices were being rebuilt and they couldn't tell me anything until May.

In the intervening years, I had become more acquainted with death than with the circumstances of my birth. In October 1998 a very good friend died suddenly of a heart attack. Then my much-loved father-in-law died on Christmas Day 1999. And in May 2000, Jon, who had been my best friend when we were seventeen, died of a brain tumour. I spoke at all three funerals and was increasingly conscious that this accumulation of grief was driving me mad.

I was becoming obsessed with death. My adoptive mother had died of a brain disease when I was ten; now Jon had left behind a little boy the same age that I had been. Your friends, it is said, are the family you choose. My friends' deaths left me no room to entertain thoughts of my birth mother . . . until, finally, I received a letter from Childlink, asking me to contact them as a matter of urgency.

So, on a suffocatingly hot day in June 2001, I found myself at their office. The meeting started uneasily. My case worker seemed rather overexcited. I found this somewhat irksome as one of the first things she told me was that my mother Kathleen was dead.

I felt my lower lip tremble slightly, and I had to remind myself that I should be getting used to this kind of thing by now. Then she handed me a sheaf of yellowing documents concerning my adoption, including a series of reports to the Board of Moral Trustees at the Church Adoption Society and several letters to and from my mother.

It had always been a piece of gossip in my adoptive family (I always knew that I had been adopted) that I had two older siblings but that my natural grandparents had not been prepared to rear a third bastard. Likewise, I had always been told that my mother was an electrical engineer with the Post Office – in fact, she was a technical assistant with the Central Electricity Generating Board – and that my father was a Canadian architect. Reading those 41-year-old records, I learned that I really did have an older brother and sister, named Andrew and Alison. I discovered, too, that my father was named Edward Burden. He had indeed been a Canadian architecture student; he had not been prepared to marry my mother.

One of the forms told me that neither of my parents harboured any Jewish, Negro or Irish blood (this was written in 1959). Another report said that Kathleen loved me and was very upset about having to give me up. The report went on: 'Kathleen promises me that this kind of thing will never happen again, but she does admit that she finds it very hard to remain celibate.' My case worker asked me how I felt. I replied, honestly, that my overwhelming emotion was sadness, for myself but also for Kathleen. I said that I doubted I'd make any effort to contact my older brother and sister. And that, I supposed, was that.

But there was more. I was told that I had a younger sister, Jan, of whom I had been quite unaware until that morning, and she'd left a letter on my file. Also adopted, she had started searching a couple of years previously.

The reason for the social worker's excitement was that never before in her experience had siblings, adopted by different families, found each other in this manner. And there was more still. After my sister Jan's adoption, Kathleen had become pregnant a fifth time. (This child was the other Martin.) This time, however, the father, an American serviceman, had married her and taken her back to California. There, they had had another six sons.

Suddenly, I had ten brothers and sisters. This time, when the social worker asked me how I felt, I replied that for the first time in months I felt wonderful. After so many painful goodbyes, from my adoptive mother's death onwards, I found myself looking forward to an almost embarrassing number of unexpected hellos. It is a cliché that adopted people don't feel quite complete, but clichés are clichés mostly because they're true. I now felt strangely complete.

Two weeks later, I spoke to Jan. After she had placed her letter on my file, she and her husband had been posted by the RAF to Cyprus. Childlink suggested that I should write first, but they also gave me her number in Cyprus. After staring at it for five minutes, I finally thought, 'Fuck it: life's too short,' and rang her.

'You've taken your bloody time!' Her response immediately confirmed she was my sister. We spoke for five hours as she told me about herself, her life, all the things she'd discovered in her searches and the contacts she'd made with our lost family. Because she had been privately adopted, she had had no access to any of the information I received by legal right. It was only because she had done so much hard work in recent years that I was able to know so much so quickly.

Then, we met and – rapidly dispatching as irrelevant the fact that she is a Christian Tory and I am not – we got on very well. We have a similar sense of humour (as does Martin) and, disconcertingly, similar gestures and patterns of speech. And she looks just like my daughter Rose.

Shortly after receiving my birth certificate, but before I discovered anything else, I was at a cartoon festival in Ireland. It was late at night and I found myself being attacked by a young Irishwoman for perpetuating English oppression of the Irish by daring to draw cartoons for an Irish paper. I listened for about half an hour before saying, simply, 'My birth mother's name was Kathleen Gould.'

'Oh, well,' replied the young woman, 'that's all right, then. You're Irish!' Except that, according to those worthy eugenicists at the adoption society, I'm not.

If my name does not define my identity, what does? By the lights of those same, perfectly well-intentioned people who, pursuing a policy of moral and social engineering, coerced generations of unmarried women into giving up their babies, I am a success. (A generation before I was born, unmarried mothers were still being locked away in mental hospitals, because their moral delinquency defined them as mad.) In this view, I have been redeemed from the original sin of illegitimacy by being brought up and loved by a respectable middle-class family who chose me and invested in me, and whom I will always repay with love and gratitude.

But I don't speak with the same accent as any member of my family I've met, acquired or genetic. Nor do I have the same politics as either my biological or adoptive families. None of them, so far as I know, draws like me or thinks in the lateral ways that a political cartoonist must.

Then again, I know practically nothing about my father. But if I did, I'm not sure it would make any difference. I was never looking for an alternative happy family. I had all I needed from the family that chose me and the family that I, later on, chose and love. What I wanted was information – some way to account for that niggling and persistent sense of a lack of completion.

This is the undercurrent that made me burst into tears recently when reading my children the end of *Tom's Midnight Garden*. When the child hero finally meets, as a ghost from the future, the old lady he had played with when she was a little girl, I think with sadness of Kathleen, giving me up to those well-intentioned and legally sanctioned child-abductors. I wonder whether all her subsequent children were not in some way compensating for that loss (first with the second Martin, and then with the last four sons who, says Martin, were each an attempt to get a daughter).

But was Kathleen herself sad? After all, she ended up in California, where, famously, people go to reinvent themselves. If she had been alive when Jan and I re-emerged, would she have welcomed us? Or would she have been horrified at this intrusion into her remade life?

We will never know, and I can only speculate. No one can change the past, and what I've discovered so far is never going to alter retrospectively the previous course of my life. Those other mes – the one who stayed with his mother (obviating the need for another Martin); and the one who lived in California becoming someone entirely different – these are merely the ghosts of what might have been.

If I underwent a catharsis that year, it was because of the information. Just knowing is a tool that helps me make more sense, however little, of why I'm the me I am. The legacy of adoption affects everyone differently; often there is the intensified sadness of failed reunions and compounded rejection. Having been denied the opportunity to be welcomed or rejected, Jan and I have very different attitudes to the mother who either abandoned us or gave us up with regret. Whatever her motivation or her character, all I know for certain is that my unknown mother is now unknowable.

A year after finding out about my siblings, in addition to Martin and Jan, I met another of the brothers who were brought up by my birth mother in California, John, who also serves in the American armed forces, and I spoke at length to my older brother, Andrew, who was formerly in the US Army. I didn't point out to any of them that the only circumstances in which I can imagine a lefty member of the chattering media classes having anything to do with an American serviceman is for sex, as I wasn't certain that we share the same irony gene.

When I told my adoptive parents, my father and my stepmother, about finding my siblings, their reaction was, as usual, supportive, although I think that my father felt more misgivings than he let on. That said, when he was in hospital briefly in December 2003, during one of the long, rambling, vaguely philo-sophical conversations we enjoyed, I told him how grateful I was that I'd been brought up by him and under his influence, rather than slugging it out with my ten siblings in a small house in California. I'm glad I raised it, as I once again became over-acquainted with death and grief the following year. In January 2004 my father died suddenly of a pulmonary embolism and through the ghastliness of my grief I felt, at least, that we'd left nothing unsaid, that we had no unfinished business. At his funeral I gave an address describing his achievements, his life, and, most of all, his wonderfully sceptical, amused take on that life, and how it had influenced me and my choice of profession so deeply. As I said at the time, another quiet little triumph of nurture over nature.

Three and a half months later, my stepmother – who'd been married to my father for thirty-one years, who'd previously been my godmother, and who'd been the ward sister in the hospital where my adoptive mother gave birth to a son, Christopher, whose death led my parents to adopt me and my older sister – died of cancer. She knew she was dying – expected, indeed, to go before my father – and after he died very much wanted to die herself, which she did with a neat dispatch which was absolutely typical of her. She was tough, and faced the end with immense, and immensely tough, dignity. I spoke at her funeral, too, and afterwards one of her cousins confided to me that we'd met when I was a baby, although I didn't know it. It seems that it was my stepmother who'd picked me up from the Mother and Baby home and taken me in a taxi to my new parents' home, and cousin Gwyneth had accompanied my stepmother and held me in her arms for most of the journey.

These were the people I'd lived my life with, who, despite all the genetic legacies, made me who I am. Since I discovered my 'real' family, I've had very little contact with them, and all of us seem quite happy with that (although I suspect that my sister Jan considers me a pretty useless instant family), and although I have absolutely no regrets about uncovering my origins – as I said above, it provided that missing jigsaw piece which made me suddenly feel whole – I also believe that my adoptive parents, my father, my mother and my stepmother, were my real 'real' parents, and that what really counts is not what you are, but who you are. The rest is merely information.

UNCLE ELWOOD

Paula Fox

The Reverend Elwood Amos Corning, the Congregational minister who took care of me in my infancy and earliest years and whom I called Uncle Elwood, always saw to it that I didn't look down and out. Twice a year, in the spring and fall, he bought a few things for me to wear, spending what he could from the yearly salary paid to him by his church. Other clothes came my way donated by the mothers in his congregation whose own children had outgrown them. They were mended, washed, and ironed before they were handed on.

In early April, before my fifth birthday, my father mailed Uncle Elwood two five-dollar bills and a written note. I can see him reading the note as he holds it and the bills in one hand, while with the index finger of the other he presses the bridge of his eyeglasses against his nose because he has broken the sidepiece. This particularity of memory can be partly attributed to the rarity of my father's notes – not to mention enclosures of money – or else to the new dress that part of the ten dollars paid for. Or so I imagine.

The next morning Uncle Elwood drove me in his old Packard from the Victorian house on the hill in Balmville, New York, where we lived, to Newburgh, a valley town half an hour distant and a dozen miles north of the Storm King promontory, which sinks into the Hudson River like an elephant's brow.

We parked on Water Street in front of a barbershop where I was taken at intervals to have my hair cut. One morning after we had left the shop, and because I was lost in reverie, staring down at the sidewalk but not seeing it, I reached up to take Uncle Elwood's hand and walked nearly a block before I realized I was holding the hand of a stranger. I let go and turned around and saw that everyone who was on the street was waiting to see how far I would go and what I would do when I looked up. Watching were both barbers from their shop doorway, Uncle Elwood with his hands clasped in front of him, three or four people on their way somewhere, and the stranger whose hand I had been holding. They were all smiling in anticipation of my surprise. For a moment the street was transformed into a familiar room in a beloved house. Still, I was faintly alarmed and ran back to Uncle Elwood.

Our destination that day was Schoonmaker's department store, next to the barbershop. When we emerged back on the sidewalk, he was carrying a box that contained a white dotted-swiss dress. It had a Peter Pan collar and fell straight to its hem from a smocked yoke.

Uncle Elwood had written a poem for me to recite at the Easter service in the church where he preached. Now I would have something new to wear, something in which I could stand before the congregation and speak his words. I loved him, and I loved the dotted-swiss dress.

Years later, when I read through the few letters and notes my father had written to Uncle Elwood, and which he had saved, I realized how Daddy had played the coquette in his apologies for his remissness in supporting me. His excuses were made with a kind of fraudulent heartiness, as though he were boasting, not confessing. His handwriting, though, was beautiful, an orderly flight of birds across the yellowing pages.

*

Uncle Elwood made parish visits most Sundays in Washington-ville, at that time still small enough to be called a village, in Orange County, New York, seventeen miles from Balmville, where most members of his congregation lived. The church where he preached was in Blooming Grove, a hamlet a mile or so west of Washingtonville, on a high ridge above a narrow country lane, and so towering – it appeared to me – it could have been a massive white ship anchored there, except for its steeple, which rose toward the heavens like prayerful hands, palms pressed together.

Behind it stood an empty manse and, farther away, a small cemetery. To the right of the church portal was a partly col-lapsed stable with dark cobwebbed stalls, one of which was still used by a single parishioner, ancient bearded Mr. Howell, who drove his buckboard and horse up the gravel-covered road that led to the church. He always arrived a minute or two before Sunday service began, dressed in a threadbare black overcoat in all seasons of the year, its collar held tight to his throat by a big safety pin. He seemed to me that rock of ages we sang about in the hymn.

After the service, we sometimes called upon two women, an elderly woman and her unmarried daughter, who looked as old as her mother, both in the church choir, whose thin soprano quavers continued long past the moment when other choir members had ceased to sing and had resumed their seats. They appeared not to notice they were the only people still standing in the choir stall.

They lived in a narrow wooden two-story house that resem-bled most of the other houses in Washingtonville. They would give us Sunday dinner in a back room that ran the width of the house and could accommodate a table large enough for the four of us. It was a distance from the kitchen, where they usually ate their meals, and there was much to-ing and fro-ing as they brought dishes and took them away, adding, it felt to me, years of waiting to the minutes when we actually ate. Summer heat bore down on that back room. It was stifling, hot as burning kindling under the noonday sun. Everything flashed and glittered – cutlery, water glasses, window panes – and drained the food of color.

When we visited Emma Board and her family in another part of the village, I felt a kind of happiness and, at the same time, an apprehension – like that of a traveler who returns to a country where she has endured inexplicable suffering.

I had arrived at the Boards' house when I was two months old, brought there by Katherine, the eldest of four Board children. She had taken me to Virginia on her brief honeymoon with Russell, her new husband. When they returned, her mother was sufficiently recovered from Spanish influenza to take care of an infant.

I heard the tale decades later from Brewster, one of Katherine's two brothers, who had lived in New York City with Leopold, one of my mother's four brothers. I had been left in a Manhattan foundling home a few days after my birth by my reluctant father, and by Elsie, my mother, panic-stricken and ungovernable in her haste to have done with me.

My grandmother, Candelaria, during a brief visit to New York City from Cuba, where she lived on a sugar plantation most of the year, inquired of Leopold the whereabouts of his sister and the baby she knew had been born a few weeks earlier. He said he didn't know where my parents had gone, but that over his objections they had placed me in a foundling home before leaving town – if indeed they had left.

When she heard where I was, my grandmother went at once to the home and took me away. But what could she do with me? She was obliged to return to Cuba within days. For a small monthly stipend, she served as companion to a rich old cousin, the plantation owner, who was subject to fits of lunacy.

It was Brewster who suggested she hand me over to Katherine, who carried me in her arms on her bridal journey to Norfolk.

By chance, by good fortune, I had landed in the hands of res-cuers, a fire brigade that passed me along from person to person until I was safe. When we visited the old woman and her daugh-ter, or any other of the minister's parishioners, I was diffident and self-conscious for the first few minutes. But not ever at the Boards'.

For a very short period of my infancy, I had belonged in that house with that family. At some moment during our visits there, I would go down the cellar steps and see if a brown rattan baby buggy and a creaking old crib, used at one time or another by all the Board children and for three months by me, were still stored there. I think the family kept them so I would always find them.

I was five months old when the minister, hearing of my pres-ence in Washingtonville and the singular way I had arrived, an event that had ruffled the nearly motionless, pondlike surface of village life – and knowing the uncertainty of my future, for the Boards, like most of their neighbors in those years, were poor – came by one Sunday to look at me. I was awake in the crib. I might have smiled up at him. In any event, I aroused his interest and compassion. He offered to take me, and, partly due to their straitened circumstances, the Boards agreed to let me go.

After he finished his sermon, Uncle Elwood would step aside from the pulpit. As the choir rose to sing, he would clasp his hands and gaze down at me where I sat alone in a front pew. There would be the barest suggestion of a smile on his face, a lightening of his Sunday look of solemnity.

The intimacy of those moments between us would give way when a church deacon passed a collection plate among the con-gregation, now hushed by an upwelling sense of the sacred that followed a reading of Bible verse. When he reached my pew, I would drop in a coin given me earlier by Uncle Elwood.

Later, when I stood beside him at the church portal while people filed out and shook his hand, and old Mr. Howell hurried by, mumbling his thanks for the sermon in a rusty, hollow voice, the feeling of intimacy returned.

I was known to the congregation as the minister's little girl, and thinking of that, I was always gladdened. I turned to him after Mr. Howell had vanished into the stable, noting as I usually did the formality of his preaching clothes, the pearl stickpin in his black and silver tie, a silken stripe running down the side of the black trousers, the beetle-winged tails of his black jacket.

It was like the Sunday a week earlier, and all the Sundays I could recall. I slipped my hand into his, and he clasped it firmly. I watched Mr. Howell, who had backed his buckboard and horse out of the stable and was starting down the road.

My unquestioning trust in Uncle Elwood's love, and in the refuge he had provided for me in the years since Katherine had taken me to her mother, would abruptly collapse. In an instant, I realized the precariousness of my circumstances. I felt the earth crumble beneath my feet. I tottered on the edge of an abyss. If I fell, I knew I would fall forever.

That happened, too, every Sunday after church. But it lasted no longer than it takes to describe it.

PARENTS

BIRTH MOTHERS

LINDA

Paula Fox

When I was two weeks away from my twenty-first birthday, I gave birth to a daughter. During my pregnancy, I had gone to an agency for financial help, Native Sons of California. A beefy-faced man looked at my swelling belly and said, pointing to a bench, 'Sit down, dear. You'll have a long wait.'

After a while, I got up and left. My labor lasted a day and a night. In the San Francisco hospital where I went for my confinement, babies were brought into the ward in their wheeled cribs. From the corridor just outside, two nurses looked in at me. I heard one of them say, 'Not her.'

I must have been on a low floor, because I could see, through a window near my bed, the branch of a tree, leaves, a small bird. All the women around me nursed their infants. I had put my daughter up for adoption.

Ten days later, I went to see one of the doctors who had been an intermediary in the adoption and asked for her back. The doctor told me it was legally too late. I didn't know any better, so I accepted his lie as truth. I had asked a second doctor who was involved in the adoption to find a Jewish family to take her. I guess to comfort me, he said jovially, 'He travels fastest who travels alone.' The world is filled with empty phrases. He hadn't even gotten the gender right, and he didn't get the family right. They were middle-aged Sicilians.

Many years later, Linda found me. One Saturday I received a thick FedEx envelope. I was sitting in my kitchen when I opened it. There was a handwritten note on the top of a letter, and it said, 'Go slow.'

I knew at once. I called up the stairs to my husband, 'She's found me.'

We wrote every day for three months, sometimes twice a day, telling, telling, telling.

We didn't speak on the telephone during that time. We both understood that our communication was to be written. She suggested we meet somewhere, perhaps Santa Fe, New Mexico, where, if we got bored with each other, there would be other sights to see.

I suggested San Francisco, where we had been parted. She agreed. Her assistant telephoned me to make arrangements, and I flew there one day in mid-May.

When the airplane was a few hundred yards from the ground, I wished it would crash. In the face of great change, one has no conscience.

It was eleven-thirty and a clear day in San Francisco. I walked off the plane and into the airport waiting room. I hadn't gone more than a few feet when I heard running steps behind me. I turned to look at the woman who was doing the running. We both laughed at the same time. We walked so closely together, I could feel her breath on my face.

'Have you got a cigarette?' she asked me. 'I quit yesterday,' she added.

I gave her one. 'Let's go in there,' I suggested, pointing to an airport bar we were about to pass.

We spent two hours drinking soda, talking. I found her beautiful. She was the first woman related to me I could speak to freely.

I have had splendid close friendships with women, beginning with Bernice in elementary school. What I had missed all the years of my life, up to the time when Linda and I met, was freedom of a certain kind: to speak without fear to a woman in my family.

We went to a hotel where we spent four days together, most of the time in the hotel, like lovers. We had separate rooms and we left notes under each other's doors. She told me she had wondered about who I was all her life. She had guessed I might be Marilyn Monroe, or a murderous old woman she had seen once on a bus.

We spent one of the days in what felt like an eternal traffic jam, headed toward Carmel. When silence fell between us, there was no tension.

She asked me again about her father – she'd written me that question.

I told her that the day her first letter had reached me I had called him up in Los Angeles, where he had lived for many years. His widow informed me that he had died a few months earlier. What did I want with him? the widow asked. I was an old friend, I said. I had yielded to him once one evening, rather gracelessly.

Linda and I went to the street where I had lived when I had been pregnant. I had rented a room on Telegraph Hill in a two-story building that was the only house left there from the forties.

We sat on the curb and looked up at two dark windows. I told Linda how a black friend had carried me to the bathroom the first day I had come home from the hospital, after she had been born.

I'll leave us there, sitting close together on the curb. Now and then someone passed by but paid no attention to us as we told each other stories from our lives, falling silent every so often.

MEN AND FISH

Lise Saffran

Men lie about fish. Catherine knew it better than anybody. During salmon season, which ran from April until October, she probably got more calls from men than any single other woman in Marin County. They called to tell her about the bait they used, the fish they snagged and the fish they didn't. She wrote the 'Hooked' column for the *Bay Journal* and the men called hoping to see their names in print.

She could tell they liked her, too, and keeping things in perspective, she liked some of them back. The older anglers, dressed alike in scruffy caps and cable-knit sweaters, put their arms around her and called her 'M'dear.' An unmarried 36-year-old woman who liked to fish was a rare joy, a daughter who had not yet deserted them for some cocky asshole who knew about computers.

The young guys called her Cath and appeared not to notice that she was a woman at all. Which was fine. She enjoyed sex with men, it wasn't that, and she knew she was good-looking in a big-ankled, wide-featured sort of way. It was just that the men she chose for boyfriends were guys like Lenny, married already with a couple kids and no desire to have any more with her. Men, she admitted to herself, whom she could despise a little.

Lenny was waiting for her at the Cantina when she got there

at four; he was sipping a Margarita and arranging the packaged sweeteners according to color. An interventional radiologist at Marin General, he was smart and nervous and, Catherine guessed, spectacularly bad with patients. They had met one morning on a party boat fishing for salmon. Before they had even cleared the Golden Gate he had worn himself out with grueling descriptions of nights on call, hours and hours of reading films, not to mention the psychological stress of having someone's life in your hands. His wife was a doctor, too, and when calls came in the middle of the night they would lie awake after and discuss possible outcomes.

'And then the girls get up and begin running around the house. Tearing things apart. We've had maybe three hours of sleep at the max at this point. It's insane. Every day is like this. Except for the days when it's worse. The dishwasher breaks down. Or the painters come to do the front room.'

'Or you spend a couple hours on a Tuesday morning with a view of the Marin Headlands shrouded in fog,' said Catherine. She was on the verge of giving up her comfortable seat and joining one of the deckhands at the rail.

Lenny was tall, with light hair cut so short he looked bald. The lack of contrast made his blue eyes appear even brighter in his thin face; like the rest of him, they were never still. At Catherine's words, he had the grace to glance at the hills and look sheepish. 'We do get a number of vacation days. That is one thing we do get.'

When he hooked a salmon he yelled, 'Oh man, oh man, oh, oh, oh,' with such unself-conscious delight that even the crew, who was paid as much to ignore the idiocies of the guests as to man the boat and clean the fish, had to laugh.

Catherine helped him net his catch and bought him a beer after, to celebrate.

He called her at the paper the next week to ask her out for another beer. The one beer had turned into two and then sex at her apartment on the couch. They had slept together a total of seven times now, always at Happy Hour. He talked about his kids and his colleagues and, rarely, his wife. Never his patients. Except for vague references to procedures, she had no idea what brought them in to the hospital.

He still complained a lot but by this time she knew that it was a kind of secret charm to keep his own good fortune from running out. To fool the gods in case they were watching. On days when she teased him about it and he laughed she guessed that perhaps one of his patients had gotten better. Sometimes he just shook his head and chewed his hangnails and at those times she wondered if maybe one of them had taken a turn for the worse or perhaps died. She respected his boundaries, though. She had her own.

For example, Lenny knew that she had grown up in the Midwest, that she broke out in hives whenever she ate beef and that she liked to make love in cars. He knew she was self-conscious about her hips and tried to choose clothes that made her shoulders seem broader; he had even brought her a colorful scarf once, as a gift. He had no idea that she had a son.

'I can't stay long today,' he said as soon as she sat down.

'Hey, Len.'

'Hey. Do you want the rest of my drink? I really can't stay long.'

'I want my own.'

'OK. Yeah. Of course.' He waved his hand toward a girl wearing a ruffled skirt and a paper flower pinned to her blouse. 'Another Margarita.'

'No,' said Catherine. 'I'll have Tequila. Straight up with a lime.'

Lenny chewed a hangnail on his thumb.

Catherine leaned back in her chair and sighed. 'Salt's on the table,' she said.

'What?'

'For my drink. I thought you might be concerned.'

'We can't do this anymore,' he said. He touched the Sweet and

Low lightly with the tip of his finger, as if to make sure that it was still in its proper place. 'Things are crazy for me right now. Just nuts. Virginia's partners are pressuring her to go back on call.' He sneaked a glance at her when he said his wife's name. 'I've got cases up to here. The contractor quit in the middle of the counters.'

Into Catherine's mind flashed the image of a guy in overalls standing on Lenny's granite counter tops and throwing his tools down in disgust. She almost laughed.

'I'm sorry, Catherine. I really am.'

She stared back coolly, wishing her Tequila would arrive. 'Don't worry about it. I was going to have to stop seeing you for a while anyway. I'm getting a visitor. My son's coming.'

'That's good then.' He nodded his head vigorously. 'Then we're both OK.'

She stared at his bobbing head. She had expected some surprise, some interest. *You have a son? I didn't know you had any children!* She watched him push stray grains of salt into a pile on the table top and thought, I will never cease to be amazed. When her Tequila came she ignored the lime and drank it down.

'I'm fine, Lenny. I don't know about you, frankly, but I'm just fine.' She dumped the sugar and sweeteners on the table and left.

She had received her first letter from Steven in April, just after he turned eighteen. It was polite and brief. He had been adopted by a family in Columbia, Missouri, he said. His father repaired heating and cooling systems. His mother worked in a law office. His little sister was adopted, too. He had sent a picture.

Catherine had stared at it for a long time. Curly blond hair. Teeth just a little too big for his mouth. She didn't own a photograph of Josh at that age (they had known each other well enough to exchange body fluids but not photographs) but this was the face she remembered. Other memories came rushing at her with an alarming physicality: the smell of her own blood in the delivery room, the baby's fist in her hand, curled tight like the spiral of a shell. How she cramped for weeks after he was gone, the muscles and organs inside her body fighting to regain their position while she sat in History of Western Civ. and took notes.

She set the picture down and called her sister in Iowa.

'Well, you have to write him back,' said Eleanor. She was thirty-three years old, unmarried and working on a PhD in history. She had never given up a baby.

'No, I don't.'

'You're a kind person, Cathy. I know you don't want to disappoint that child.'

Catherine picked up the picture again and peered into it. 'He's not a child,' she said.

'Of course he is. He may have a man's face and a man's body but eighteen is a kid. You know it is. Of all people, you should know.'

She did know and the knowledge scared her. Eighteen is a great time for expectations that have very little to do with reality. She had expected dates to the movies, study sessions, midnight conversations about film. She had expected to spend her four years coasting through school like most of the other kids in her University of Iowa freshman class. What she got was pregnant after hurried sex at a frat party her very first semester.

This boy would march into her life wearing that face and expect what? A mother? A friend? His letter said he just wanted to hear from her but she knew better. She sent a short note and waited. He wrote back asking if he could visit her in the summer before he started college. Out of curiosity and because she wanted to be the person her sister seemed to think she was, she said *Yes*.

Why didn't you say no, her father had asked over and over, his voice rising each time. Catherine had sat stiffly on the couch, five months along. She couldn't blame him for yelling; when she thought of that girl now she wanted to do more than yell at her. She wanted to shake her, wag a finger in her face, pour cold water on her head. Eighteen-year-old Catherine hadn't answered his question; no answer had been expected of her, really. The best she could have offered at the time would have been, *Because I wanted to say yes.*

In the years since then she had picked those few hours clean for clues to her own mind and Josh's. She remembered his hand on the small of her back as he led her up the stairs. The way he lifted the blue keg cup out of her hand and set it on the night table. At the time he must have seemed confident and manly, like someone who could take care of her. She blushed at the memory of herself that night: closing her eyes with each drunken kiss and speaking only in whispers. Definitely the behavior of someone who wanted to be taken care of. When she thought of those two kids now it was with humiliation tinged with anger. What movie did they think they were in?

The day after Lenny dumped her, Catherine went by Caruso's about the time the boats came in. She was warming her palms through a plastic cup of coffee by the time the first unshaven anglers began swaggering through the door.

'They're thick as fleas out there, Cath.'

'Whatja catch, Sam?'

Sam Martindale crewed the party boat, *WharfRat*. He was a big, blonde kid who talked with his eyes on the floor.

'I landed a twenty-pound striper, but I saw this guy off Stinson Beach pull in a gargantuan smoker. He said it weighed in at forty. Don't know about that, but I judged it over thirty-five. It was a pig, Cath.'

'Name?'

'Sorry.'

She chewed on the end of her pencil and then wrote, 'unidentified angler, thirty-five, Stinson,' on her pad.

Wally 'Low Tide' Greer crowded in behind Sam. He was handsome and knew it; the only guy she had ever seen show up at the docks at 4:30 AM with mousse in his hair.

'There were diving birds, anchovies, big fish busting the top –

it was incredible,' he said. 'I had a halibut on so big it bent my hook straight.'

'So where's the bathrobe?'

The men laughed, remembering how Wally had run out of plastic bags one time and brought a salmon into Caruso's to be smoked wrapped in a pale green paisley robe.

'Hey, Sam,' she called. 'Got room on the *WharfRat* for Sunday?' Steven's plane was arriving Friday afternoon. She would find something for him to do Saturday while she worked and then Sunday would be the big finish.

'We can squeeze you on.'

'There'll be two of us.'

'That nurse gal?'

She smiled, remembering how the deckhands had fallen over themselves to net a fish for her friend Janine.

'Nah. A kid I know.'

'Yeah, sure. Bring him down.'

Catherine collected a few more tidbits for the column before leaving: Captain Jimbo of *Larkspur* logged a 38-pounder using big herring threaded on flexible 'cable baiter' rigs. Raymond Berry nailed ten stripers with a fly rod and flies tied by Parker Bigs at Western Boat. Halibut were hitting at Seal Rocks.

The guys chorused their good-byes to her when she left, her pad full of notes and a couple ounces of fresh steamed shrimp in a bag. She got in her car and revved the engine. Opened the bag and popped a shrimp into her mouth. Drove by Lenny's.

There were trucks parked out front. *Allessandro's Yard Care. David Birk Contracting.* The front door was open and men were going in and out, dragging orange cables and carrying large pieces of wood. She looked at the carefully landscaped yard, the wide front door. A little table with a Cinzano umbrella sat on one of the two upper balconies. She tried to imagine herself living in that house. It would be nice to have a perfectly silent high efficiency dishwasher, she admitted. Not to have to worry so much about money. Though Lenny worried plenty. About everything.

She sat in the car at the end of the cul-de-sac and finished the shrimp. The truth was she would rather house-sit than live there, she decided. She'd rather screw Lenny every now and then than be married to him. It was a fabulous set, the Cinzano umbrella was a very nice touch indeed, but the movie she was in was called, *Soon to be Middle-Aged Writer with Enough Worries of her Own*. The person who could best take care of her was herself.

Catherine wore a white carnation to the airport. The idea had come to her the night before when she was on the phone with Steven and she had blurted it out. She had hoped the ironic gesture would break the ice a little, highlight for both of them the absurdity of their situation.

'A white carnation,' he had repeated. 'Oh great. Thanks a lot. I was wondering, you know . . . Well, that's a relief.'

She stared out her kitchen window at the illuminated parking lot, the enormity of what she was facing just now hitting her. His extreme youth. *Be careful*, she told herself. One hard push at that age could send a person reeling onto a whole other course. She knew she had a tendency to be flip.

The plane landed and wheeled toward the gate. Catherine leaned against a support beam; her mouth felt like it was carpeted wall to wall. She knew him the minute he emerged through the gate. Since taking the picture he had sent her he had cut his hair short. He wore a basketball jacket. His backpack hung loose from his shoulder with a studied casualness and his eyes darted around the room. Saw her. Dropped to the flower at her breast. He smiled briefly and jerked his head back in a gesture of acknowledgment she recognized from TV shows about juvenile delinquents and gang members.

'Hi, Steven.'

'Hey.'

She didn't know whether to shake his hand or give him a hug. At the last minute she gave his back a quick, comradely pat.

Her palm cupped his shoulder blade. She stuck her hands in her pockets.

'Good flight?'

'Don't know.'

'Were you asleep?' She pointed in the direction of the parking lot and they started walking.

'First time I ever flew.'

'No kidding.'

Their bodies clanked and bumped in and out of rhythm as they walked side by side, like pistons in a rusty machine.

'Hungry?'

He turned his face to her and smiled a familiar toothy smile. 'I'm starved.'

'I know a great Chinese place here in the city.' She glanced at her watch. 'If we hurry we can make Dim Sum.'

'Ummm. Sure.'

'Or is there something else you'd like better?' She unlocked the car door, glad that she'd stopped at a gas station on the way to vacuum the floors.

'Just American, I guess.' He ducked his head. 'Sorry.'

'Don't apologize,' she said, her jaw tightening. 'You have nothing to be sorry for.'

She studied the traffic ahead of her and searched her mind for something to say. Over the past several days she had struggled to condense whole years of her life into several amusing anecdotes. She wondered if she could possibly start with the one where her parents lost her on the Paris subway. Eleanor was a clingy hand-holding ten-year-old and so when they stepped out on the platform she was right alongside. Catherine was absorbed in watching a man with pierced ears and a lapdog. It had been amusing when she imagined telling it but now sitting next to Steven she suddenly remembered how unfunny it had been to her at the time. How terrifying to see those glass doors close between her and her family.

'So you have a sister, you said.'

'Yeah. She's fourteen. Emily.'

'That's funny. My sister's name is Eleanor.'

'You have a sister? Cool.'

'She doesn't live that far from you, actually. Iowa City.' She pictured Steven showing up at Eleanor's apartment and smiled. *I knew you'd let him in*, she imagined herself saying. *You're a kind person.*

'Hawkeyes.' He nodded. 'I thought about going there but then I got into Chicago. And well, you know. University of Chicago is a better school, all around.' He glanced at her shyly and then looked out the window.

He wants me to be proud of him, she realized. She thought with surprise, I *am*. She had to concentrate to keep a goofy smile off her face on the way into the restaurant. Maybe this wouldn't be so hard after all.

They sat down across from each other and ordered Cokes. Catherine lifted the laminated menu into her hands and began to consider the choice between Caesar salad with chicken strips and a fresh fish fajita.

'My father lives in Chicago.'

'I didn't realize your parents were divorced.'

'My birth father.'

She set the menu down and studied the boy's face. She wondered why the idea hadn't occurred to her until now that he'd tracked her down to exact his revenge.

'If you mean Josh, he couldn't have placed himself farther from your birth if he'd gone to India.'

'It's just an expression.' He looked at the table, bravado slowly leaking from his face.

'Have you talked to him?'

'To him and his wife.' He raised his eyes.

'My.'

'They have two boys. My half brothers.'

'My, my.'

'Have you all decided on lunch?'

Steven glanced at the waitress, blushed slightly and nodded. She grinned and brushed hair out of her eyes with her pencil. Catherine gazed at them and chewed the inside of her cheek. She imagined throwing a lit match and watching the air between them combust.

'I'll have the double Texas burger with cheddar. Side of fries.'

The girl scribbled. 'Ma'am?'

'Just a cup of soup.'

Their waitress gathered their menus and smiled at Steven before she left.

'I told him I was coming to see you,' Steven said. 'He said to say *Hi*.'

She laughed, a short, sharp burst of expelled air.

'You know, Steven. Steve? It's really great to be with you. To meet you. You seem like a great guy. Really great.' She sipped her Coke. 'And I can understand why you'd be curious about your *birth parents* but I have to say, and I hope you won't take this the wrong way, that this is all a little *much* for me at the moment, do you know what I mean? It's a lot to take in.'

'Sure, I understand.'

When the waitress brought their food Steven looked away from her, almost, thought Catherine, as if he were hiding his face.

She twisted her napkin in her lap. 'You know I'm a writer, don't you? I do a column for the paper, some newsletters. I even wrote some poetry for a while. I had a poem published in the student newspaper in college.' Steven ate his fries without looking at her. 'Well, anyway, I was thinking maybe you could take a few minutes later and write down some questions that you have. About me or my family. Whatever you wanted. No censorship.' She laughed nervously.

'OK.'

'OK.' She nodded. 'How's your burger? Is it all right?'

'It's fine.'

'Good. This is a good place, I think. I like this place.' Catherine took a sip of her tasteless, cream-based soup and felt like throwing up.

'Let me get this straight,' said Eleanor. 'You asked him to submit his questions *in writing*?'

'He told me Josh said to say, *Hi*. To me. Josh. Loving husband and father.' Catherine wrapped the phone cord around her finger and took a sip of the wine she had poured herself seconds after Steven left for the video store.

'Didn't you think he might be married? It's been twenty years.'

'In the abstract he might have been a lot of things. He might have been dead.' Her finger was starting to turn red where the phone cord cut off the blood flow. "What does he think he's doing, acting like he didn't split the scene like a scared dog when I told him I was pregnant? Stepping in as Mr. Birth Father as if he didn't have that to answer for?'

'Maybe he's trying to answer for it now.'

'What? By saying, tell her I said, *Hi*?'

'Not to *you*, Catherine.'

Catherine pinched her nose and blinked her eyes. She said, 'There's nothing worse than a know-it-all little sister.'

Eleanor laughed.

'Look, Steven's been gone twenty-five minutes and Video Drone is only five minutes away. He might be trying to call.'

'Hang in there.'

'I guess it's better than the alternative.'

After forty-five minutes Catherine started to get worried. After an hour she began to imagine his body twisted around the steering wheel of her car. The Jaws of Life. She pulled her knees up to her chest on the couch and thought, *if something has happened to him what will I say to his mother*? When he walked in after an hour and a half she was on the verge of calling the police.

'I got *Edward Scissorhands*. That was one of the ones you hadn't seen, right?' He threw his jacket on the chair and smiled at her as if nothing was wrong. His cheeks were flushed.

'Was it crowded?' She kept her voice even.

His brow furrowed. 'No.' He seemed to be thinking and then he smiled. 'I did meet a girl there, though. Zoë.'

Catherine ran through a list of possible responses in her mind. Each of them seemed slightly hysterical or shrewish. The kind of thing a wife might say to a husband who came home late. Or a mother to her child.

'*Edward Scissorhands* is fine,' she said and got up. 'Want a Coke?'

'Oh yeah. Thanks.'

She held a can out to him and when he took it she sat down beside him.

'Josh didn't believe me when I said I was pregnant,' she said. 'Or he pretended not to. He was kind of a lightweight emotion-ally." She glanced at Steven's face and then looked away again quickly. "Though maybe he's changed. Anyway, he switched schools as soon as it was obvious I wasn't lying. Iowa State, I think.' She fingered the remote. 'The Cyclones.'

Steven shifted on the couch. Swallowed. 'Did you know right away you were going to give me up for adoption? Or did you ever think about . . .?'

Catherine sighed. She remembered sitting in the girls' toilet and staring at that little bit of blood on the paper. Convincing herself it was a period. Hoping for the next one. She started to say something about waiting too long for an abortion but then stopped herself just in time. She realized that was not what he meant.

'I was a kid,' she said. 'Both of us. We knew nothing at all.'

'You were my age,' said Steven. 'I know some things.'

Her smile was brief and tired. 'Yeah? What do you know?'

'To use a condom, for one thing.'

Catherine's eyes rested on his hands. They were bony and oversized, still out of proportion to the rest of his body. She imagined those hands on the bare shoulders of a girl and shivered. 'Is this where I'm supposed to congratulate you for being responsible? The fact is the idea of you having sex with anyone at this point depresses the hell out of me.'

He started to say something, to protest, but then stopped himself. He chewed the inside of his cheek. 'Don't get too bent out of shape,' he said. 'Doesn't happen all that often.'

She laughed. 'Want to watch the movie?'

Lights out, they sat in the glow from the TV and watched Johnny Depp slice suburban hedges into shreds.

The last call of the afternoon was from Arlen McKeon who hammered a forty-pound smoker using a red rotary killer at Rocky Point.

'Remember, that's Arlen "Grammy" McKeon,' he said.

'Wasn't that Grammy thing like twenty years ago, Arlen? Besides, the only person I've ever heard refer to you by that name was you.'

'Oh and I guess Randall "Two Fish" Birnbaum was given that name by the Pope himself.'

Catherine held the phone away from her face and gave it a disbelieving look.

'Forty pounds, huh, Arlen? You sure about that?'

'Got a picture of the fish on the scale.'

Catherine submitted the column and hopped in her car. Steven had said something about shopping for some new jeans while she was at work; he said he could spend hours at the mall. She pictured him wandering through the stores, wanting things. Perhaps she should buy him a small present before he left. She decided to pull Sam aside on the boat and ask for suggestions.

The apartment seemed empty when she first walked in the door; it was quiet and the lights were off. She reached down to flip the switch on the reading lamp and almost tripped over a canvas backpack. It was full of books and deep purple like the inside of a wound. She picked it up. It smelled like patchouli. A girl's, she decided, but which one? And where were they? She heard a muffled laugh from the guest bedroom and remembered 'Zoë' from the video store in the same second. Her heart began to pound.

She saw herself setting the backpack down, turning around and walking out her own front door. She could come back later when the girl was gone. There was no law that said she had to look Steven's mistakes in the face as well as her own. Perhaps she had judged Josh too harshly all of these years, she thought. The real difference between them hadn't been the desire to run away, it had been that he had been able to and she had not.

She knew the exact level of disarray she would find inside the guest room. Still she was pulled in that direction. It was more than the fact that she suspected that leaving now wouldn't make her free. Josh, after all, suddenly had an extra son. She wanted to see what recklessness looked like from the other side of the door.

'Catherine! I thought . . .' Steven sat up and swung his feet to the floor.

'I got done early.'

'Oh, God. This is so embarrassing.'

The girl buttoning her shirt didn't seem all that embarrassed to Catherine. She had purplish red hair not unlike the color of her backpack. In high school Catherine had carried a blue pack with buttons stuck in it. A sun saying, Nuclear Power, No Thanks. What's wrong with a nice leather book bag, she could remember her mother asking. Why do all you kids have to look like you're running away from home?

'Ummm, could we have a second?' Steven gestured toward the door.

Catherine raised her eyebrows thinking, *haven't had time to get her pregnant?*

'To get decent,' Steven added.

'Sure thing.' Catherine backed out of the room, sat down on the couch and waited.

'I'm Zoë.' The girl stood in front of her with her hand out.

Catherine shook it but did not stand up.

'How old are you?'

'She's seventeen.' Steven emerged behind her.

'Not even close,' said Catherine, wishing she had held her column until Arlen had *shown* her the picture of his fish on the scale.

'I'm fifteen,' said Zoë. She glanced back at Steven and then looked at the floor. 'I'll be fifteen in September.'

The surprise on Steven's face was both comical and heart-breaking. This is just the beginning of what you don't know about each other, she wanted to say. She thought of all the times she had wished she could live those years over again, the hours spent designing scenarios in which she skipped the party, went home early, called student health. It took Steven and Zoë blushing in her living room to make her realize that she wouldn't go back under any circumstances, for any amount of money. The realization made her want to give them a break.

'Are you guys hungry? Do you want to go out for ice cream sundaes or something? Baskin Robbins is just around the corner.'

A look passed between them and Zoë shook her head.

'Thanks, though.'

Steven and Catherine were careful around each other that evening. Polite. Although he had been half-dressed and she fully clothed, it was as if each of them had caught the other in an embarrassing situation, one they discreetly avoided mentioning.

I might have made it through the three days, thought Catherine, if the boats didn't leave so damned early in the morning. She had set her alarm for four-fifteen and promised to wake Steven by four-thirty. Still half asleep in old jeans and a sweatshirt, she turned on the hall light and opened his door. Steven's head had migrated off the pillow and was lying flat on the mattress, his mouth open slightly. She could see his teeth. She wanted, with a force so powerful it almost buckled her knees, to put her face close to his and feel his breath on her cheek. She wrapped her arms tightly around her middle and backed into the hallway. Knees drawn up to her chest she sat on the floor, chewed the sleeve of her sweatshirt and cried. So many mornings lost, she thought.

'What time is it?' Steven stood in his long underwear rubbing his eyes.

'Quarter to five.'

He looked at her. 'Are you all right?'

'I'll be fine.' She stood up. 'We've got to hurry.'

They hustled out to the pier holding bagged lunches and steaming coffee in styrofoam cups. The sky was lightening slowly from black to gray and the air was wet, halfway between mist and drizzle. Sam was loading the boat dressed in a hooded sweatshirt and down vest. He smiled broadly when he saw Catherine.

'Remember that pain-in-the-ass doctor from the last time you rode the boat?' he asked.

She nodded.

Sam jerked his head toward the cabin. 'He's in there eating a donut.'

'He's going out with us?'

'Evidently so.' Sam chuckled, attributing the horror in her voice to her memories from that day on the ocean. 'So who's this?' He smiled at Steven.

Catherine hesitated.

'I'm Steven.' He stepped forward and shook Sam's hand.

'Hey, Steven. Let me get this gear on and I'll show you the boat. Meanwhile you can stand over there,' he pointed to a spot by the rail, 'and drink your coffee.'

'I'll join you in a second,' said Catherine and headed for the cabin.

Lenny was perched on a padded bench near the window.

'What are you doing?' She stared down at him with her hands on her hips.

'That's your kid, isn't it?'

'It's my new boyfriend.'

'I called your office yesterday and they said you had the day off. I figured you'd be here.'

'And you wanted to know because . . .'

'I want us to be friends again.'

'We weren't *friends*, Lenny. We were never friends.'

It began to drizzle in earnest when they left the dock. Sam passed out rain hats but most of the passengers chose to huddle inside the cabin and watch the water splash against the windows. Catherine and Steven shared a bench near the back.

'Weather sucks,' said Steven.

'But it can mean some great fishing,' said Catherine. 'The bait swims up near the surface when it's overcast.' She was trying to avoid looking at Lenny who sat alone and was uncharacteristically quiet.

They entered the wake of the San Francisco ferry and the boat rocked. Steven gripped the fold-out table and Catherine looked at him carefully. Was he a little green? She hoped not. This was supposed to be the best day of his visit, the one he would look back on and remember.

They passed under the Golden Gate Bridge, rounded the coast by Kirby Cove and hit the swells. The boat pitched back and forth, leaning in and out of the gusts of rain in a jerky rhythm. Catherine knew it was just some rough water, nothing to worry about, she turned to Steven to tell him so.

'I gotta puke.' Steven pulled himself off the bench and stumbled outside onto the slick deck.

Sam grabbed his arm on the way to the railing and steadied him while he spilled his coffee and donut over the side. As Catherine reached for his other arm Steven began to straighten up and then buckled over again suddenly, retching.

'Got any Dramamine?' Sam asked.

Catherine shook her head; no. Steven's pale face glistened in the rain.

She said, 'Let me go ask Lenny.'

'No, I'm sorry I don't,' said Lenny, avoiding her eyes. 'I never get seasick.'

Catherine started to say something clever but then stopped herself. 'Thanks, anyway.'

'Wait.' Lenny fished in a bag and pulled out a plain donut. 'Try to get him to take a few bites of this . . .'

'Thanks, Lenny.' Catherine stepped forward and took the donut.

The rain stopped after a while. Sam guided the passengers to rod holders along the deck. They baited and let their lines out and sat swaying in deck chairs. Steven let Catherine fill his mouth with a couple bites of donut. She placed them carefully on his tongue as if she were giving communion; he chewed them as if he were eating paste.

Every twenty minutes, donut or not, Steven pulled himself over to the rail and hawked into the water. You could set a clock to the frequency with which the human stomach produces bile, thought Catherine. In between bouts of vomiting he leaned against her on an outside bench, his eyes carefully closed. The wind began to dry his hair in tufts. A pot-bellied man in a Giants cap shouted that he had a fish on the line. There was the usual slapping of feet on deck, the splash of the net into water, the otherworldly flash of scales emerging into light.

Catherine sat as still as she could on the bench to support Steven's weight and she talked in a low, soothing voice, stopping only to guide him to the rail and back every twenty minutes. She told him about the Iowa State Fair when she was four, her first conscious memory. He might be interested to know that they were related to John Paul Jones, the one who said *We have not yet begun to fight*, on her mother's side. His grandmother. She told him about her terror on the Metro in Paris. The French commuters rushing by in their scarves and nice shoes, not a single one stopping to help a sobbing American girl. High school. Her first days in college. Meeting Josh.

She talked and talked while the men reeled in fish and the

gulls whirled overhead. Lenny hovered near by, listening, and still she talked. She talked as the boat chugged back under the towering shadow of the Golden Gate. She talked for hours on end until they reached smooth water.

THIS IS THE DAY WE GIVE BABIES AWAY

Priscilla T. Nagle

The Placement.

Here is one way to give away your baby.

First, you go see Mrs. Bronston at the Children's Home, three days out of the hospital. You're still so sore you can't sit up straight, and the chair is a hard wooden one so you have to sit crooked, on the edge. You're still too fat for non-pregnant clothes, so you have to wear a smock over a skirt. Your hair looks awful. You didn't know you were seeing her in time to set it. You're feeling pushed. They're really rushing you, you think, because they're afraid you'll change your mind. And everybody there knows, 'It's best for the baby' – that's all you hear. This is the most important impression you're ever going to have to make, because Mrs. Bronston chooses the parents for your baby. And you're not ready. There is no way you can feel 'at your best.'

You hate Mrs. Bronston, you hate her questions, and you're sitting there giving the wrong answers to most of them: 'Do you want your baby to have a Catholic or Protestant home, or does it matter?' 'Protestant.' 'Do you think your son should be placed in a home in which the father is in the professions?' (Because she knows you're very bright.) 'Oh yes, that would be very nice . . .' 'And what are your plans, dear, for the immediate future?'

So you tell her something impressive, mention a career that

shows how ambitious you are and how much you care about humanity; later you want to bite out your tongue because you mentioned a local university – now she'll probably send your baby off somewhere and definitely rule out a professor at the university because you might *find out*. Everyone is always worried you'll try to find out. It never occurs to you to mention age, and later you regret it. Mrs. Bronston is sitting there looking totally together, and you know how you look, and she is making a living out of finding a home for your baby. It's supposed to be a nice thing to do. But it absolutely doesn't feel that way. And you hate her not only for that, but also because you have to sit there and be so nice to her, and try to get her to think highly of you . . .

Mrs. Bronston, I want my son to have a home with a lot of love and warmth and caring in it. Parents who are secure about themselves and can be open and intimate and very understanding and supportive about the differences in people – especially their children. Why didn't you say that? *I want them to be able to play with, talk with and enjoy my son for who he is. To teach him by example how to live life. I don't care if they have a religion or not. Or even how much money they have, as long as they have enough for good food. I want their spirits to be in touch with a power for good, whatever that is.*

Why didn't you say that? You weren't prepared. And that isn't what she needed to know to fill out the paper. You never forgive yourself for not thinking clearly there. Never. But for a long time, you think it's her you're not forgiving.

The Visit.
Next, if you request it, you go to the Children's Home to see your baby the morning before you sign the papers. Two of you go together to see your babies. You feel watched the whole time, and you are. Everyone around is watching you, but trying to be subtle about it. So they bring you your baby, who starts to cry just before your twenty minutes are up. You don't know if there is an actual time limit, but that's about the longest anyone ever

stays there. You didn't know that he was still technically yours until that day, that you could have visited him all along – of course it's pretty obvious why no one has told you that. It could be too upsetting.

Anyway, now you're holding him. Memorize his features. Some little kid who lives there keeps talking to you. The other mother keeps talking to you. You wish they'd all shut up so you could really see and feel him. He doesn't seem to like you. He doesn't want to cuddle. Your hands are as cold as death. No wonder he doesn't like being held by you. Both babies start to cry (oh no, you didn't get to undress him and look at him all over); you walk over to the doorway that opens down a long, long hall where you can hear other babies. Some woman who seems nice, but harassed and uncomfortable, takes him from your arms and goes away.

This twenty-minute picture never leaves you. You always wonder if they hold them and give them loving back there, down that long hallway, while they're waiting to be born again . . .

You step outside and look to the treetops, where you always have found solace. And suddenly the pain hits. Deep and unbearable. All you can think is, Who will show him the beauty? Who will show him? . . . You realize years later that that was the first time it had occurred to you that you might have something special to offer him that others did not. That maybe you had the right to him, after all, and that this was a terrible mistake. But those thoughts are so out of your experience that you can't respond to them. All you can do is feel the pain.

The Signing.
That afternoon is the paper signing. You go to the Children's Home shortly after lunch and walk into a room with a table in it and two ladies sitting to the side. Mrs. Bronston is sitting at the table. You are introduced to the two ladies, who are there as witnesses. Your social worker is with you. Everyone is looking very uncomfortable. You are trying to look poised and lovely

(someone tells you later you were white as a sheet). You are trying to make everyone feel at ease and to treat them graciously, because it's obvious they don't want to be there and that they're just doing this for you and they know you hate it.

Mrs. Bronston has you read the paper, but first apologizes for the language, says it's just a necessary legality. You correct the spelling of your name and the name of your hometown. You sign a paper that says, 'I hereby abandon and neglect my child, (his name), and request that he become a ward of the court . . .' They all stand up and half smile. You say, 'Thank you,' though you're barely breathing, because you want everyone to think you're wonderful so they'll work very hard to find your son a wonderful home.

The Hearing.
You walk into a giant courtroom, with the social worker, Mrs. Smith, and the nurse, and you're thinking, *Oh my God, it's as big as a church!* And indeed, it feels like a funeral. Your mind is numb, your body is cold, your hands are so cold they have no feeling. There are other people there. Teenagers and parents, all looking glum. *Oh no, are they gonna do this in front of everybody?* But you can't get out the question loud enough for anyone to hear.

Finally, you see this room's only used as a waiting room, because way up in front at an elevated desk someone comes out and calls the next case.

So you sit. And wait. The judge comes out once and calls Mrs. Smith up to him and talks to her – something you can't quite understand, though you hear words echo against the walls.

It's time. They call you, though you never remember what they said. Did they say your whole name? Probably not, for no one has said your last name out loud since you arrived at the home.

The three of you go inside to a normal-sized courtroom. You're all dressed up in your brown suit, wanting to look as nice as possible, still wanting to impress everyone so they'll make sure your son gets an especially good home. There's a young man there, in the benches at the right. Who is he? The nurse and Mrs. Smith seat you between them in the second row, right in front of the judge's high desk. He speaks kindly, but there's an edge of anger you can hear quite clearly.

The judge introduces himself, then introduces the young lawyer over on the right. You stand, the lawyer stands, you swear to who you are, and to tell the truth. It's all outside of you somewhere. The only word that's repeating in your mind is 'horrible.' The only feeling is 'hurry.' There seems to be no air inside you. All your insides are frozen.

The young lawyer keeps saying things to you. Something is terribly wrong. He's saying, 'Are you aware that this will no longer be your child? Do you promise before this court and these witnesses that you will never seek to find him, or any information regarding him, again, for as long as you live? If you understand and agree, please answer, "Yes, I do so promise."'

'Yes, I do so promise.'

He goes on and on . . .

'Yes, I do so promise.'

They keep asking you to speak up. There is nothing to push your voice out. A scream is starting. Deep inside of you. Something is dying there. Something wants out.

The judge: he's supposed to just declare whatever it is he declares. But he starts asking you questions. He tells someone later he wanted to be sure you knew what you were doing, that you didn't look as if you were sure of what was happening. 'How long had you known the father of this child? Was he aware of your pregnancy, and did he offer to help? No? Why didn't you inform him?'

'He had stopped seeing me. He had already graduated and left, and I didn't know where to get in touch with him.' You don't tell him that your mind helped you deny you were pregnant for five months. You don't tell him that you thought you had to go out and change the world with your intellect, but now that your baby is real to you, he's the only thing that matters, and it's too late because you've already set the wheels in motion. And nothing in your whole life has shown you that you have the right to what you want just because you want it when it might hurt others. Nothing in your life has prepared you to believe that you have anything to offer your son that is special enough to keep him from what everyone says is 'the best thing for him.'

What is he doing? You have to get out of there. You're starting to lose the numbness that's holding you in one piece. You're starting to lose control over the screams.

It gets worse. He declares, banging a gavel, something wrong and terrible. You hear as you are leaving, '. . . that (your son's name) is now a ward of this court, and that he is no longer your son.' Something else declares to you as you are leaving, *I will never be happy again.*

Run. Run and scream – where is the door? Outside. Outside the door you can run because the screams are overtaking you. But outside, there is someone waiting for you, and there is no place to run . . .

The screams never die. They just get locked away, driving deeper inside you. You learn to unlock them sometimes, to keep them from growing stronger and destroying you. But they never die. You live your life, you learn to find love and beauty, again. You raise your other children, you bury a child, but this one is always alive, and you don't know where, and you don't know how.

And you learn that there are decisions that are not right or wrong, they are just decisions. But if they are not natural to your deepest being, they change you forever, and the problem remains unsolved. He is real. And, alive or dead, he never dies to you. He is out there somewhere . . . lost to you . . . as you are to him.

ILLUSIONS

Hannah wa Muigai

It was that dreamed of season. A levels were done, and the first year of adulthood stretched out. We had spent six years of school speculating about the lengths we would go to, the things we would do. The nightclub, Illusions, was just that – an illusion of a tropical paradise. Fake palm trees, made of green styrofoam, hung from the rafters. Reflections from the giant disco ball at the centre of the dance floor sent speckles of light all around. Every few minutes somebody drunk would get ejected, or leave the club to chew Miraa (khat). Within a five-metre radius I recognized at least five people I knew. Nakuru was a small town, and this was the only decent club.

It was after midnight; suddenly smoke rose from the dance floor as the DJ pelted out yet another dance hit. 'Come on up, people, it's Cool and the Gang,' his mellow voice called out over the music.

I had been on the dance floor for almost half an hour, but I could have carried on for ever. My friend, Chep, waved at me from our table. Squinting at my dance partner, Kangethe, I wondered, Is he always so energetic?

At seventeen I was no longer a virgin, but my sexual experience was limited. Kangethe had been after me for years, and I had always put him off thinking him too 'serious'. Now, as we danced to the eighties R & B music, I thought I could give him a chance.

'Now let's slow it down,' the DJ's voice came through again, as a slow number began to play.

Typically, most of the singles on the floor walked back to their seats. Kangethe held my hands and drew me close. Hey, what the heck, we were both dripping with perspiration, so it was nice to slow down the pace.

And he could actually dance! I recalled my old lessons in the waltz as he took me through the paces. Now I was really impressed.

Later, we headed back to join Chep, who was making really small talk with Njoroge, Kangethe's pal.

The waiters carried around hotpots full of sausages, samosas and dubious kebabs, ever ready to serve. I downed my Guinness, not cold any more, and signalled to one.

'Leta round' (bring us a round). I made the order knowing he did not expect me to pay him in advance. Chep and I were well known at the club and we always settled our bill at the end of the evening.

'So?' She grinned at me wickedly. 'You two going somewhere tonight?'

'Shut up and let's go pee,' I answered, trying hard not to blush.

There were two sets of washrooms at the club. Those of us who knew better used the more hidden ones, which were relatively clean.

I tidied up as Chep went on and on.

'You see, I keep telling you the guy likes you,' she whispered. 'What do you think, will you go out with him again?'

I busied myself in front of the mirror, making sure my unpractised hand did not smudge my make-up.

'Chep, if he makes love the way he dances, I am going back to his place tonight,' I stated, and no stage whisper for me.

If anyone in the ladies' room had a problem with what I had to say, shauri yao (it's their problem).

Chep was, for a change, speechless.

We made our way through the crowded club back to our table. Kangethe politely stood up as we took our seats. Njoroge seemed irritated at our arrival, as though we had interrupted them. Shauri yake (that's his problem) – he goes clubbing to have serious discussions?

The DJ kept the music mellow; Kangethe and I took to the floor again and again. After a couple of hours, Chep was clearly ready to leave. Kangethe walked us out of the club to the waiting taxis.

Our usual arrangement was to take a taxi back to her parents' home, as it was easier to sneak in undetected.

'Hannah, are you sure I should leave you?' she whispered, hugging me close.

'My dear, I will call you tomorrow, sawa (OK)?' I replied.

Kangethe gallantly dropped Njoroge off at a nearby suburb, and then we came back into town to his flat. I had been to Kangethe's house several times with his sisters, but had never imagined this kind of scenario.

He hooted at the gate for the dozing nightwatchman. The man could not help but take a second look at me as he opened the gate to the parking lot. I felt a bit nervous as we finally got into the flat.

'Relax my dear.' He read my mind. 'You know your way around, feel at home.'

I headed for the shower, eager to wash off the night's sweat.

He joined me.

'Baby that was wonderful,' he whispered, all toothpastey breath. 'You are incredible!'

My mind drew a blank. And what man wakes up to brush his teeth before you do? Bits and pieces of the night before started to come back to me.

'Uh, let me use your bathroom,' as I hopped out of bed.

The bathroom was stark and smelled of pot-pourri air freshener.

A flowery shower curtain was draped across the bathtub, where a plastic telephone shower hung. I blushed as I remembered taking my clothes off, feeling daring, seductive, and heading for the shower before joining Kangethe in bed earlier that morning.

Thinking about it as I looked at myself in the mirror above the sink, I figured, why not go with the flow for as long as it lasts? That way it wouldn't be a one-night stand.

I saw the used condom wrappers in the bin, and felt warm all over again.

At seventeen you see yourself as steam, gas, ever rising, ceaselessly changeable. I was not at all certain what sort of career I wanted, but felt ready to take on any undergraduate programme that would allow me the time to decide.

I had a desk job at a local petrol station to help pass time as I waited for my A level results. Every day I would get a ride into town with my father. My duties included manning the switchboard, but with only three extensions and one incoming line I was hardly overwhelmed with work. The daily banking was the highlight of my day. The walk to and from the bank was as much exercise as I ever did. I strolled out of the office at mid-morning and always stopped off at the yoghurt man, with his ice-cream-like pushcart full of ice-cold sachets of strawberry yoghurt. Sticking an extra fat straw into the sachet, I sipped greedily the thick, tangy drink faithfully every day.

Qualifying for a university degree in Kenya would take another six years, given all the disruptions caused by overloading of limited universities. During this time, attaining financial independence would not be easy, as the few jobs available paid a pittance. I saw myself still heavily reliant on my parents at the ripe old age of twenty-five.

I barely thought about my affair with Kangethe, except when we were together. We would meet almost every other day at his flat. It was a typical bachelor pad, with a leather settee placed bang in front of the 26-inch television. The kitchen only had an old electric kettle, and tins of hardened instant coffee. His ancient fridge hummed away; all it ever had in it were cartons of milk, none of them fresh.

He lived on take-away food. And there was always the smell of cold nyama choma (grilled goat meat) in the mornings. Coming back from our 'regular' pub around the corner one evening, he surprised me by saying,

'What would Daddy say if you spent the night out again?' (Strict as my parents were, it had not been possible for me to spend the night with him again, since that first time.)

He put his arms around me, grinning wickedly.

'Put that thought away. You have to take me home in time for dinner, you know that,' I replied.

He knew as well as I did that I did not want to expose our affair. I was not in love with him, yet, and was rather nervous about the age gap between us. I enjoyed making love with him; he was patient and experienced. But it was important to me that he did not intrude on my life at home, so that I did not need to lie to my parents about having a much older boyfriend. Often he was with his 'best friend'. I had never realized men, too, have that category in their relationships. Njoroge was quiet and reserved; when I arrived at Kangethe's flat and he was there, he would quickly find a reason to leave. All the better for me, I always thought. Three's a crowd.

Brushing my teeth one morning, I suddenly felt bile rise up my throat.

'Shit!' I thought.

We always used a condom, but one night the bloody thing had burst. I was, at the time, hysterical with laughter.

'Shit!'

It was the morning of my seventeenth birthday. I left home determined to maintain high spirits. My brother, Thande, had promised to take me out to lunch, for pizza!

At noon I left the office and went to the only restaurant in town that served pizza – frozen, but delicious all the same. After waiting for half an hour I confidently made my order, knowing that my brother would be there before long. As I got to the last slice a twinge of worry hit me, as he had not yet arrived and I did not have enough money to pay the bill. I decided to call my father from a payphone nearby. When I heard his voice something inside me snapped. I wept as I asked him to please come bail me out. He was there in ten minutes.

'Are you OK?' he asked. 'Did anyone give you trouble?'

After getting back to my office, I could not stop crying. My boss kindly did not pressurize me and transferred all calls to his line.

'Your brother called, just after you left,' said Mr Raja gently. 'He said he would meet you in the evening, rather than for lunch.'

'Sir,' I asked Mr Raja. 'Could you please allow me the rest of the afternoon off?'

He nodded without looking up at me.

'No problem, you go get some rest.' He probably thought I had 'female problems'.

I smiled through my tears and thanked him.

There was a small pharmacy just around the corner. I walked in and asked to speak to the pharmacist in confidence. Ignoring the knowing looks, we stepped into a cubicle.

I asked for a pregnancy test. Time stood still as I watched the indicator turn pink. I was definitely pregnant.

Now to tackle my partner in crime. I had to let Kangethe know.

It was with more excitement than trepidation that I headed off for his flat.

Surely this meant that I could expose our affair, as he would definitely do the honourable thing and ask me to marry him. My mind did not go beyond that point, to wonder how much I would miss out on as such a young mother, and wife.

Kangethe always left his key hidden above the door for those in the know, like Njoroge and me. I let myself in, and promptly wished I never had.

Kangethe lay above Njoroge on the floor, both naked; their bodies glistened with sweat. They looked up at me in shock.

My heart stopped beating.

I turned around and ran out of the flat, out of the building, and only stopped when I realized people were staring at me.

I slowly walked towards a payphone nearby. I rang Chep, knowing she would be at home. On hearing the coins drop into the slot she said, 'Hey, have you left the office already?' We were supposed to meet for dinner that evening.

'Chep, I have to go home, I have nasty cramps,' I lied, suddenly very composed.

I still don't know why I lied, as at that point I really needed to confide in someone; but how? Admit to having slept with a gay man, and never noticed? Homosexuality in Kenya is still against the law. I imagined Kangethe and his partner worrying that I could get them into trouble with the law for 'acts contrary to the laws of nature'.

It was the longest walk home I had ever taken. When I got there I rang my father.

'Hi, Baba.' I forced a cheerful note into my voice. 'Please don't pick me up; I am already at home.'

'Are you feeling better now?' he asked, still worried about my lunchtime misadventure.

'Yes, thanks. I want to get ready and go out with Chep later.'

'I thought we would all go out to dinner,' he said. My parents did not approve of Chep and me going out in the evenings.

'Baba, we made plans already. We will be home by eleven.'

'OK,' he relented. 'Just let your mother know your plans.'

Waves of guilt washed over me. A few minutes later my mother came home.

'Hey, you home already?' she asked. 'What are you wearing tonight?'

Every year on my birthday the whole family would take me out to dinner. Mom had clearly forgotten that I had told them

I wanted to launch my independence by going out without them.

I busied myself in the bathroom, knowing she would notice my distress just by looking at me.

'Mom, I am going out with Chep,' I called through the door. 'Please drop me in town when you deliver the milk, OK?'

Her latest venture was dairy cows. I thought the cows were really pretty, from a distance, but the smell of their manure lingered in every breeze coming through the windows. Or was I just extra sensitive to smells, already?

She did not respond as I got myself ready. Having a job meant that I could indulge my own aesthetics. I had on tight black pants and a matching sweater. Going to her room, I knocked gently on the door.

'Mom, are you almost ready to leave?'

'Come in, we need to talk,' she answered.

Typically she started by criticizing my outfit.

'Why don't you wear something more ladylike?' she asked.

'I picked this outfit because it is what I want to wear.'

'Where are you girls going?' she asked.

'Mom, please. We are having dinner at Gilanis Restaurant. Just the two of us,' I replied, pre-empting her next question. They always assumed we were going out to meet men.

'I thought we could all go out to dinner. Your father has already promised to join us.' She spoke without looking me in the eye.

'Mom, can we just go? It's my birthday, please let me enjoy it the way I prefer to.' My voice broke with unshed tears. I stood up and walked out of her room, resisting the urge to slam the door behind me. I needed the ride into town, after all.

The telephone extension in the hallway rang out as Mom used the phone to call Baba for advice. He must have been feeling sorry for me still, as she came out after a few minutes.

'Hannah, are you ready?' She walked swiftly to the car.

We didn't speak during the ten-minute ride to town.

Gilanis was a well-known restaurant above a supermarket. Chep and I enjoyed meeting at the bar tucked away from the prying eyes of diners.

We imagined ourselves to be all-knowing and sophisticated, seated at the counter.

The barman, Otish, welcomed me like an old friend.

'Kawaida, na tumania bhajia (the usual, and a plate of bhajias)', I ordered, knowing Chep would soon join me. Nothing like the spicy potato dish to help line our tummies for all the beer we would drink.

The bar was relatively empty, but a few people were seated at the scattered tables at the far end.

Chep breezed in as I finished my beer.

'You look chirpy!' she said. 'Had a good day? Lots of presents?'

'Actually, yes,' I lied. 'Where's yours?'

We laughed as we ordered more drinks. It was always nice to have a friend you knew so well; Chep was sweet. We had grown up in the same neighbourhood and shared many girlish confidences. But I found, as the evening wore on, that I still could not share with her what had happened to me.

Day by day I pondered over my dilemma as I carried on with my routines. While in boarding school I had rounded out well and was easily a size 16. As my belly grew I found it easy to camouflage my pregnancy. My heavy bust helped most of all.

My brother Thande assumed my cold attitude towards him was because of the failed birthday lunch, and he too cooled off towards me.

Just as well, as he would have picked up on my stress and worry.

My biggest fear was AIDS. Clearly Kangethe and Njoroge did not worry about contraception, and I figured he couldn't possibly be using condoms with his best friend and lover of God knows how many years.

I felt as though my life had stopped, and someone else had taken over. A voice far away tempted me to try for an abortion. But this was not an easy venture. Abortion is against the law in Kenya. Horror stories of botched operations scared me. Beside all this, the town had only two practising gynaecologists, both of whom were known to my family. I could not take the risk of exposing myself to such trauma and the possibility of permanent injury, arrest or even death at the hands of an abortionist.

The days turned into weeks, and weeks to months. My tummy grew huge as my appetite increased.

The yoghurt man doubled his rations for me. Those who now know about this wonder how I kept the baby to myself for nine months. It was easy. Nobody in our home expected that such a thing could possibly happen; and I simply took each day at a time. Sometimes I felt powerful, that I had something that was irrevocably my own, for the very first time.

I erased from my mind what to do when the time came to give birth.

Kangethe called me at work incessantly. Each time I heard his voice I hung up.

Before long I noticed my breasts were tender, and when I squeezed them a thick liquid oozed out.

'Milk,' I thought. I could not imagine breastfeeding a child. I did not once look at my naked body in the mirror.

The months had gone by so fast. It was easy to save money, as I had few expenses. I took time off from work; after all I had been there close to a year. The plan was to get to Nairobi, far away from my family.

Staying with an aunt, as I usually did, was not an option. A friend from school, Amina, had always asked me to visit with her. This was the perfect time.

'Amina,' I rang her one evening, 'you feel like having me over?'

She screamed into the phone, 'Girlfriend, where have you been?'

I explained that I had been working and needed to get away from home. We planned to meet that Friday evening; she pointed out that I was welcome to stay as long as I wanted. Her parents were more liberal than mine, and were used to hosting her friends from time to time.

During the two-hour trip into the city I felt like I was going to a place I could never come back from. The drive to Nairobi is full of twists and turns and climbs, and there was much to think about. My life would never be the same.

Amina was waiting for me at the bus terminus.

'Hannah!' she tried to embrace me but I evaded her by handing over my little suitcase. 'How are you? Wow, you are so fat!'

I had thought my swollen feet and legs were well camouflaged in my baggy jeans. It was typical of Amina not to hold back her feelings.

We took a bus to her parents' home. Carefully coordinated pink and purple covered just about every surface of Amina's room. It was the eighties.

'So, who's the man?' she asked as she freshened up for her Friday night out on the town with her boyfriend. She was surprised I was not interested in going out clubbing.

'Who said I had a man?' was my answer. I felt a moment of panic – had she figured out my condition? Although I had intended to confide in her that evening I was not quite ready to do so.

'Why don't you want to come out tonight?' she asked. 'You know Tim and I will enjoy having you around.'

'Honestly, the trip wore me out,' I replied. 'You guys go have fun; I'll join you tomorrow night.'

She left, assuring me that I could help myself to an early dinner whenever I felt hungry.

I felt rather tired, and had no appetite for a change. At about midnight that night my waters broke. I always imagined a flood of liquid would gush out of me, but it felt more like peeing on myself ever so slightly. Half an hour later, a pain crept across my stomach. Was that it? I wondered if dawn would hold off until I was ready to give birth. The slow pain came and went; came and went. Each time it felt sharper, more intense.

Then I felt the urge to sit on the toilet and shit. I worried I would soil the bedclothes.

Ooh, the urge to shit intensified. And there she was, all wet and slippery. She cried. She was beautiful. The pink bedcover was now a mess of blood, thick blood everywhere.

Time folded, and Amina's mother stood there, wearing a pink nightgown.

'Oh, God! Oh, God! I heard a baby cry!'

Coming to the bed, she picked up my little girl, holding her close.

'Where is Amina?' she asked, as she realized I was on my own.

Amina's brother appeared from nowhere, looking slightly tipsy. His night out had ended earlier than his sister's. What a welcome home.

'Salim, we mlevi (you drunkard)!' Mama Amina called out. 'Go get your father to drive us to hospital, and be quick!'

She placed the baby carefully beside me, and her voice quietened to a whisper as she asked, 'Has the afterbirth come?'

Well, there was a detail I had not taken into account. She pressed me down against the bed and massaged my stomach none too gently.

I was amazed at how flat my stomach suddenly was.

'You girls take such risks!' she chided. 'Why didn't you tell us you were expecting?'

Soon afterwards, I was in an operating theatre. Bright lights blinded me as I shivered.

'Be careful, this is a young girl,' the gynaecologist said as they cleaned up my privates. I felt the icy liquid sting me.

'My dear, relax, we are going to shave you,' said yet another hazy shadow looming over me.

I had torn pretty badly, apparently, and needed stitching. It was a strange sensation as the doctor stitched me up – no pain, just numbness. They drew blood for an HIV test.

When I came to, I was in a ward, a white curtain separating my bed from the others.

As I looked around me I saw from a distance my brother Thande, larger than life as he strode purposefully towards me. Behind him was my mother. Thande smiled at me.

'It's OK, we are here!' my mother whispered.

I felt warm tears slide out of the corner of my eye; drops fell past my nose as I reached up to wipe them.

'Why didn't you tell me?'

So much for the hysteria I had anticipated. My mother held her so comfortably; I wondered when I would ever learn. The poor thing was so tiny, her golden skin tinged with pink. I felt woozy and can't recall much of the conversation. I just knew that Mommy was with me and all would be well. My blood pressure had to be stabilized so I stayed in hospital for two days.

I got my HIV test results after a stern talking to by the matron.

'Never be too afraid to face the truth,' she said. 'All that stress can actually kill you.'

I was relieved. Now I could breastfeed little Wangeci.

A nurse tweaked my breasts to see if I had milk. She then brought the little baby to me, placing her in my arms so I could feed her. She looked like a little rabbit as she struggled blindly to secure her mouth onto my nipple. I felt a strange tugging as she began to suckle.

'Let her feed for ten minutes, then switch to the other breast,' the nurse instructed.

Well, that was it. I was nursing my baby.

My brother had rented a furnished apartment for my mother and me to use. My father sent word that I should not worry but focus on getting well. He never came to see me. I was not ready to face him.

My mother was constantly with me, and my brother called on us every day to make sure we had all that we needed. Wangeci was not as noisy as some babies I knew. She fed well, and spent most of her time punching her fists in the air. That gave me a chance to do her laundry. Nappies, vests, little dress, bibs that were constantly in need of changing. I was so paranoid about germs that I sterilized the laundry water. My days were typically busy and I rarely went to sleep before 11 p.m. Fortunately Wangeci slept through the night, so all I had to do was change her nappy in the early hours of the morning.

Single motherhood was and still is a big stigma in Kenya. The few single parents I knew suffered under patriarchal laws that gave you no right to financial support from a man who was not your husband.

It would be even worse for me as I could never tell this child the truth about her father. A fairly common option is to have your parents bring up your child. I knew of a family who brought up a 'younger sister' thus. She believed that her grandmother was her mother and her mother, an older sister, and when she learned the truth she was devastated. To this day she cannot relate to her real mother. Even if my parents had offered this as an option, I could not even imagine such a scenario. I needed to get back to living the life of the young adult I now was. While depending on my parents to support me through university was hardly independent, at least I was investing in my future. Without a degree, my chances of getting a job were extremely low.

Before a full week had ended, I knew I had to give her up for adoption. My mother broached the subject.

'You know, before I married your father I fell pregnant,' she started. 'If we had not married, I would have opted for adoption. You have not told me who your boyfriend is.'

'It was such a mistake. I can't talk to anyone about it,' I whispered. 'Please, help me plan for adoption.'

She embarked on her new mission with her usual zeal. It took about three weeks for the process to be completed.

It was a Tuesday morning when I had to give her up. I don't like the month of August any more. Every year, Wangeci makes her way into my head, into my life. Not knowing seems as dangerous as finding out. I wonder if Wangeci simply is a baby, always will only be a baby. Whatever it is we can be together, it is not mother and daughter. There is nothing we have shared together. And yet, she is, oddly, the most important thing. She is seventeen this year.

I barely slept the night before, gazing at her as she slept. I looked at the size of her things by my bed, and wondered how it is that this assortment of things, so small when packed, was the size of a whole world I was about to close to myself, and her, for good. My whole life remains pivoted around those months.

'How do we know you will not change your mind and start crying for your child?' one of the social workers asked, as I held Wangeci close to my chest. The small room smelled of ink and old paper. There was a pink baby shawl draped over one of the chairs. From another baby left here, I thought.

'Do you know the father's name?' another asked.

I gave Kangethe's name. It was the last time I ever voiced it out loud.

'Mnyonyeshe (breastfeed her), it's your last chance,' spoke out yet another social worker. 'You don't know the next time she will get fed.'

I began to wonder if I had made a mistake. These were the people I would hand my baby over to. Why were they being so mean?

She sucked at my breast until she fell asleep.

I handed her over. We went for lunch.

A LOVE DIVERTED

Lynn Lauber

Here are some of the things you can do when you give away a baby: you can deny it, you can dissociate from your body, you can mistreat yourself or seduce someone to do it for you; you can over eat, you can drink, you can smoke whatever is ignitable, whatever you can sear into your lungs.

You can sublimate, you can become ambitious, you can be terrified of ever again being pregnant. You can study faces in shopping malls, catalogs, over your shoulder. You can talk about your loss and, by doing so, convince yourself that you are doing something beneficial. You can develop chest pains, you can have a neck lift, a nose job, a blepharoplasty. You can not show up; you can show up early. You can refuse to take care of anything, even yourself. You can dream; you can have nightmares; you can establish unreasonable attachments; you can be attached to nothing at all. You can have an odd affect; people can say you look sad. Men can say, 'Hey, it can't be that bad.' You can start crying and be unable to stop. You can feel as if you have a straight pin lodged in your face so that it hurts when you smile.

Twenty years after I was pregnant, I found a 1949 book at a garage sale called *Pedigrees of Negro Families*, by an Englishman, R. Ruggles Gates, F.R.S., who wrote of racial traits with the offhandedness of a cattle breeder. I read randomly from page 231: 'Kinky or wooly hair is found not only in the Negro but also in the Negrito, Melanesian and Tasmanian. The pepper-corn hair of South African Bushmen and Hottentots differs only in being knotted together in little clusters, with bare patches of skull between them.' Hottentots!

I studied the photos of these lost subjects: Fig. VI.8 with her tightly kinked African or *cuculaxtl* hair, Fig. 116 with her longer second toe, displayed against a worn Persian rug. I read how vio-lent temper is inherited as a simple dominant without a skip, how inheritance of artistic abilities resembles that of an allergy, that there is a lower frequency of nontasters in the Negro race. I read a quote from a former Justice Hughes who said that 'by applying one tenth as much science in mating human beings as we do in mating animals, we would probably add more to the health of our children and grandchildren than can be done by all the medical discoveries of the next hundred years.'

I studied the interior of Fig. 69's mouth, with his small upper lateral incisors, a disharmony, along with malocclusion, 'which occurs in racial crosses,' the author notes. A strong whiff of disapproval hung over these descriptions, but I was accustomed to that.

In 1969, when I was sixteen, I had given up for adoption my baby by my African-American boyfriend. I had given this child up without a peek or a hug, the method of choice of both the Friends Home for Unwed Mothers, where I had spent seven sodden, lethargic months, and the Methodists' Children's Home, who had placed my child, promptly and peremptorily, with a sniff of righteousness. I had been strongly advised that this was the preferable way to proceed – without sight or sound. Several girls from the home who had resisted and nursed their babies once or viewed them once became troublesome about signing relinquishment papers and developed pesky separation prob-lems. But it had been borne in on me what a heartache and

trouble I was, and I was eager to impersonate the pleasant, mal-
leable girl I'd been prior to my rebellion. So I signed the release
forms, I had my breasts bound, I did not speak of what I felt or
thought. But I couldn't do anything about my face, which had
developed during my months of pregnancy a grave and melan-
choly cast, or the injured point in the center of my eyes.

No matter what you do, pain bleeds through, like a stain.
And I still had my imagination. No one could take that.

Deeper in *Negro Pedigrees*, I read about the B family, which
began when a Scotsman married a Negro. 'When the elder
daughter married a Hindu, their five children showed a wide
range in hair form.' Studying the results of this union, I began to
construct an elaborate jigsaw of what my own lost daughter
might look like, taking an eye from here, a jowl from there.
I knew dark skin was dominant to pale and, according to
Mr. Ruggles, that curly hair was dominant to wavy and wavy to
straight. I hoped long bones and slimness were dominant, too,
for my daughter's sake – my line were long-torsoed Germans
with a tendency toward ruddy skin and pastel eyes, but not lithe
and lean like my old boyfriend's side.

The photos of the now dead subjects in *Negro Pedigrees* were
beautiful to me with their crinkled hair and soft-toned skins.
They looked made of chocolate and cream, buttery, umbery. I
had always admired the mulatto offspring in my boyfriend's
neighborhood, their magnificent curled heads and golden skins.
I was aware of formulating a belief that this toss of the races created the most sublime of creatures, the best of everyone.

With my dark tan and wide features, I even impersonated
being a mulatto for a time, saying I was adopted, in an amazing
foreboding of what would soon actually occur in my life. In
what must have seemed to my boyfriend an odd reversal of the
usual pattern, I passed for a season as half black.

My boyfriend was another casualty of my pregnancy; three of

us were lost, in all. Although he offered marriage, I took this only as a courteous gesture and declined his mother's offer to keep the baby, convinced that it would be the same as keeping it myself. There were hard feelings after that, and a separation; I received a phone call from him occasionally, usually on the birthday of our child. He always believed we would find our daughter, even though I – the one who made sporadic searches – remained doubtful. He prayed for this, he told me, along with his mother, for whom I'd developed a soft spot. He had done what I had done, what you seem to do when you have a child with someone and all is lost – romanticized our past. That our relationship had only lasted a few months, that he had originally been more interested in a girlfriend of mine than in me, that half the nights I spent at his house were with his mother, listening to her tell stories and eating her cake – these facts became lost to us, glossed over by surplus feelings; the conception of our daughter had gathered around itself a holy, redemptive light. Who had known what a monumental act we were performing behind the shower curtain of his bedroom, when instead of algebra, we turned and studied ourselves. Neither of us could help what we did with such material later. For a long time he constructed a fantasy of what the two of us had been to each other. And for twenty years, using various voices and angles of approach, I wrote about that window of time.

That same year, from two different sources, I came upon another arcane book, *The Game of Life and How to Play It*, written in 1925 by Florence Scovel Shinn. I discovered it first in a house on the Greek island of Santorini where I was staying with friends. The house was hollowed into the cliffs and featured a walled-off courtyard where I sat in the sun listening to a tour of nuns wander by; the sea – and their habits – were just visible through chinks in the wall. I discovered this book tucked in a bookshelf in the bedroom I had been arbitrarily assigned, and I read it through one stormy night, adrift in the sea.

Back home, out of the blue, I received another copy of this same book from a former boyfriend who was by then a neurosurgeon in Hawaii. In *The Game of Life*, Shinn wrote about the power of words and imaginings, how every desire, uttered or unexpressed, is a demand.

She told a little story: 'One Easter, having seen many beautiful rose-trees in the florists' windows, I wished I would receive one, and for an instant saw it mentally being carried in the door. Easter came, and with it a beautiful rose-tree. I thanked my friend the following day, and told her it was just what I had wanted.

'She replied, "I didn't send you a rose-tree, I sent you lilies!"

'The man had mixed the order, and sent me a rose-tree simply because I had started the law in action, and *I had to have a rose-tree.*'

There were other such stories, hilarious to me in their mundaneness: of people desiring hats, fur-lined overcoats, houses not intended for them.

Still, one night soon after, I said out loud to whoever might be listening: 'I want to find my daughter.'

It was this same neurosurgeon who also provided me with the next link in my search, my labor records, which I asked him to request from the hospital and forward to me.

I tore through these faded pages, reading about myself as if I were the fictional character I'd turned myself into all these years – the she, the her, the distant I.

I was amazed by the eloquence of facts, how many clues there were to savor:

The ballpoint words written across the glossy pages: BFA – Baby for Adoption. The signature of the nursery nurse, Frances Lombardi, R.N., who had seen more of my baby then I had. The signature of the delivery nurse, Mary Loomis, R.N., whose wrist I had bitten at one point during my prolonged and ignorant labor. (No one had given us breathing tips at the puritan home for unwed mothers; they'd rather you suffer, better to remind you of your sins.) I read that a sixteen-year-old female, whose leg ached when it rained, had a low-forceps delivery with an ROA vertex presentation and a 400 cc blood loss and that the final diagnosis (for a pregnancy, on these forms, was no more than an illness) was this: next to the word *viable*, someone had drawn the woman sign. This hieroglyph was the only real evidence I had of my daughter. It shook me deep, as symbols can, and concentrated my resolve to find her.

Throughout the years, whenever I tried to imagine my daughter's life, I envisioned her living amidst a family of brisk, competent 'professionals,' the term that was used to soothe me at the time of her adoption – erudite professors or anthropologists, who wore horn-rimmed glasses and lavished her with World Books and oxblood shoes. I expected this fantasy to be further fueled by the letter I received from the adoption agency a few months later, after I discovered I was permitted to know nonidentifying information about the adoptive family.

In this note, Margaret Eufinger, L.S.W., caseworker of the United Methodists' Children's Home, informed me that my daughter's father was a psychiatrist and that her mother had been a case aide in a psychiatric hospital.

Then she reached into the bag of all she must have known, and pulled out one little narrative to tell me – an emblematic story to stand in for all the rest. It concerned a month spent by the family on a farm with friends where the father helped with the harvest and the mother helped with all the cooking for the farmhands. The mother had described a lovely room with a canopy bed and antique furniture that their daughter occupied when they were there. Their success and family happiness were such that they planned to adopt another biracial child.

I was forty-one by the time I had this little plate of tidbits handed to me, but it did not produce the gratitude I'd expected. And what about my daughter? Couldn't Margaret Eufinger have given me one shard, one descriptive fact, the shade of her hair, or the size of her shoes, something, anything? All along, I had been given to think that whoever was raising my daughter, there were at least two of them, while there was only one callow me. But now that I had this whole panorama of family felicity typed up on cream bond, I felt suspicious. It only enticed me further – my faceless child in a canopy bed!

Of course, by the time the caseworker doled out this thin gruel, she was writing about a vanished version of my daughter, one I had been unable to conjure up in the aftermath of my pregnancy, wandering lost and logy through my late teens. There was something profoundly damaged about me after my pregnancy, as if I had abandoned not only my baby but some central internal organ, a nameless monitor or clearinghouse without which I was running amok. I developed a veneer, a scab, a husk, a hull, and was callous most of all toward myself.

But now I felt something else, a belligerence not necessarily aimed back at myself: Mrs. Eufinger may have thought she was quieting me down with her dull letter, but in fact she was stirring me up.

The letter ended:

'I don't know whether you were aware that since 1985 it is possible for a biological parent to file the form I have enclosed which gives permission for the child to find them. If you want you can fill out the form and send it to the address given. The only problem with this process is that most parents and children born long before it was passed don't know about it. But it certainly wouldn't hurt to send it in.'

It certainly wouldn't; and no, I wasn't aware, having not kept up with the nuances of Ohio state law, having escaped, in fact, the state of Ohio as soon as I was able.

But I filled it in; I began filling in many forms.

I discern now what I couldn't then, what we never can make out till later, a pattern; after years of floundering, abortive efforts, I was making inexorable progress.

The next link was simple: a friend gave me a magazine that contained a letter from a birth mother who'd found her daughter in Ohio; she urged readers to call if they wanted further information. I placed the letter on a table and looked at it, then covered it with junk mail, and then found it again. Finally, one evening, I called the number and talked to the birth mother, who told me about a group of women who worked as sleuths, using a computer database, to reunite adoptees and their birth parents. The cost was nominal; she gave me the number.

I called, filled in the forms, and paid the money; I waited weeks, which, after decades, seemed too long. These searchers were housewives working out of midwestern basements. I didn't know – or care – about their methods. If they were breaking into office buildings with machetes, with machine guns, it was all right by me. In my mind's eye, I envisioned a locked file cabinet bulging with all the facts that I'd wanted to know all these years – starting with my daughter's name – her name! of which I had not an inkling. If I'd had a stick of dynamite, I would have blown it up myself.

The searcher finally called and said she had narrowed it down to four girls who had been born and adopted the correct day and place. She read them off to me, a smorgasbord of possibilities, and I tried to sense some recognition, but there was none. The Deborah sounded the same to me as the Sherry – none of them were names I would have picked (what would I have picked? It was one of the many things I'd never allowed myself to consider), someone else's idea of a daughter.

The searcher left me to ponder the names; she would get back to me when she pinpointed the girl who had been born at the correct moment on that day in July. I waited again, but with a different taste in my mouth. I knew that I was going to find out now, and I could sense just beyond that knowing the wealth of information that was going to pour out.

And then everything happened at once: the searcher called

and told me she'd found my daughter lodged even deeper in the midwest than I'd been myself – in Missouri, a state I'd never even thought of before. I ripped through the almanac to study its portly shape. Why hadn't I had a feeling about this? On what sublevel had I been living, dumb and numb and factless?

The searcher had been able to locate only the phone number of the adoptive parents. She was going to call them and present the situation; hopefully, they would be agreeable to giving my number to their daughter and letting her decide if she wanted to make the call.

Another day of waiting; and another report. The mother, who turned out not to be the original adoptive one, was willing to talk to me.

Everything was in my throat when I called her: I dimly realized I had to represent myself well or I might lose my daughter again. But I couldn't hold myself back to prepare a statement, a press release of who I was – instead I rattled off a welter of my professional and personal history and could hear, even as I was saying it, that being an unmarried writer wasn't sitting well in Missouri, a state, I was to learn, where they seem to marry – and divorce – more than they do anything else.

Still, after my recitation, she offered me my first facts, they rolled out of her mouth and into my ear like marbles, so many that I could hardly contain them.

As it turned out, my daughter'd had several mothers in her life before I found her, but no central mother, none who had stayed, starting with me, the original, central fleer.

From a selfish point of view, this lack of a central mother meant there was no major maternal figure who might resent me and withhold access. In fact, the latest wife, perhaps because she had children of her own, was the one who kindly sent me the first views I ever had of my daughter, X-ray-like baby photos rolled off the fax machine in my pharmacy, a toddler face bleeding into a glamour shot where she looked like an old-fashioned movie star, bleeding into an honor roll list of 1983 – even upside

down I could discern one A after another: smart *and* beautiful.
Deep in my secret heart, this was exactly what I'd expected.

The next milestone was when my daughter called me: one afternoon in April while I was folding clothes – the simplest of
scenes! – the phone rang, and the inevitable happened: like water
seeking its own level, we were connected again. But only by
words, and I'd made do with words long enough. Now I wanted
the concrete, the three dimensional; I wanted to see the breath in
her chest. At the airport, a month later, I searched for her face in
the blur of arriving passengers. And then there she was, striding
toward me on the most delicate ankles, ankles that had once
been folded inside me like a colt's.

That first visit blurred by in a series of concentrated moments –
it was almost too much to apprehend her all at once. I looked
at her baby photos for the first time while she sat across the
table, studying me. I left the room and walked back in again,
just to see her anew, sitting there, plain as a lamp in my living
room. Her cheek collapsed on the pillow the first morning
was just like my mother's. Heard from another room, her voice
was an echo of mine. I couldn't represent this to anyone – you
would have had to be there, you would have had to be me –
but I had already begun developing a brisk, breezy veneer that
belied what was going on inside, a fountain of feelings from
the clogged center of my heart. I'd heard of a reunited mother
and daughter who slept together and constantly held hands.
But I didn't do this – I was careful how I touched her, in case
she vanished like smoke. In fact, I felt to my surprise a tug of
holding back – the same holding back I was always so scornful of in Ohio. On one occasion when she stood in front of me
weeping, I hugged my own arms in frozen inertness; I couldn't
do what I longed to, take her in my arms and hug her back.
    The truth was, thrust all at once into the costume of a mother,
I was unsure how to act. I was the one who had always been the

daughter – it had been my most enduring role; encountering her shook up my sense of myself. It made me aware of how mature, how solid I was; not having children can keep you adrift in a perpetual late adolescence. But now I was confronted with the fact I had produced this complex creature, taller and more beautiful than I ever was, even if I hadn't raised her.

While women around me were going through fertility agonies, I felt a sense of serenity at what I'd already – however inadvertently – accomplished.

Seeing my daughter for the first time was like walking into the middle of my long-ago affair with her father – into the living room of it – that autumn of her conception: chitlins on the stovetop, Smokey Robinson crooning, jumbled bedclothes, a surprising kindness. Out of less than this are children born.

Why hadn't I become pregnant before? For I had been at this for some months then – making love in the blind plain way of our old beagle Missy, who we sometimes caught in the act, her muzzle averted, looking abstracted at some far-off place. I don't remember enjoyment so much as the powerful salt and liquid of it all. Quickly over, wordless; procreation like in the biology books, which I dozed over shortly – pregnant, more than I had ever been anything. Who would have thought someone so inauthentic, so unfinished, could be something so concrete, so legal – that without a driver's license, a guidebook, I had managed such a serious, elemental state?

I never got over the surprise of my condition and for the rest of my fertile life avoided pregnancy like the dread disease it had once been made to seem. Whatever maternal impulse I might have had was effectively blocked by this experience; to be pregnant without the prize at the end is a cruel trick on more than the body. I rarely lingered over babies; whether I was genuinely uninterested or couldn't afford to, I never knew for sure. In any case, I never considered having another. If I couldn't have her, I didn't want anyone else.

*

Here are some of the frightening stories you hear about reunifica-
tion: a child is found, a girl, with bad skin and a reform school
record; she slouches into your unmarried life smoking Salem
Lights, demanding funds, hoisting grudges that she plops down on
your living room rug. There are recriminations, tallying up of old
debts, and you are the one who owes. Or this: a young man knocks
on your door, a tall dusky man – you answer in your apron, your
married life shimmering behind you . . . your appliances, your children, your husband, pale and innocent of your ignoble past . . . Hi,
Mom, he says, through corroded teeth. Guess who?

These are the stories you hear of adoptive reunions – only bad
stories, because what is adoption deep down but a love diverted?

They are cautionary tales. You don't hear stories like mine
without waiting for the twist, the other shoe to drop, as I do.

I worry that my daughter will disappear again – that some
words I say will be wrong, that she will all at once express the
outrage I fear she feels, deep down – and deprive me of the great
privilege of knowing her.

When I don't hear from her for a while, I fear the worst; I
have no faith, there being nothing to fall back on. The years
between us are not only unaccounted but unaccountable; they
cannot be made up no matter how many photo albums I drag
from my closet. My face lies flat under plastic, one dimensional,
finished – she cannot get to me at sixteen, when I had her, or
twenty, just as I cannot reach out now and fathom the scent of
her as the infant I never saw. Her baby photos call up in me a
well of nonrecognition – there she is beribboned with tiny teeth
and eyelet collar loved by someone – while I was where, doing
what? Because I did not take her into my arms, there was no
early bond, no scent to enrich my torment. It was a plain loss,
unexplored, unremarked.

My daughter was twenty-five by the time I met her, a beautiful,
pragmatic, efficient young woman. While I, in my forties, work
freelance and manage a certain aloofness to tradition, my daugh-

ter owns property; she owns crystal; her purses match her shoes.

In these traits, she has jumped a generation to my decorative mother, who was always too much for our hometown. My mother, who is always trying to give me appliquéd gloves and embellished tea towels. These can now go directly to my daughter.

'She's just like us!' my mother cried happily the first time she met her, meaning she was just like her.

I persist in this too; happily counting the ways she is just like me. Unknown to us for so long, we search her face and yearn to find ourselves there, embedded.

Over time, my daughter and I have developed between us a bantering, easygoing manner. I seem to have emerged as an intimate pal, a veteran of life and love, not the role I might have imagined, but what was there for me to be? It was too late for an apron, too late in a number of ways. What could I teach this woman, who already had an M.B.A., who could already choose a stock fund better than I? About novels? Flowers? I did help her plant a garden the third year, bringing nasturtium seeds in my carry-on bag. It was a fine thing, digging in the earth with her under the flat midwestern sun, just as it was good to devour fried catfish with her, to sleep with a fan in the room with her, to be hypochondriacs together. These are the odd traits I seem to have passed on to my daughter, but I am thrilled to have passed on anything at all. It seems now that I spent the whole first year happily affirming her questions. Yes, I grind my teeth at night; yes, I pee all the time ... yes to cheesecake, Laurence Olivier, Alfred Hitchcock. Yes, yes. Finally.

ADOPTIVE PARENTS

BRINGING HOME BABY

Tama Janowitz

Days 1–2

We are in Beijing, en route to adopt our baby. Our group consists of eight couples and two single women, along with our leader, a woman named Xiong Yan, who will serve as tour guide for two days in Beijing before we fly down to Hefei to collect the babies and where Xiong Yan will do our final adoption paperwork.

Even though I had been anxious, even desperate, to get our baby when I was back in New York, for some reason I calmed down the minute we arrived in China. The other couples are all frantic to get to the kids, most of whom are around nine months old and whom we have seen only in photos. Now, after more than eight months of excruciating waiting and paperwork, now that we have landed, I suddenly begin to wonder – what's the rush?

The endless adoption process has been like a scavenger hunt: the FBI, for example, needed fingerprints to prove we weren't on their most-wanted list. Birth certificates with original signatures had to be acquired, then sent to city departments, taken to state departments, federal departments, then to the Chinese consulate. Medical exams were required, along with tax returns and letters of recommendation. Our heads even had to be probed and analyzed by therapists.

During that time, it seemed we would *never* get our baby. After all, she was getting older by the minute, and in the only picture we had, taken when she was two months old, she already had a surly expression – a positive attribute, by my standards.

I might have adopted years ago, even before I met my husband, but I had never been entirely certain that I had maternal tendencies toward babies. I knew I had maternal tendencies toward dogs. And since I always knew any child of mine would have doggish qualities, I wasn't too concerned. I was a novelist and worked at home, so I had plenty of time on my hands. Since I could never write for more than a few hours a day, when I was finished all I had left to do was to stare at the ceiling, wondering why I had picked novel writing as a career. Fourteen years ago, I came to Manhattan in search of other human beings and found myself, only a short time later, on the cover of *New York* magazine in a meat locker with a lot of animal carcasses, the author of a hit novel. Now, I felt, I was on to even bigger adventures.

I knew Tim would make a wonderful father, but I rarely picked up friends' children, since whenever I did, they usually burst into tears. Also, I never could believe that anyone would let us adopt – for one thing, we lived in a small one-bedroom apartment. Two adults, three dogs, and both of us fanatical collectors of books (Tim is a curator). There was scarcely any room left. But the adoption agency assured us that two rooms were an improvement over a crib in a crowded orphanage, and that once we were driven out of our minds, we would double our efforts to find another place to live. Soon we would be a family – or whatever they call it at the end of the twentieth century. So I was thrilled that, once I was in Beijing, my anxiety and apprehensions had disappeared. We were taken to see the Great Wall and the Forbidden City. In Tienanmen Square a woman got run over by a taxi – not someone in our group, though.

I loved everything about the place – the sights and the shopping (cashmere sweaters were $100, and they came in the richest, lushest hues I had ever seen; huge cashmere shawls for $150; and dresses of fantastically patterned silk for $30). The antiques market had beautiful old Chinese elm chests lined with camphor ($50), and brilliant vermilion lacquer and leather trunks ($40). And the restaurants! We ate in our hotel, which was a modern skyscraper – our last night alone as a couple – and I couldn't get over the menu, which was the most fabulous menu I had ever seen. Under the category 'Danty of Sea Food' was listed: Fried Fish Maw with Stuff and Green Cucumber; Sautéed Cuttlefish with American Celery; and Sea Blubber with Cucumber Shreds. Under 'Vetable,' I found Braised Hedgehog Hydnun and Fried Whole Scorpion.

'Let's stay away from the Dry-Braised Dick Strip in Brawn Sauce,' Tim said.

'OK,' I said. 'But why don't we try the Fried Whole Scorpion? It's only ten cents, and it can't possibly really be a scorpion – it's under the Vetable heading.'

The waitress seemed astonished that we wanted Fried Whole Scorpion. 'Maybe scorpion's out of season?' I said.

'Only one?' She shook her head. 'Only one?' she repeated.

'OK,' said Tim, to placate her. 'Two.'

A few minutes later two fried, whole black scorpions – claws outstretched, tails curled – arrived at our table, each dramatically positioned on a rice cracker.

'Do you think people usually order a whole platterful?' I said. Tim was looking at the scorpions appreciatively. 'Well, here goes,' I said, shutting my eyes and putting the scorpion in my mouth. Under normal circumstances, I probably wouldn't have done this. It might have been my last attempt at extricating myself from a situation – getting our baby – which, as the hour grew closer, I was beginning, far too late, to question.

The scorpion was crispy but did not have a distinctive scorpion flavor nor any instantaneous venomous effects. I really did want a baby, as long as it was quiet and gurgled to itself in a crib. Anybody I ever knew who had a baby always said, almost continuously, 'You should have a baby. It's the most fantastic thing that can happen to you.' I could never figure out why they kept saying this when the look in their eyes was that of a survivor of an airplane crash, but I figured it was something I would understand later.

Day 3
Everyone is impatient on the flight to Hefei. One father-to-be says he feels like we are Elvis fans, waiting for a glimpse of Him.

I am beginning to get to know our group a little bit. Everyone is in their mid-thirties to mid-forties – a physiologist, a pediatrician, a photographer, an editor, an insurance agent, an education researcher, a marine engineer. One or two of our group have grown children from a previous marriage. Two couples already have four-year-olds waiting for a new sister. In China, it's the girls who are abandoned. Chinese couples are allowed only one child, and girls just don't have much cultural status. In addition, it's the boys who look after the parents in their old age: in other words, no son, no pension plan. In the future, China will be like New York City, only in reverse: men will outnumber women one hundred to one. When a single Chinese woman walks into a party, she will be as desirable as a movie-star-handsome billionaire bisexual bachelor is in Manhattan.

Under normal circumstances, the people in our group wouldn't have much in common, but the fact that we are all joined together in this adventure makes me feel like a timid opera buff who has signed up for a packaged Perillo tour to La Scala.

At the hotel in Hefei – another modern skyscraper – we all disappear to our rooms, still laughing, smiling. The next time we see one another, we will all be with our smiling, adorable, happy little babies. I only wish I had brought other clothing. All the women seem to be dressed as Mothers, in long floral-print dresses or crisp linen outfits. A glimpse in the mirror as we all get off the elevator reveals a sophisticated crowd of parents-to-be and one hippie type with hair like black scrambled eggs, wearing a T-shirt Tim found in Beijing that reads CDLVIH-KLEIN, with smaller letters beneath that explain it is UHDERWEQR. (The Chinese love T-shirts printed with English words. They don't seem to care that they are almost always misspelled and that they make very little sense.)

Two o'clock, 2:15, 2:30. Tim and I pace back and forth, as if our wife were in labor next door in the delivery room. I keep running to the bathroom to brush my teeth. If the baby detects even a whiff of stale breath, it could put a damper on our relationship for years to come. Finally, around 3:30, the call comes: *she* is on her way.

After months of arguing, we have decided to name her Willow. I had wanted to call her Thomasina, or Letizia. Tim was thinking more in terms of Hortense or Hattie. It no longer matters. Maybe the name Willow is a safeguard: after all, the background information and photograph we received several months ago indicated that – for her age – she was extremely short and fat. With a name like Willow, this will have to change. The doorbell rings: Xiong Yan and a baby-nurse from the orphanage arrive with Willow.

Willow is very cute, dripping with sweat (the Chinese believe in keeping their babies bundled up even in the heat), with giant ears. When the nurse hands her to me, she smiles, even though she and the other babies have been riding for six hours in an unair-conditioned bus from the orphanage. 'This is the first baby I've ever held who didn't burst into tears,' I say, smiling.

'She doesn't cry,' says the nurse in Mandarin. Xiong Yan translates. 'She likes to play.'

'She's just been fed,' Xiong Yan adds. 'When you give her food, make sure it's boiling hot – that's what they're accustomed to. She should be fed at six a.m., nine, twelve, three, six, and then she goes to sleep and gets fed again at eleven at night. Keep her warm – never let her stomach be uncovered.'

Then, handing us a box of rice cereal and a bag of formula that we are to combine in specific amounts at the next feeding, Xiong Yan and Willow's nurse leave.

Immediately, the smiling happy baby in my arms bursts into tears. The nurse was right, Willow doesn't cry, as long as she is played with – every single second. This baby doesn't want to cuddle; she wants to be bounced, rocked, swooped around the room, then turned upside down to stare grimly while adults flap their arms and hop around the room like parrots. Because Willow has been confined to a crib for the past nine months – ever since she was abandoned in a park at two days old – she has no muscle tone, so all the swooping, jostling, and jiggling has to be by the person holding her. The minute that person stops tossing her around, she screams.

Despite her physical weakness, she has an abnormal amount of energy. I'm wondering, hyperactive? Her head has been shaved – another Chinese custom, to assure thicker, more luxuriant growth – and she definitely has sideburns. It really may be that Baby Elvis, complete with all the troubles of his past life, has been reincarnated. I wonder if they selected her for us after they saw the picture of Tim and me that we had to send with our application.

She cries nonstop, and since I have read somewhere that babies cry only for a reason, Tim and I decide to change her diaper. We put her on the floor and try to get her out of her clothes. Though she is weak, she is able to fight like a wounded fox in a leghold trap. Even with the two of us working hard, the task is next to impossible.

My face is bright red; sweat is pouring off Tim, dripping onto the sweating baby. We look at each other. 'Is it too late for her to catch the bus back to the orphanage?' I ask.

This diaper changing takes around an hour. When Willow is back in her clothes with a diaper haphazardly strangling her midriff, the sobbing diminishes somewhat, which makes us realize it is time for her bottle. Trying to get the lumps out of the gruel with the lukewarm water in a thermos provided by the hotel takes almost another hour. By then, I can tell, she is really angry and bored – obviously this was not what she expected.

The hotel has provided our room with a purple metal cage, a crib with bars that are spaced just far enough apart to trap a baby's head. Willow doesn't like the crib. Being in the crib makes her very upset. If she was angry before, now she is furious. The toys we brought from the United States are lousy; any fool would have known. But finally, after several hours of strenuous entertainment – songs, the hora, arm wrestling – and another feeding, we are able to get her to sleep. By now it's quite late, though how much time has passed it's hard to say. I was ready for bed hours ago.

Unfortunately, though she's already snoring, I can't sleep. What if we have unwittingly killed her, and each snore is her last gasp? A kid who survives being left in a park, only to be murdered by two witless foreigners. If she lives, though, I don't know what we are going to do: it will be eighteen years before she's ready for college. I suppose we can send her to summer camp and boarding school in the meantime.

At least I know she's not dead when she decides – at three a.m. – to take a second look at some of the toys. She discovers that if she pounds a button, the tinny electronic version of 'It's a Small World,' a song I have always loathed, will play over and over.

Day 4

Dawn. First there is the feeding, the bathing, the changing, the attempt at cheering her up while the other adult member of our family unit tries to shower and put on some clothes and vice versa. At no time must she be ignored. The kid has no inner resources – can't read, write letters, put on nail polish – and seems to have nowhere to go.

It is now eight – it has taken us only three hours to get ready for breakfast.

In the lobby, large groups are patrolling the halls, and I see that – although they are speaking Norwegian or Swedish, or have Canadian accents – every single one of them is lugging a sobbing Chinese baby. No wonder the place was so noisy last night. What I thought was simply bad singing coming from the karaoke bar downstairs was a hellish chorus of babies.

A woman approaches Willow in her stroller. Willow looks up at her and coos appreciatively, as if she is about to be rescued from what is obviously a mistaken placement. 'Oh, what a cute baby!' the woman says. 'I was supposed to get mine yesterday, but she's not going to be delivered until today. It's like torture, waiting for her!'

'You could take this one,' I offer.

Our group has already gathered in the dining hall for breakfast. Tots in their strollers are lined up in a ring around the table. 'How's everything going?' I ask weakly, expecting a response similar to one I would have given.

Instead, and in unison, they shout, 'Great!'

Day 5
The horror. The horror.

Day 6
By now the other parents also appear to have aged ten years. They're so worn down that at last they, too, are willing to admit everything is not perfect. Two babies cry constantly and even if they can be stopped will start again the moment anyone looks at them. One baby is on a hunger strike. Two babies have been given the wrong ratio of rice cereal to formula and are severely constipated.

I have definitely bonded with the group, if not the baby. There is nothing like discussing techniques for relieving constipation over breakfast to make one feel close. But then at every meal we have the most fascinating conversations on topics ranging from diaper rash and diarrhea to baby dandruff.

Day 7
How could I have been such an idiot? It was Tim who had his doubts and apprehensions about adopting, but it's he who has

bonded immediately with Willow. No wonder she looks at him so adoringly. He is a natural: strong enough to throw her around, adept at changing diapers, and he laughs with honest delight when she viciously inserts one sharp-clawed finger as far up his right nostril as possible.

When she tries to pull out my hair by the roots, I can't help but believe her intent is malicious. My arms are too weak to toss her into the air. For this, it is obvious, she will never forgive me. And I will never forgive myself for believing all those girlfriends who kept telling me, 'You should have a baby! It's so great!' I see now that it was their method of revenge. I must remember to encourage others to do this marvelous thing – adopting a hyperactive, sweating lunatic unable to change her own diaper.

The Chinese paperwork is complete; our next stop is a week in Guangzhou (formerly Canton) to complete the American immigration process. After that, we fly back to the United States, where, I suppose, the real nightmare begins and where Willow will soon begin demanding Barbie dolls, Nintendo, and pure-white Arabian mares, start taking drugs, contract sexually transmitted diseases, insist on attending the fanciest, most expensive private schools, and sob uncontrollably when she doesn't get into the college of her choice.

Postscript: Four Weeks Later

Despite what my journal predicted, we have been extremely lucky. Our baby is so easygoing; she's laughing, laughing, laughing all the time. Sometimes she laughs so much, staring at her beautiful little rosebudlike face in the mirror, that I, too, begin to cackle uncontrollably.

Honestly, no matter how many times anyone insists I wrote those earlier entries in my diary, I truly can never believe them. It must have just been the jet lag. Or something. Willow is so sweet! Just the other day our pediatrician told me not to worry – hopefully by college age she won't need a bottle and will be on to the harder stuff. Having a baby is the most fantastic, wonderful thing a person can do. And Willow is so cute! So smart! I'm thinking maybe in the fall I'll look into adopting one from India. Yes, I can see her already: perhaps a bit older than Willow, one of those gypsy/street-urchin/waif types, with dark skin, gold bangles at her slim wrists and ankles, and thick, wild hair. I wonder just how long it will take to convince Tim . . .

MY DAUGHTER'S BIG BROTHER

Matthew Engel

I met my first child in roughly the way most fathers do. It was late spring in 1992, warm and humid, as I recall. We were in a small room off the maternity ward of a slightly underfunded hospital in an English provincial city. It was a difficult birth, and my son's cry was more than normally plaintive. We called him Laurie, after his maternal grandfather, who did not live to see him.

I met my second child on 25 January 1999. We were in the nursery room at the Tyumen Municipal Orphanage, Siberia, which is very underfunded indeed. Outside, it was close to −30°C. Our daughter was already eight months old and crawling. She immediately beamed at us. We called her Victoria, because someone already had. We are a bit hazy about her original maternal grandfather.

Fathering my son took a couple of glasses of wine, and a raise of the eyebrow. Fathering my daughter took twenty months, mostly spent battling against a bureaucracy that was often intrusive, inefficient, uncommunicative and unfeeling in a way the Tsars would have recognized. But that wasn't in Russia – the Russians were fine. It was in Britain.

This country has turned the adoption of a child into something very close to a crime: the perpetrators are harried, if not actually punished.

In Britain, you have a slightly better chance of adopting a baby less than a year old than you do of winning a million pounds on the lottery. But only slightly better (175 lottery millionaires a year; maybe 300 babies adopted). For various reasons, few babies are available here. But across the world, orphanages are full of babies and older children all literally crying out for a loving family. Almost 16,000 go to the USA every year, and around 4,000 to France. Here, only about 200 children were adopted from overseas in 1998. I can find nothing in our law or our culture to explain this, but everything in the implementation of the law by local authorities, civil servants and social workers.

I believe we took Victoria from a situation in which she had no hope and gave her a chance of a happy and fulfilled life. From Russia to love. Happiness may elude her, of course – that can happen to anyone – but we will always do our utmost for her. Thus, something miraculous has already happened, for her and for us. Yet British officialdom sees things differently. Adopting a child involves indignities that should be unacceptable in a free society. But it has also given us the most extraordinary adventure of our lives: an emotional thriller, an epic.

We married late, that was the thing. We knew of each other for years, because we had many friends in common. When we did meet, it was on a professional basis: Hilary was a high-powered publisher, and I was a recalcitrant author. By the time we managed to change the subject from books, we were starting to straddle forty. We'd had good times separately: I'd knocked around the world for the *Guardian* and Hilary had risen to be editorial director of Pan. Our previous entanglements had managed to stop short of marriage and children.

We married quickly, and moved out of London to Herefordshire. Laurie came two years later. We wanted two, but there were three miscarriages, and time started to run out. Late at night, I would say that nobody had it all, that we were lucky to have Laurie, and should be satisfied. But Hilary never agreed. The turning point came on a Sunday afternoon in the summer of 1997. We were with friends in Oxfordshire, Nick and Fanny Arbuthnott. Another couple was there, the journalist Charles Nevin and his wife Liv O'Hanlon, writer and director of the pressure group Adoption Forum. Each couple had two children, all plucked from hopelessness in Latin America, all visibly bright and vigorous and thriving. It was Laurie, the singleton, who seemed the odd one out. A few days later, we rang social services.

The first representative of Hereford and Worcester County Council wanted us to consider fostering, not adoption. It was clear that we were far too old to be allowed to adopt a British child, and we thought hard about what they said. But then we wrote and said we wanted to adopt from overseas. (Some local authorities have until recently forbidden this. It is surprising that such a crucial matter can depend on who empties your dustbins, but we soon stopped being surprised by anything.) A month later, in early September, we got a reply telling us that before we could start on the 'home study' (cost in our area: £1,510) that is crucial to any adoption, we would have to go on a course. The next might be available the following spring. Not merely were we old, we were likely to get a great deal older before we could even get started.

We did have a social worker assigned to us, though. And this was our first stroke of luck. We have heard many horror stories about cold-fish social workers, especially in London, where home studies are habitually contracted out. But we had Sue Curren. She was friendly, caring and conscientious. And when Hilary found us a place on a course scheduled for Sutton Coldfield in November, Sue agreed to start the home study at once.

The huge county of Hereford and Worcester, a mad invention of the Heath government, no longer exists. But it did in 1997, and poor Sue had to drive the seventy miles from her office in Droitwich to our home in the lee of the Black Mountains countless times. It is essential for the state to assess prospective parents. Overseas governments require such an assessment before they will release a child. But what they require and what Britain gives them are somewhat different. The Martell family from Montana, who we were to meet in Siberia, had a home study, too: their social worker came round one morning for coffee and carrot cake. Sue put us through twenty-eight hours of questioning. And that was before she grilled four sets of referees for two hours each.

What is the state's legitimate interest here? There is a potential immigration issue, but no one is worried about Britain being overrun by Russians with snow on their bootees. I accept that they ought to make sure we are not bankrupts, bandits, bullies or buggers, although none of that would prevent us having children in the normal way. They need to assess the risk of us rejecting the child after adoption, though with babies this is very rare indeed. Then they have to ask whether the whole thing is in the interests of the child, which is the cornerstone of British family law.

On all these points, Sue – backed up by police checks – might have made up her mind after two or three coffee (and maybe carrot cake) sessions, if not one. Hilary and I fumble through parenting no better than most, but it would have been clear to anyone that our home was already child-centred, and that our existing child was well adjusted within normal limits and short of only one thing, a sibling. British adoption practice has become so obsessed with finding perfect parents that the best has become the enemy of the good.

Of course, I was worried about risking Laurie's happiness. But he was five already, knew exactly what was going on and was involved at every stage. It was sort of his idea: he would have preferred a brother, but you can't give children everything they want.

We wanted a girl. And, after much investigation, we settled on Russia. It was Liv O'Hanlon's suggestion. The Russians have large numbers of children in orphanages, which grow harsher as the children get older. Adoption is rare there, too, partly because people are hard up and live in tiny flats, and partly because of a cultural taboo – the few mothers who do adopt have been known to stuff pillows up their jumpers to fake pregnancy. The Russian government is not averse to children going overseas, and dozens go to the USA every month. It is an intriguing twist of history, and there is a continuous rumble of discontent about it from Communists in the Duma. My own grandfather had trekked west from what is now Poland, which provided a kind of cultural affinity, the sort of detail both the Russians and British social workers liked to hear. I never mentioned that he was escaping the beginnings of anti-Semitic persecution and the threat of conscription into the Tsar's army.

Maybe it was the East European in me, but I had my own taboo against adoption. Who knows where nature ends and nurture takes effect? Somewhere in the back of my own mind, there was a masculine prejudice against couples who adopt. (Don't they do it, then?) And life, quite frankly, was comfortable as it was. Laurie was old enough to be a pal as well as a son. Did I want to change a baby? Did I want a baby to change me? There were other worries. We had heard of unscrupulous Latin American lawyers alleged to snatch babies, and of East European gypsies alleged to sell their kids. But we know the world is full of genuinely unwanted kids who desperately need homes. And the system soon ensured that positions became entrenched. Hilary was not going to be beaten by them. And nor was I.

I enjoyed the first home study session. I began to understand why people go to psychotherapists. It offered the chance to talk about oneself without the cocktail-party obligation to break off and ask about the other person. And we did learn a lot about adoption theory, about the importance of bonding, and the possibility of 'attachment disorder', when an institutionalized child becomes unable to form relationships. This heightened our resolve to get a child as young as possible. Hilary read a lot, and we absorbed and embraced the prevailing belief that adoption should never be a secret from the child.

But, as the sessions went on, and every single aspect of our life together was investigated, I began to get increasingly irritated. If Sue didn't actually ask how often we had sex and in which positions, she got pretty close. (Some social workers, I hear, are less delicate.) Any irritation with her was mitigated, however, by the course. It was run by the National Children's Homes, and it was good of them to take us. However, four November days in Sutton Coldfield, separated from our son, was never an attractive prospect. And it got worse.

One of the things I love about my profession is that I never (well, hardly ever) feel trapped. My job is to extract information quickly. If I'm bored then, *ipso facto*, newspaper readers will be bored: it's time to terminate the interview or leave the room. I haven't had to sit somewhere and be talked at since school. I had to sit in Sutton Coldfield. I doodled a lot. I got by until Day Three, which was devoted to race and sex. Then I flipped.

Prospective adopters in Britain are required to learn three things about race. 1) Racism is wicked. (I was even obliged to write an essay to this effect.) 2) On the other hand, it is 'culturally inappropriate' to adopt a child of a different race. 3) No good will come of suggesting that these propositions might be contradictory. Indeed, expressing opinions of any kind is dangerous . . .

. . . As I discovered during the sex session. Of course, all parents need to be aware of the dangers of sexual abuse. Anxious to contribute in class, I remarked – uncontroversially, so I thought – that this was not a matter of absolutes: that there was a difference between someone buggering a toddler, and a sixteen-year-old having sex with a fifteen-year-old, even though both are criminal offences. I also mentioned, merely because it had been in the paper that day, a case of a fifteen-year-old girl who had seduced her 47-year-old headmaster. Again, I said, this was not to be compared with paedophilia. I was howled down by two social workers.

I shut up after that, but it was too late. The social workers shopped me. My file, I came to understand, complained about me 'doing other work' (the doodling) and about my attitude towards sex abuse. I am willing to back my record on paedophilia against that of, say, the National Children's Homes. Humility, however, was not the strong point of the people who had power over us. The prevailing orthodoxy among social workers might change next week. In the meantime, it was never to be questioned by the likes of us.

By New Year 1998, Sue was ready to complete her report. She was anxious, on our behalf, to present it to the local authority's adoption panel on 2 February. However, this was not possible – the chairman was skiing that week. We would have to wait another month. I wrote and protested, very mildly. (I was, after all, paying heavily for this service.) I was brushed aside. Again, we were lucky. Many applicants are turned down. This panel – a mixture of social workers, councillors and others – decides on who may and may not adopt. When it finally met, it found in our favour, but not unanimously. I believe two or three out of ten said we were not fit and proper adoptive parents. There were various areas of concern: our age (a lot older than when we started), my attitude to sexual abuse and the panel's view that 'our expectations for the child were not as realistic as we said they were'.

It is tempting to say I don't know what they meant. But I do. An adopted child, and a foreign one at that, was bound to be useless, whereas we, as middle-class parents, would be disappointed if she failed to win a scholarship to Balliol. We had explained, over and over, that we believed success in life was not to be measured by exam results. But we were obvious liars. Though we were approved, we still had to answer sixteen (yes – sixteen!) further supplementary questions, all of them, in our view, irrelevant.

I find it hard to fathom now that three people in England could seriously believe that little Victoria would have been better off starving in a Siberian orphanage than at home with us. Lord knows how they manage to recruit all of them to sit on this ludicrous panel.

The next phase was meant to be straightforward. It involved a notary public, a massive pile of documents to be passed from us to the notary to the Foreign Office to the Department of Health and back again, a remarkable number of phone calls and faxes, regulations that seemed to change all the time, and an extra £144 demanded out of nowhere. Anyone less determined than Hilary would have given up. The purpose of all this was for the Department of Health to validate the council's decision. It was supposed to take ten working days. It took two months. We were told later that there had been bank holidays. Perhaps they have more of them in Whitehall than we do.

In early June, our papers were finally sent – notarized, legalized and approved – to the Cradle of Hope adoption agency in Maryland. It is a further irony of history that the only way a British family can adopt a Russian child is through the USA. But every other method seems untenable.

Hilary talked to other American agencies. One got straight up her nose. Another told her that it was impossible for a British family: the Russians would not grant an adoption order until the child was granted entry clearance to Britain and vice versa. This was wholly believable, though not, it turned out, actually true. Cradle of Hope sounded reassuring and optimistic. Another family had recommended them, impressed that their offices were scruffy – always a good sign with a charity.

Cradle of Hope deals with orphanages throughout Russia. If a child is given up for adoption there, the name is kept on a database for three months. The mother can change her mind in that time, and has to sign away her rights on two separate occasions. Then the child is offered for adoption inside Russia, which hardly ever happens. Only then can the child be offered to foreigners. We asked for a girl who was as young as possible, and healthy. The agency said it might take them three months to offer us a child. It took six weeks, and it happened in the most dramatic circumstances imaginable.

*

All year, my mother had been getting more and more frail; 7 July 1998 was her eightieth birthday, and she was clearly unwell. On the following Sunday, we held a party for her and, with a mighty effort of will, she was radiant. Her seven grandchildren were all there, but she was never to meet the eighth. The next day she went into hospital. Three days later, her condition deteriorated.

I had spent that day researching a *Guardian* column about John Toland, the eighteenth-century Irish theologian, and his concept of Deism: the belief that, though God exists, He does not intervene – the world operates rationally. The Open Golf Championship was going on at the time, and American golfers kept insisting that God helps them sink their putts.

That evening, Helene, our social worker at Cradle of Hope, rang up. She had a child for us: a healthy eight-month-old baby called Olga, who was in the orphanage at Achinsk. Early next day, Mum lapsed into unconsciousness. Before she did so, my brother was able to tell her the news. I don't believe anything could have made her happier. She died that afternoon.

I never wrote the column on rationalism. The *Guardian* allowed me time off on compassionate grounds. And, anyway, here was something wholly irrational: one life ended and yet being replaced. Suddenly, I began to be sceptical about scepticism. Three days later, we were just leaving home to go to the funeral when the phone rang. It was Helene. She was dreadfully apologetic, because she knew what a terrible time this was for us. Something had happened that hardly ever happened. Olga had been picked out for adoption by a Russian family, and they had preference.

The workings of the universe seemed clearer to me once again. It was as I had always imagined: complete fluke leavened with the Law of Sod. But Helene was on the phone again a week later. She was, I thought, tentative. They had another baby to offer. Her name was Natalya, from Khabarovsk in the Russian Far East. She was already fifteen months old, small, behind in her development, rather reticent. Somehow, we felt none of the surge of excitement that had accompanied the first phone call.

If a child is available for adoption, the orphanage sends photos or a video, and medical information, not always complete, but usually – in our experience – honest, designed to help you decide whether or not to proceed. Russian doctors seem inclined, if anything, to maximize a child's problems rather than minimize them. This is partly because a problem that might seem insuperable to them can often be treated in the West. It may also be that the orphanage can wheedle more money from the state for a sick child. The video of Natalya was quite long: it lasted ten minutes. A nurse tried to attract her attention with a succession of toys. She failed every time. The baby never smiled once.

We had thought all this through. We did not expect to adopt a child prodigy, though it might be nice to have one who could ram the county council's brand of genetic determinism back up their fundaments. The object of the exercise was to give a child the best chance of flourishing. There was no point in doing that if the baby was already damaged beyond repair. A paediatrician friend saw the video, and supported our instincts. Reluctantly, we rang Helene. She was extremely nice about it. We were entitled to reject a child – indeed, if we felt uncertain, it was the right thing to do. 'We will find a home for this child, and a child for your home,' she said, and sounded sweet and sincere, even if it was a well-worn mantra. But I sensed that the agency's guilt about Olga had been expiated. Now we would have to wait.

The autumn was wretched. There was no more news from Maryland. Hilary and I grew tetchy with each other. Laurie, just five when this started, was heading for six and a half. He sometimes talked eagerly about his sister's arrival. But she can hardly have seemed very real to him.

It was an even more wretched autumn in Russia. The stories of economic collapse and political instability made us fearful. Perhaps the crisis could wreck all our plans. It was late November before the phone rang again. There was a baby. She was healthy. She was in Tyumen, a city in Western Siberia where adoptions worked particularly smoothly. Her name was Victoria.

On the video, taken in September when she was four months old, she looked huge, with lots of dark hair, a hint of Russian bear- ishness mitigated by a luscious Cupid's-bow mouth that kept breaking into a smile. Never mind Toland or Sod. We just knew, knew, that she was the one.

We arrived at Tyumen Airport one evening two months later. It was cold beyond all imagining. The hotel, however, was four star, and could have been anywhere. I felt just a little cheated, having spent my last morning in England following guidebook advice, and trying to buy a bath plug. Actually, a Siberian winter is very hot, as long as you don't attempt to go outside. Indoors, even in ordinary tower-block flats, the heating (assuming it is working) is always full-blast, and the only way to reduce it is to open the window, which, at −30°C, is not recommended.

This applies to orphanages, too. Next day, we were driven there, and in a bright, pleasant but stiflingly hot nursery sat Victoria. At once, she beamed at us, as if to say, 'Ah, I've been waiting for you.' But, though she smiled on schedule, she had very little hair, and a pale, monkeyish face. I began to sense the problem when they gave me a bottle to feed her. It was sugar water. The video, in which she looked so healthy, had been taken in September. What had changed since September? Russia had gone broke. Who is likely to feel the pinch first in this situation? Answer: an orphanage. We were shocked and needed time to adjust. But events had their own momentum. The Martells of Montana were also in Tyumen and set on adopting their little boy, Gregory. They weren't faltering. The following day we were due in court, to adopt Victoria under Russian law. Who knew when we would get another court date? The consequences would be horrendous. And how could we leave her? Clearly, the baby had been neglected. There were 150 children in the orphanage, but we hardly saw any except the dozen in the same nursery. It may have been significant that whenever I mentioned seeing the rest of the orphanage, the subject got changed. But I wasn't there as a journalist. If this was a Potemkin room, designed to fool the visitors about conditions, then my role was to get fooled. And the devotion of the staff seemed unquestionable. I believe they did the best they could.

I got one glimpse behind the lines. The babies were meant to sleep in a back room behind the nursery for ten hours at night with three two-hour naps a day, whether they wanted them or not. But they were tucked up for their midday nap twenty minutes early – perhaps for the staff's benefit, perhaps because we were disrupting routine, who knows? We had brought Victoria her first cuddly toy, a puppy, and wanted to leave it with her. I went into the dormitory. There were thirteen children in cots. One looked asleep. The rest, toyless, were in various stages of baby-wakefulness. Victoria was rocking herself furiously, backwards and forwards, in a desperate search for stimulation. At that moment, I was certain. We were going to get her out of there.

Court No. 4 in the Tyumen District Court was a small room, with a buzzing electric light. There was nothing intimidating about it, except the fierce-looking Russian double-eagle crest. In a high-backed chair sat the judge, a mumsy, middle-aged woman wearing a leather jerkin and a lot of lipstick. The hearing was private; no one was allowed in except the court officials and our interpreter – not even the child's natural mother. Especially not the natural mother.

The low number of adoptions in Britain is partly because the relevant acts require families to be kept together whenever possible. A birth mother has rights. The Russians have no truck with this. This one had given hers away, three times. And that, as far as they are concerned, was that. Sue Curren's report, translated into Russian at vast expense (to us), sat on the judge's desk. But the hearing was ritualized, even formulaic. We were asked why we wanted to adopt Victoria. I said we had room in our home and our hearts for a baby. I promised we would do our utmost to ensure she fulfilled her potential. The judge went out and, twenty minutes later, returned to give her consent on behalf of the Russian Republic. That afternoon, we went back to the orphanage and cuddled Victoria on a different basis, as our daughter. There were no second thoughts now.

Which was lucky. A new birth certificate was immediately issued in her new name by the city registrar, a matronly lady who made a little speech about how grateful the city was to us. Did we want to change her name? We had no plans to call her anything other than Victoria and the nurses had nicknamed her 'Vika' (which has stuck). We changed her middle name to Betty, after my mother, and her last name to Engel. Under Russian law, her old birth certificate was destroyed. We were even given the option, which we declined, of changing her birth date.

We know quite a bit about Victoria's background, and why she had to be adopted. It will be no secret from her. As she grows, we will let her absorb it. But it is her story, not mine, and for her to tell when she chooses, not me. For her, the past is another country.

The following morning the nurses took off her orphanage clothes, dressed her in the warm outfit we had brought, and handed her over. A couple of them were crying. 'The merriest girl in the orphanage,' one sniffled. Everyone kissed everyone else. We took Vika back to the hotel room and, as instructed, put her down for her nap at noon precisely. She finally dozed at teatime. Most of the time she was just guzzling. Between whiles, she would stare up at us both, and grin toothlessly. It took me a couple of vodkas to cotton on. All along, I had been thinking of Victoria as a series of problems that had to be overcome. But she wasn't a problem. She was a solution.

We flew to Moscow – the three of us. We sent joyous word to Laurie, staying with friends back home, that he had a sister. But the last part was something we had been dreading all along. We had to gain entry clearance for Vika to come home with us – we had to deal with the British again.

There also needed to be a medical report. Children being taken to America for adoption have to be accompanied by a simple form, in keeping with the coffee-and-carrot-cake spirit of the enterprise. They are checked to ensure they are free of terrible diseases, then go off to the embassy, are processed rapidly, and welcomed to the Land of the Free.

The Land of Bossy Officials requires a form of infinitely greater complexity. The American Medical Center in Moscow, which deals with the ailments of expats and the local rich, said it had to be handled by a senior paediatrician, who agreed to see us on the Friday morning. This was no bad thing: we needed reassurance about Vika's condition. And there would be just enough time to rush the form over to the embassy before it shut for the weekend. There it would join the twenty-two other documents that had to be faxed to London before permission could be granted.

I should have seen the blow coming. I had approached the business of adoption as I approach life: with constructive pessimism. Expect the worst, I believe, and you can spend a great deal of time being pleasantly surprised. Anticipate trouble, and it may not happen. I never anticipated this.

A nurse took Vika's measurements, the doctor consulted his charts, and watched her crawl across the floor. He asked a few questions. Then he started an involuntary nervous titter. She has a very small head, he said. She was way off the bottom of his charts, not even in the lowest percentile of normal development. That, he felt, meant that she would probably be educationally subnormal. Then there was the question of the leg. The leg? It's spastic, he said. That was the word he used. But look, we said, she's crawling much earlier than most babies. And pulling herself up. That wasn't unusual, he replied. Babies with a stiff leg often did this quickly – it was a form of compensation. Again and again, I asked him questions designed to get him to back off a little: to say he might be wrong, that head size wasn't the answer to everything, that many things were still mysterious. But he didn't think anything was mysterious at all. He was sorry.

Why? Why? Why? Why hadn't we checked her out properly

in advance? Physical handicap, I could perhaps accept. Mental handicap even. But both? How had we let this happen? At the first opportunity, I stormed out of the clinic in the hope of leaping in our car and just being driven, fast. But at that moment, perhaps the worst of my life, Gennady, the driver assigned to us by Cradle of Hope, the sort of bear-like Russian you don't pick fights with, had decided to shove off. He was gone for twenty minutes, the longest piss in history. We had to be at the embassy by 12.30 p.m. or we couldn't get the papers there till Monday. Helen, the translator, said it would take forty-five minutes to get there. Gennady came back at 12.05, muttering.

It was an awful journey, with Helen, not quite reading the mood, pointing out tourist sights. But we got to the embassy in time. And there the staff were terrific: friendly, helpful, content to sort the twenty-three documents and fax them to London as fast as they could. We were a bit of a novelty: no British family had adopted a Russian child in six months. And through the day we had a slow recovery.

A senior Cradle of Hope official was in Moscow. He dismissed the bad news at once. Small head? Not uncommon in orphanages. Bad leg? Physiotherapy will fix it. He arranged for a Russian paediatrician to come round the next day.

By then, Hilary and Vika had been billeted in a small flat with a local family, while I had gone back home to look after Laurie, to a chorus of reassurance – led by the Martells – that the American Medical Center was notorious among adopters for precisely this kind of diagnosis. And indeed we kept getting little droplets of better news. The Russian paediatrician re-measured Victoria's head, found that it was a centimetre larger than the Americans had said and that they had not taken prematurity into account. That made her head small but not tiny. Vika then crawled across the floor for her. There was no sign of stiffness. Something occurred to Hilary. At the clinic, there had been a cold lino floor and Vika had been wearing only a vest. Hilary decided that she had been trying to keep at least one of her knees warm.

Next day, Hilary took her to another Western doctor who examines a lot of orphanage children. He concluded: 'The child is bright-eyed, alert, curious, social and active . . . I think full and easy weight-bearing, and crawling, at eight months practically rules out serious neurological or orthopaedic problems. I have no reason to believe that the child is other than perfectly healthy.' And that remains the consensus to this day. That does not make the original opinion wrong. It still haunts me. But five experienced doctors have seen her, and none has agreed with it. Our health visitor at home was the briskest on the subject: 'This child has been over-analysed. Just look at her. She's fine.' That's jumping ahead. We couldn't really do anything with Vika until we got her back to England. And, on the Monday morning, I rang the desk officer at the Department of Health to see if the papers had arrived. They hadn't. They had to go from the Moscow embassy to the Home Office to the Department of Health Adoption Unit to an inspector and all the way back again. 'My wife's in Moscow where it's twenty below zero, staying in a tiny flat with a tiny baby. I have a small son who's desperate to see them. Can you please help?' In a fifties Carry On film, the desk officer would have been played by Joan Sims at her most nasally contemptuous: 'You knew all this in advance, Mr Engel. You could have sent your legal representative to Russia instead.' My legal representative happens to be my brother. What was he going to do with Vika in Moscow? Breastfeed her? The desk officer then posted me the department's official guidelines: she highlighted the section that said it might take six weeks for temporary admission to be granted. And still the papers were nowhere to be found. The Home Office was undergoing a complete reorganization. Never famously supple, the operation had apparently seized up. I believe the original 23-page fax from Moscow had lain where it landed in an empty office. The official listed as being in charge of the section did not, according to the switchboard, actually exist.

Curiously, their chaos probably worked to our advantage in the end. The Moscow embassy was brilliant – phoning and chivvying, even re-sending the 23-page fax three times until it finally found a human. From that point, the Department of Health were highly efficient, and I'm grateful. And the Home Office gave the embassy delegated powers to make a decision. I think that meant 'Oh, crikey. You bloody sort it out then.' Which they did, rapidly. It took six days, not six weeks. It would have been six hours if we were Americans. But, as with so many other aspects of this story, we were a great deal luckier than we might have been.

Hilary and Vika didn't have such a bad time, actually. The journalistic community of Moscow, led by the *Guardian*'s James Meek, his wife Yulia, and the Reeves family of the *Independent*, wrapped them against the worries of the wintry city. On the same Aeroflot flight, a week after me, they were at Heathrow. And the moment he saw her, Laurie fell head over heels in love with Vika. 'The best present I've ever had,' he calls her.

So now we were four, and it was wonderful. No bureaucrat would split us now. The process of love is a mysterious one, but it seems as instinctive with an adopted child as with any other.

Vika ate like crazy, and grew fast. Our relatives and friends were all besotted with her, because she was such a happy and responsive baby. Some of our acquaintances (male, mostly) had more difficulty. One of my colleagues put the phone down on Hilary when she said we had adopted a child. Another said, with genuine puzzlement, 'Am I supposed to congratulate you?'

But Vika knew she was extra special. When she was a baby, I had a game with her that only Daddy was allowed to play. I lifted her up to the ceiling and she held her arms out wide. I asked her how she got here and said, 'By aeroplane!' And she beamed.

Vika is now six. She is blonde, beautiful, beguiling and bloody-minded. She learned to speak more quickly than her English-born contemporaries, which knocks to hell various developmental theories we were told as fact.

And it was soon obvious she had a natural sense of how to shape language to charm, flatter, get a laugh or (especially in the case of her parents) get up someone's nose. There are times, especially on school mornings as she pads reluctantly downstairs tossing her mane, when she seems – heaven help us – more like a teenager than a six-year-old.

She is tall and strong and fit; in the playground she matches strides with the boys yet still fantasizes that she is a Red Indian princess. The Herefordshire countryside is her adventure playground, and she adores animals. Sometimes she still doesn't quite grasp the difference between a pet and a fluffy toy. Sometimes she wants to be a Dalmatian more than she wants to own one. But she is already a fearless rider and we won't be able to delay for ever the day she has her own pony.

No one doubts now that Vika is intelligent. (As a local shop-keeper put it: 'She's got all her buttons done up, that one.') But her intelligence is of the restless, wayward, questioning kind that does not necessarily appeal to the fustier kind of schoolteacher.

She knows her own story, without yet fully understanding it. It remains to be seen whether she will become obsessed by it, or find it irrelevant; it can go either way. Sometimes, we look back and think how things might have been otherwise, but not often.

The problems the professionals warned us about have not become a factor. Five and three-quarter years on, nothing in the parent–child relationship has been substantially different than it was for us the first time around. But we never make the mistake of believing Vika is in any sense 'ours'. She is, very obviously, her own woman.

HOW WE MET

Sarah Cameron

Wearing a white and royal blue Babygro and matching tam-o'-shanter perched at a rakish angle on the back of his head, Joe looked as if he had staggered home from a Burns' Night celebration and passed out. Eyes screwed shut, hands by his ears, black hair. 'This is your son,' said Jenni and withdrew discreetly, but not without the flash of an instamatic, making a photo I now have which shows me leaning over the cot like a garden visitor poring over the label on a rare herbaceous plant. I knew I should be feeling something momentous, and almost magically tears came to my eyes as if they at least knew how to do the right thing, but the truth is I felt surreally detached, an actor in a play I still wasn't sure I wanted to be in.

I had arrived in America a couple of hours before, reeling from a week of to-do lists and gnomic instructions, scribbled down and making no sense an hour later. 'Take sling', 'bebe confort good'. We had heard about Joe's birth eleven days earlier, the first of many transatlantic calls at odd times of day, and with each conversation, each anxious question, each confusing response, the possibility of this baby being our baby had become stronger and more strange. Leaving my husband behind to deal with putting everything – work, pets, plans – on temporary standby, I got on a plane to Seattle. Looking down on mountains

and lakes I thought of Joe moving more slowly to our ren-
dezvous. Through the snow and the high passes I imagined him
wrapped in a papoose like the baby sucking on a rag in *Children
on the Oregon Trail*, my favourite book as a child. A real baby
in a real car seat on his way from the hospital on the borders of
Oregon and Iowa in a social worker's SUV – that seemed the fictional thing. I looked again at the bag on my knee, full of the
sacred talismans, totems and medicines that would magically
transform me into a real mother: the white newborn ballet cardi-
gan, vests, cloths, bottles, nappies and gripe water. A small
knitted rabbit regarded me with a sceptical eye.

Out of the airport, in a hired car, the rabbit and I negotiated
the skein of motorways and slip roads looking for the suburb
where Joe and I were to meet and spend our first few days
together. Driving through a Stepford Wives set of ramped drive-
ways, astro lawn and shrubs, I saw the house. Draped across the
front a huge banner read 'The Teddy Bear Motel Welcomes the
New Mom'. Balloons attached to each corner of the eaves gave
the impression that this vision might at any moment lift off and
float upwards into the cloudless sky. Jenni, professional foster-
mother of newborns, and her daughter Bethany were on the
steps anchoring the house to the ground. We hugged and went
in, through rooms themed for maximum impact, one full of pictures and china figurines of geese, the next of angels, our feet
silent in thick shagpile, to the room where Joe slept, immune to
any sense of occasion.

There followed days of bathing Joe, dressing Joe, making bottles for Joe – lining them up in the evening like skittles in a
bowling alley ready for the night's entertainment, and roaring
through them between snatches of oblivion. My I-have-not-been-
through-childbirth veneer of health wore thinner. With Joe in
public those first days I felt buoyed by a kind of silent applause
which buzzed like static all around me at the huge supermarket
or the second-hand baby clothes shop in the mall which was
Jenni's Mecca. 'Look at that bright-eyed mother with the darling

baby,' I congratulated myself as I scooped him up and laid him down in his pod-like portable car seat with growing expertise. Now, five days later, I looked more the part: black circles under puffy eyes, greasy hair, woolly brain, my qualification for the role ever more tenuous. Couldn't all these people tell that he wasn't really mine, that he just wasn't happy with formula milk, that he seemed to be sicking up half I fed him, that he was surely sleeping less than other babies? Jenni's and my social worker's soothing words about how good he was, how calm, how much weight he was putting on, even the hard evidence of the postnatal weight chart at the local clinic did nothing to convince me I wasn't going to be found out soon. Joe knew. Every time he opened his eyes and looked at me with an intense yet unfocused gaze his separateness seemed to shout at me.

A week later we went to meet my husband at the airport. I allowed hours but arrived only just in time, my brain unable to absorb directions or decipher the map. As I dashed in, a plaintive wail rose from the wobbly sling attached to my front. Like a Hyde Park nanny determined to present her charge to his best advantage I galloped into the toilets with my kitbag of equipment. Late, so late now, we flew out again desperately looking for instructions to Arrivals. Were we meeting here, by the train which beamed you out to your satellite like *Blade Runner*, or over there at the other end by Immigration Control? Leaping onto the train as the doors glided shut we arrived in an empty terminal, no one coming through clutching a British passport, nothing but some luggage sitting abandoned by a carousel. There was no one to ask but an immigration official, his boredom masked by an icy politeness, who advised me to return, Ma'am, to the main terminal. Suddenly this situation was unbearable. I was the wrong person, in the wrong place, doing the wrong thing. Joe, having regained his unerring ability to sleep whenever I was awake, made no comment. Hearing English voices, two BA hostesses clack-clacking through the empty hall chatting about the evening ahead, I flew up to them weeping hysterically, spilling out my tale of a father who had never met his son and was now lost, lost, in this unfeeling place. They doled out comforting words like gulps of brown sugary tea and I was taken back through the airport to an obvious spot where Tom finally found me, slumped and undone, a perfect example of new motherhood.

A few days later Jenni suggested that Tom and I might like to spend some time alone together. Visions of a sci-fi flip to a tiny table with a white tablecloth and candles, Tom and I bending towards each other wearing cashmere with mood music in the background swam in front of me. A powerful desire to book two rooms in a hotel for twenty-four hours' sleep was reluctantly banished. The prospect of a conversation, let alone rediscovering some pre-parental quality time, was inconceivable. We seemed, the three of us, to have become a sort of three-headed mythical beast, one who has taken up permanent, paralysed residence on a sofa, joined in some organic way but profoundly unconnected mentally, gazing mindlessly at *Seinfeld*, *Friends* or *Falcon Crest* on late-night TV.

Jenni's second husband Lance, who had lived in seven states before he was grown but whose heart and soul had never left Texas, kept two horses a couple of miles away. Jenni's first husband, Bethany's father, who still lived upstairs and worked in computers, lent Tom some large yellow boots. We tacked up outside a big red barn set incongruously at the end of a suburban street. At first riding along roads and numbered drives seemed strange, like a compulsory leisure activity for the terminally exhausted, but soon the houses thinned out and at the end of the streets rose the vague outlines of mountains covered in pine trees. It was hard to imagine Joe, at the house with Jenni, his routine of bottles and naps and different outfits proceeding calmly without us. Much easier to imagine was a scene in which our sleepy horses sped up to a Western movie gallop and headed for a distant horizon, through a landscape of campfires and starlight, sagebrush and snowy peaks, with cowboys and dusty rodeos, and no parents or middle-class anxieties about post-natal bonding in sight. We clop-clopped on through the suburbs, and the mountains remained aloof.

That evening Jenni and the husbands took us to their local church, shaped like a slice of cake in streaky concrete, with pale-suited greeters with orthodontal smiles at the door. I could feel my anti-evangelical antennae quivering as we were ushered in, could hear myself describing amusingly to friends at home the moment we met fundamental right-wing America in grey polyester. But, at the end of the service when we were asked to stand, Joe in my arms proudly wearing Jenni's latest acquisition complete with satin bows and rosettes, and the congregation were called to pray for this new family in their midst who had come all the way from England to their church, I felt the tightening throat of genuine emotion. It was as if the sentimental side of me was now getting the hang of motherhood – I felt all the irrational pride and exhausted happiness. It was a self which collapsed with increasing ease in tears. But my anxious brain constantly questioned these feelings. I played the role but felt all the time it was a role, and searched desperately for responses both in me and from Joe who – unsurprisingly in a baby of less than a month old – betrayed no sense of ownership, and seemed to show me no special favour. We were cheered for, blessed and hugged and went back to the Teddy Bear Motel for microwaved turkey with jello salad and creamed potatoes. First husband Bob gave Joe a baseball mitt and ball and a cricket bat to cover all the sporting bases, which he had ordered specially on the Internet.

A month later we were staying in the Marriott in the middle of Seattle waiting for the final papers to come through for the court appearance which would finalize everything. We had spent a draining but exhilarating day with Joe's birth mother Mary and Joe's half-brother and sister, sharing photographs and stories, and soap bubbles of information, most of which I failed to capture beyond the moment. I remember half sentences about Joe's father – 'All I can tell you is that he was really cute' – and dramatic country-and-western song tales of bad boyfriends and dangerous lovers, stories which all seemed to end with state troopers on the doorstep. Unexpectedly, Joe's birth mother had done more to give me a sense of my place in his life than anyone else had been able to achieve. Her vulnerability, her bravery, her wit, her laugh and her faith in us carved out a place for me, gave me a part which felt chosen for me, entrusted me with a mission I felt bound to try to live up to. When we got back to the hotel, tired from the long drive, I offered to go to the I Love Sushi across the street for supper. I left Tom bathing Joe in the hotel basin, carefully wrapping the hot tap in a towel and laying out the No Tears shampoo and baby bath with a barman's professional air. As I came out of the lift bearing bento boxes and cold beer I could hear Joe's protests, loud demanding cries which grew steadily in volume as I walked down the long corridors towards our room as if they were being turned up on a dial. That baby wants something I thought; he needs me. Yes. He needs me.

DEAR DJENEBA

Meg Bortin

Dear Djeneba,

The first time I saw you, you had no hair. They had told me you were nine months old, and said you were nearly walking. But the child thrust into my arms at the orphanage was tiny and light as the red dust that rose in the African air. You were terribly thin. You seemed too frail to hold up your head. And you were completely bald.

It was 1 November 2000. I'd left Paris that morning and landed in mid-afternoon in Bamako, capital of Mali, the land of Timbuktu. The flight had seemed interminable, yet I'd been grateful for the few hours of passage from cold damp France to the African heat, from the longing for a child that had pursued me through adulthood to the thrilling, terrifying moment of encounter with the little girl who was to become my daughter. I emerged onto the baking tarmac ready but nervous, hopeful but wary. Who would you be? How would you like me?

Maître Diallo, my Malian lawyer, appeared at my side, smiling broadly and welcoming me. We chatted on the ride into town, but I couldn't keep my mind on the conversation. My heart was pounding as we drove past parched fields and long-horned cattle, twisted trees and low ramshackle buildings, across the broad silver band of the Niger.

We pulled into the orphanage grounds at dusk. A sullen aide in a pink smock came to greet us. Nene Ouattara, the orphanage director, had gone for the day; the children were already going to bed. She sat me in a chair while they changed your clothes. 'Don't bother,' I said, 'just let me see my child.' But she made me wait, about ten minutes – the longest ten minutes of my life. Then she returned and held you out to me.

'C'est ça?' The words came out of my mouth as soon as I saw you: 'That's it?' I had seen a lot of Malian babies when I'd visited six months earlier, but none had looked as woeful as the limp bald girl I took onto my lap.

They had dressed you in a little white cotton dress with a navy pattern and a bow at the back that hung on your thin frame pathetically. Your eyes were dull and conveyed no emotion. You stole a look at me, then hid your head away, burying it further down when I talked to you. You tugged at your ear – a habit, I was to learn, when you were anxious. Your skin had a papery feel as though you could blow away.

My visit with you lasted about five minutes. I kissed your naked head when they took you away. You reacted not at all. Were you scared? I was.

Maître Diallo took me to a hotel and left, saying he'd see me in the morning. Someone showed me to a box of a room with a tiny window and a bright striped bedspread. Night had fallen but it was suffocatingly hot inside. I dropped my bags, sponged my face and pulled the window open to try to get some air. Then I put through a call to Paris. My friend Nicole and I had been over and over my decision to adopt at fifty. As a future single mother, I wasn't prepared to take on a child with physical or psychological disabilities. I wanted to give a chance in life to a normal child. I felt capable of it, despite questions of age, race and the absence of a father. But now I was alarmed. The child I'd just left behind did not seem normal. Nicole tried to calm me. 'Wait and see how she looks in the morning,' my friend said. 'In any event, you don't have to take her.' We hung up. Night sounds drifted in, African voices and music. 'That's right,' I thought, hardening my heart. 'If there's something seriously wrong, if this child is damaged, I don't have to take her.' Then I lay down on the bed and wept.

It is almost incredible to me, as I sit writing this in Paris, to think I ever had such doubts. On the mantelpiece is a photo of you shortly after our arrival home. Your bright brown face is the picture of health. With your two little teeth poking through your smile, your eyes full of mischief and your fuzz of dark hair, you're the image of a happy baby. That was just six weeks after I first saw you. No one could tell, looking at that photo, that you almost didn't make it.

The next day, when Maître Diallo drove me to the orphanage, I told him I'd been shocked at your condition and asked why you had no hair. He said the heads of baby girls were shaved sometimes to make the hair grow in more thickly. He dropped me off, and someone took me to the room where you spent your days. I peeked in from the doorway. It was a large space with light filtering in from two windows at the back, screened against the malaria-carrying mosquitoes that are endemic in Mali. Toddlers were scrambling over each other, some playing and squabbling, some lying listlessly on the tile floor. An aide watched dispassionately, chewing on betel nut.

You didn't notice me. You were across the room beside some shelves where toys were kept, trying to pull yourself up. You couldn't quite stand on your spindly little legs, but you kept a grip on the shelves, trying again and again.

Eventually I approached you, and now I got a better look. Your head curved back dramatically like an African sculpture. On your right arm was a bracelet: five rings of tiny blue and white beads. Your ears were pierced, the left twice and the right once, in the Malian tradition, but you wore no earrings. It went a bit better this time. I picked you up, and was again startled by how light you were. You let me hold you, but you looked away and tugged your ear.

I watched the aide who looked after your group bring your lunch – rice with a peanut sauce. There were about ten of you. She washed each child's hands in a pail of water, then sat you in a circle on the floor and gave you each an enameled metal plate with the food. A couple of the children had physical handicaps; those she fed. The others ate their rice Malian style, with the right hand, in mouth-sized clumps.

You sat there, the youngest child in your group, so fragile you could barely hold up your head, and slowly lifted the rice to your mouth – one grain at a time.

I had to steady myself against the wall as I watched you try to eat. It was almost unbearable. Now I understood why you were so painfully thin. You were too weak to feed yourself, and you had no one to help you. After a while the aide collected the plates. The other children had finished their food; your plate was still full. You'd fallen asleep on the floor, exhausted. You had eaten maybe fifteen grains of rice.

Once you'd been moved to your crib, I went to see Nene Ouattara, the orphanage director, and told her I was concerned about your health. She gave me certificates showing you'd tested negative for AIDS and had been vaccinated against a string of illnesses. I asked her why you were bald – had they shaved your head? She looked embarrassed. Nobody at the orphanage had shaved you, she said. 'Well,' I asked, 'did she have hair when they found her?' Nene admitted you did indeed have hair when you were brought to the orphanage, three months earlier, after being found on the side of the road by the Bamako police.

Djeneba, you have every right to ask me about your Malian roots, but there's not much I can tell you. What happened, why you were abandoned, can never be known. According to the orphanage records, you were admitted on 9 August 2000. The police report describes you as a female child about eight months old found in the Bole district of Bamako. In most cases, I was told, when Malian children are abandoned it's because their parents can't afford to feed them. This is most likely what happened with you: your Malian parents were too poor to keep you and hoped you'd have a better future with somebody else. I'm sure, if they're alive, they continue to think of you. But there's no way to find them.

Under Malian law, the police conduct a three-month search for relatives before an abandoned child becomes eligible for international adoption. That search is inevitably fruitless, I was told. In your case, the investigation was closed on 20 October 2000. The state adoption commission met one week later, on 27 October. That was the day I learned you had been chosen to become my daughter.

This for me was a miracle. As far back as I can remember, what I had wanted most in life was a child. As a young woman I'd assumed I'd have kids in a couple. But as time went by and my relations with men proved rocky, I'd considered other possibilities. Reproduction through artificial means did not appeal; among other things, I didn't want to go through pregnancy alone. I thought about adoption, but rejected the idea – as long as I was physically capable of bearing a child, I continued to hope I'd find a man who'd want that too.

Then, when my mother died of cancer at the relatively early age of seventy-five, four years after my father died, my feelings shifted as my own mortality came sharply into focus. While still grieving, I'd learned it was possible in France for a single woman past childbearing age to adopt. This was a revelation. Then forty-nine, not daring to hope, I applied to adopt a child.

Under French rules, only married French couples may adopt French babies – all other candidates are channeled toward international adoption. As a single American woman, that was clearly my only option. At a bureau attached to the French Foreign Ministry, a friendly young woman fed some data about me into a computer, and out came a list of countries where I could apply to adopt. Three of them, the woman said, were most likely to accept the candidacy of a single woman my age: Russia, Romania and Mali.

The decision was easy and instantaneous. During my five

years in Russia as a journalist, I had seen how the Russian orphanage system left children traumatized. In Romania, by all accounts, the situation was far worse. Although I had never been to Mali, I was familiar with the French West African community in Paris. The people seemed warm and generous. With their tradition of extended families, children were likely to get plenty of attention early in life, I thought. And adoption in Mali was straightforward. I would simply apply to a branch of the Malian government. There was no agency or intermediary, and expenses were minimal.

I first had to apply for French authorization to adopt; that took about six months. With that in hand, it took a few more days to finish the paperwork for Mali. I sent off my application to Bamako on 26 October 1999. So it was a year and a day later, a few days before my fiftieth birthday, when I got the news that a girl named Djeneba Kone was waiting for me.

On my second morning in Bamako, I arrived at the orphanage armed with a baby bottle, mineral water, powdered milk formula I'd brought from Paris, and what turned out to be my chief weapon in the battle for your survival – a spoon. At snack time I sat with you on the floor, and when the aide, Fatoumata, put the plate of rice between your tiny legs I was right behind you, feeding you. Though you ate slowly, you did manage to swallow more than before. Still, the effort exhausted you and you fell asleep in my arms.

After your nap, Maître Diallo's driver picked us up for your first visit with Dr. Coulibaly, a young pediatrician who had trained in the United States. As we waited on a torn leatherette bench at the clinic, you on my lap getting used to me, and me to you, a nurse walked by. 'That child has no hair,' she scolded. 'She's suffering from malnutrition.'

I was taken aback. Somehow, despite everything I'd seen in the streets of Bamako, where some of the world's poorest children live and play, I was quite unprepared for the word 'malnutrition.'

It seems ludicrous now. But Nene Ouattara had assured me you were fine, and I'd believed her. 'Are you sure?' I asked the nurse. 'They told me her head might have been shaved to make the hair grow in more thickly.' She stared at me. 'Of course I'm sure,' she said. 'Just look at her. She's all skin and bones and her hair's fallen out. It's about time she saw a doctor.'

Dr. Coulibaly confirmed her diagnosis. You were sixty-eight centimeters long, about twenty-seven inches. That was normal. But you weighed only six kilos, about thirteen pounds, not enough for a child your age – in fact, I later found out, it was the average weight for a baby girl just four months old.

He prescribed vitamins and chocolate-flavored iron powder and told me to feed you rice and the French baby food I'd brought from Paris. 'She'll have to fight, but she can make it,' he said, telling us to come back in a week.

Back at the orphanage, I went to see Nene. I was frightened, and my fear came out as anger. 'Nene,' I said, 'I told you from the beginning that I wouldn't take a damaged child.' I broke down and wept. She was upset. 'We thought she was right for you,' she said. 'If you don't want her, we can try to find another child for you.' I wasn't ready for that. 'No,' I said, 'let's wait and see how it goes.' I had known you then for less than forty-eight hours, and you were already becoming my girl.

That night, on returning to the hotel, I went straight to the baby books I'd brought from France. They had everything you needed to know about childhood illnesses. Well, almost every-thing. There was nothing on malnutrition. It was simply assumed, in our Western world, that children would get fed enough. How ethnocentric we were, I thought.

I felt utterly at a loss. I had so many questions, chief among them whether – assuming you became healthy again – there would be long-term consequences of the malnutrition. Would it affect your brain? Your growth in later years? Dr. Coulibaly had laughed away my doubts, but I was scared.

*

Before arriving in Mali, I'd been told the adoption procedures would take three weeks – first a hearing, then a two-week appeals period, and then a few more days to get your passport and French entry visa. Now, stuck in a hotel and not knowing whether I could feed you properly, I wanted to get you back to France as soon as possible. But I received bad news from Maître Diallo: the adoption hearing would be held a week later than expected, putting everything else off by a week. It was to be the first of many frustrations. I phoned Air France to reschedule our tickets home.

The next day, our third together, you surprised me by giving me your first smile – it turned out you had dimples! We were getting along well, and I decided to take you to the hotel for lunch and naptime. But on the ride out, the fierce noontime heat turned the car into a furnace. When we arrived, you took a look at the hotel and panicked. I tried to feed you some baby food but you just spit it out. So I tried a bottle. You wailed and wailed before finally succumbing to sleep. After your nap we went straight back to Fatoumata. You seemed relieved to see me go. Our first afternoon alone together had been a fiasco.

But in time, we developed a routine. Most days I was at the orphanage with you from nine to five, with a break for my lunch while you were napping. I would cradle you in my arms to give you a bottle of milk in the corridor before putting you into your little crib. Although I spoke French to you most of the time, I'd sing you a lullaby in English: 'Hush little baby, don't say a word, mama's gonna buy you a mockingbird . . .' Do you remember? You slept easily, for a couple of hours, and I'd be there when you woke up. In the afternoon, you played again until suppertime. Then it was quickly to bed.

Fatoumata took care of all the children in your group, feeding you, dressing you, changing you. A handsome, proud woman, she often sang while she worked. Do you remember her special song for you? *Biso biso biso biso biso lo, Djeneba biso biso biso*

biso lo. Over and over. I chattered to you constantly, calling you my little Djenebaba from which you later named yourself, Baba.

Your playing space was roomy and full of donated toys – building blocks, rocking horses, stuffed animals and a little cart on wheels for children learning to walk. You loved pushing that cart around as your legs gained strength, and soon you were toddling on your own.

I had talked the chef at the hotel into preparing little meals for you in the morning, usually poached fish and a vegetable puree that I'd feed you at lunchtime. After a week I took you back to Dr. Coulibaly, who was pleased with your progress. And – was I imagining it? – on your beautiful head, a dusting of hair appeared to be sprouting.

Like a little wilted flower that wanted watering, you'd perked up once you got what you needed. In less than a week, your bright little eyes returned my approval when I cooed your name, your dimpled smile returned my smile, your love returned my love. You came back to life and began to bloom. It was the most moving thing I've ever experienced.

Our lonely initial period together lasted ten days – then Nicole flew in with her daughter, Léa. They were utterly charmed by you. I took you to see them at the Hotel Mandé, a lovely place along the Niger with sculptured grounds and a pool. You were so attached to me by then that you'd wail each time I went for a swim. It was as though when I swam to the end of the pool you feared I'd never swim back. You needn't have worried. We were at last nearing the day of the adoption hearing and I had no more doubts. My initial panic had passed. You and I were already family. I wasn't about to swim away.

The courthouse where the hearing took place was on a rock-strewn mud lane on the opposite bank of the Niger, a drab yellow building reminiscent of Soviet architecture at its worst. We went upstairs and waited in a stifling antechamber.

Eventually the presiding judge, Hameye Foune Mahalmadane, called the adoption lawyers into his chambers; he wanted to look over the documents they'd brought. Maître Diallo emerged, crestfallen. It appeared the dossiers did not contain the children's 'original' birth certificates, without which the judge would not hold the hearing. He was threatening to postpone the proceedings by another week – or two.

Pressed by me and another adoptive mother, Maître Diallo went back and told the judge he'd fetch the birth certificates right away. Would the judge then hear our cases? Maybe. I sat there in the wilting heat as the hours crept past. It wasn't until mid-afternoon that he called me into his chambers.

Our encounter was mercifully brief. The judge asked me about my family, and I told him about my brother, Bruce, your uncle in California. He liked the idea that you'd be visiting America and would be bilingual one day. I told him my parents had passed away – and so you unfortunately would not have grandparents. But I said my network of friends formed an extended family that could substitute rather well.

By the time we finally left the court I was exhausted, but ecstatic. The judge had given his approval. That day, Djeneba Kone became Djeneba Rosa Barbara Bortin – my daughter.

But it turned out the victory had a sting in its tail. The judge dated his decision 15 November, not 13 November, the day of the hearing. This put off our departure by two more days. With the fifteen-day appeals period before the ruling could be signed, we wouldn't get out of Mali until December.

On the following Monday morning, I arrived at the orphanage to find Nene waiting impatiently for me. 'Meg,' she said, 'Djeneba was up all night crying for her mama. You have to take her with you to the hotel.' 'Fine,' I said, struggling to get my thoughts in order, 'but there's no baby bed there.' Nene gestured across the courtyard. 'We're moving her bed to the hotel,' she replied. A couple of men were loading your pink metal crib into the orphanage van. 'Now?' I said, overwhelmed by what was happening. Nene laughed at my confusion. 'Right now.' Right then, on 20 November, you moved permanently into my life.

For you, the hotel was no longer a problem. You enjoyed the attention from the staff and liked dining outdoors on the patio. But for me it was daunting. I was now fully responsible for the well-being of a tiny individual. Yet our first night together went smoothly, and I'll never forget the next morning. When you awoke I plucked you from your crib and brought you to bed with me. You looked around at your new surroundings, cooed with delight and flung yourself into my arms. I'd been afraid you'd miss the orphanage, but you never looked back.

A few days after you moved into the hotel, you fell ill. You were listless in the morning, and at snacktime, when I gave you a bit of banana, you examined it dubiously, ate it and spat it out. I took your temperature and, sure enough, you had a fever. I gave you a rehydration formula I'd brought from Paris, but you couldn't keep anything down. And you were coughing a lot.

I sponged you down. You had a touch of flu, I told myself, trying not to worry. I gave you baby paracetamol to keep the fever down. The hotel staff brought my meals to the darkened room. Somehow we got through that day, and a difficult night.

The next morning I phoned Maître Diallo, who came to see us with his brother, a lung specialist. Dr. Diallo diagnosed you with bronchitis and an ear infection and prescribed cough medicine and an antibiotic. He told me to feed you mashed bananas or apples and plenty of water, with the rehydration formula. But nothing worked. I spent hours in the chiaroscuro of our room poring over baby books, searching for a word of comfort, but the more I read the more my disquiet grew. Fever, vomiting, diarrhea and coughing added up to trouble.

That night you slept fretfully and woke often. The ear infection, in particular, was bothering you. Periodically you howled in pain. I'd feed you more baby aspirin and rock you and hold

you, counting the minutes until the painkiller kicked in. Then
you'd calm a bit and I'd sing you back to sleep. But not for long.
With each of your screams I felt more frantic. Then I remembered the apple I'd ordered after Dr. Diallo's visit. Maybe you
would eat that. Trouble was, I had nothing to chop it up with.
And you had only two teeth, so you couldn't chew it.

There in the hotel room in the middle of the night, with you
wailing in my arms, I did the only thing I could think of.
Working as fast as I could I peeled some skin off the apple with
my fingernails, took a small bite, chewed the flesh into a pulp
and fed you a fingerful like a mama bird, forcing it into your tiny
mouth. You seemed to like it. You stopped crying and opened
your mouth for more. So I continued into the night, skinning the
apple, chewing and feeding you, willing you to get better.

On Monday I took you to see a French pediatrician, Dr.
Catherine Cissé. She confirmed you had an ear infection and
said to continue with the antibiotic. She also prescribed a non-
dairy milk, hoping that would help clear up the diarrhea.

I was increasingly desperate to get you home. But although the
appeals period was nearly over, I learned that same day,
27 November, that Judge Mahalmadane had refused to sign the
final adoption ruling – due to typos – and had left town for two
weeks. As he was the only one who could sign it, we wouldn't be
able to leave until mid-December. We now had tickets for 5
December. I phoned Air France to see about changing the date
again and to my chagrin learned there were no seats left for Paris
until Christmas Eve. It looked like we'd be stuck for another
month.

By Wednesday, your condition had not improved. You'd been ill
for five days. We went back to Dr. Cissé, who was appalled to
see how much weight you'd lost. She wanted to hospitalize you
immediately.

This was a moment I'd been dreading. Of course I wanted you

to get the best medical care possible, but at the same time I desperately didn't want to expose you to what I feared might be unsanitary conditions at the hospital.

For the first time, I worried that you might not make it – that you might actually die. Like the day weeks earlier when I'd heard you were suffering from malnutrition, I felt a sense of disbelief – this can't be happening to my child. What have I done wrong, I asked myself over and over. Why are we still marooned here? If only we'd been able to go home to Paris, where you'd be safe.

Dr. Cissé told us to go straight to the Clinique Pasteur – a modern hospital with a first-rate pediatrics department, she assured me. 'I'll let them know you're coming,' she said. 'Hurry.' At the hospital, the pediatrician frowned as she checked you. Dr. Tatiana Keita, Ukrainian by birth, was all cool efficiency. She upbraided me for waiting to hospitalize you. She said you had otitis, bronchitis and gastroenteritis; you were in a state of severe dehydration and would have to be hooked up to an IV. You took one look at her and howled, but I was reassured. I stood there, holding your hand, as she barked out orders. Your life was in danger. It was a huge relief to let someone else take charge.

They put you in a metal crib, a stiff white bandage around your tiny hand, the IV hanging beside you. We were in a private room with a bed for me beside yours. You eventually calmed down and drifted off.

Djeneba, I want to break off from your story now to say something about motherly love. Early on, when we were first getting to know each other, I worried about this. Once I got over my initial shock at your appearance – bald and scrawny as a newborn chick – I quickly grew fond of you. You delighted me with your curiosity about the world and your readiness to learn and your eagerness to love and be loved. And I did love you, but I asked myself whether what I felt was motherly love. After all, I had loved many children throughout my life. Even after the adoption ruling that legally made you my daughter, I wasn't sure my love for you was different. Well, Baba, the trip to the hospital solved that. I remember weeping as I lay there beside you, praying you'd stay alive. Any doubts I'd had were resolved that night. The scrawny chick who'd frightened me so when I first laid eyes on her had become my dimpled baby, my brightness, my joy, my little Djenebaba. I couldn't bear the thought of losing you.

As I lay there beside you in the hospital, willing my life to pass into your tiny body, I felt attached to you as though by an umbilical cord. Although I hadn't given birth to you, our lives were linked, and so they still are, my darling girl, now and forever.

Two mornings later, for the first time in days, you smiled at me. You were getting better at last, eating and gaining strength. It was 1 December, one month since we first met.

I went off to the French Consulate, armed with a medical certificate stating that I should take you home at once. I wanted to cut through the bureaucracy and get us on a plane. You needed a French entry visa, but the French demanded a signed adoption ruling. The vice-consul shook his head as I told our story. He'd heard of cases like this before, but none as preposterous as our tale of the disappearing judge. He scheduled a meeting with the Malian justice minister to discuss your case: your future had become an affair of state.

Back at the hospital, Dr. Keita pronounced you well enough to be unhooked from the IV. You could return to the hotel. I took you back there and went straight to see the chef. Like many a cook, he was a strong-willed character. While he'd been quite happy to prepare the little meals I took you at the orphanage, he'd also made clear that he was the chef and I was not welcome in his kitchen.

But now things were different. Was I a Jewish mother or wasn't I? The chef came to the kitchen door. I planted myself in front of him. 'You *have* to let me cook,' I demanded. We faced off for a moment, then the chef stepped aside.

On the way home, I'd bought a chicken and some vegetables. I borrowed an apron, found a knife, a cutting board and a pot.

Soon, there I was at the stove of the Al Mounia, making my family's remedy for everything – chicken soup.

When the sun came up on Monday, 4 December, I was ready to do battle again. We still held air tickets for the next day. I couldn't wait to hear what had happened with the justice minister. But the vice-consul had bad news: the Malians would not waive Judge Mahalmadane's signature and give us the adoption ruling. We'd have to wait another week for the judge to return before you could get your French entry visa.

I protested, saying this was an emergency. What about a medical visa? Not a viable option, he replied. Suddenly I had an idea. What if I was able to get hold of the final adoption ruling without the judge's signature? Surely the secretary had managed to correct the typos by now.

The vice-consul thought this over. Clearly it was irregular. But this was an irregular situation. All things considered, he indicated, if I managed to get the unsigned ruling, maybe they could make an exception.

I hailed a cab for the courthouse. Yes, the judge's scribe said, the adoption ruling was ready. But she couldn't show it to me. I'd have to wait and see the judge's deputy the next morning – the morning of the day we were supposed to leave. The day went by in a tense blur. I didn't dare pack. Would we be able to fly out of Bamako the next evening, or wouldn't we?

I was up early again the next day and headed straight to the courthouse. Another person was ahead of me in the drab waiting room. I watched the time tick by, wondering how I'd get everything done if, by some miracle, the judge's deputy agreed to give me the unsigned ruling. Thank goodness it was a late night flight.

I was deep in my musing when the door opened. Judge Mahalmadane's deputy showed me in. Forcing myself to smile, I told him what had happened. I showed him the hospital certificate saying you should leave at once: the delay due to the unsigned ruling had become injurious to your health. I asked the deputy whether he had children. Yes, he said, and told me a little about them. 'Put yourself in my place,' I said. 'If your child had been hospitalized and nearly died, wouldn't you do everything in your power to ensure the child got better? In exceptional circumstances, wouldn't you ask for an exceptional solution?'

The deputy looked troubled. He excused himself, saying he needed to look at the ruling, then returned – with the document. I knew then that we had won. First, he lectured me about how irregular this was. Then he wished me luck and, with a smile, gave me a copy of the unsigned ruling. I felt like leaping across the desk to embrace him. My girl, we'd fly to Paris that night!

So there we were, Djeneba, alone together in the no man's land of the air terminal. You were bright-eyed and excited, observing everything. Eventually they called our flight. I carried you out onto the tarmac in the balmy night. I strapped you in with me and held you tight as we taxied down the runway. We were airborne!

They served champagne and you and I shared a toast. We'd waited a long, long time and we were ready to celebrate. Our Malian chapter was finished, our life in Paris about to begin.

My darling Baba, we were going home.

Djeneba, it's been four years now since we left Mali. All the anxiety and turmoil of our initial meeting seems far behind us. We've settled into our Parisian life. You've grown strong and tall and are more beautiful every day. Four years into our adventure together, life with you is endlessly fascinating, and I see no reason why this should change.

In the nature–nurture debate, you seem to be living proof that a child's environment is at least as important a factor in development as what nature has provided. You resemble me in ways I find absolutely uncanny. I'm thinking in particular of your strong personality, and I'm afraid to say you've picked up the bad with the good. You can be stubborn and willful and brash.

You have a sharp tongue. But you can also be heart-meltingly endearing, like the day you blew kisses to everybody on the bus. Like the way you run to hug a child who gets hurt. Like your tendency to sing as we walk down the street. Like the way, in the dark, you repeat your bedtime stories to your teddy bear.

I'm so interested to see how you'll develop as you grow older, what paths you'll take, who you'll turn out to be.

If my life had followed the traditional path, we might not have found each other. Yes, there were obstacles – but look how things turned out. I wake up in the morning – or, I should say, am awakened, like today – with you jumping onto my bed, clambering over me and giving me a dimpled smile, then a big kiss. 'Come on, Mama,' you demand, tugging at the covers. 'Get up and make my breakfast.' That smile and that kiss are worth everything to me.

So, Djeneba, now that you know the story of your beginnings, I hope you'll be able to go forward in the years ahead confident in your ability to make things work, no matter what the challenge. Already at your tender age you've proved that you can do it. Whatever life may throw in your path, you are a survivor. Don't ever forget it.

It's true that you have difficulties awaiting you, not least having to deal with me for the foreseeable future. I'm not the world's most perfect mother. I make lots of mistakes, just like everybody does. And I can't give you everything you want.

But the bottom line is, you're a scamp and a rascal and a cheerful, happy kid – full of spice and full of life. Yes, my darling Baba, after a very rocky start you are now full of life. You made it. And I love you madly.

Mama

THE PANDA GAME

Emily Prager

My daughter LuLu and I had our first real conversation about adoption when she was three and a half. I know exactly, because it happened at a 'multicultural' Thanksgiving dinner held at Red Apple preschool in Chinatown. We were the 'multicultural' part. Everyone else in the class was so Chinese that not one parent spoke a word of English.

The other mothers tried to be nonchalant. But even as little as three years ago, Westerners didn't go down to Chinatown and march into fully Chinese institutions. And there was not much consciousness of Chinese adoption then, among Americans or Chinese.

It didn't help that I was a lot older than everyone else. 'You're like a grandma,' LuLu said to me one day, and she was quite right.

I was forty-five when she said that to me, about the age of the grandparents who often picked up her classmates at the end of the day. Most of the mothers were in their twenties.

But it wasn't until the Thanksgiving dinner, that LuLu seemed to fully grasp the oddness of our situation. Faced with a classroom full of young Chinese mothers and me, a light bulb seemed to go off over her head.

She began to run aimlessly but frantically around the room.

Then she started to bring me food from the table, as if trying to find a way to include me. She refused to sit at the table where all her classmates were sitting. She sat apart from them or just ran to and fro. She was clearly profoundly uncomfortable.

When we left and were out in the street, I bent down to her in the stroller. 'Are you embarrassed that I am not Chinese?' I asked.

'Yes,' she replied.

I felt a terror in my heart that I tried to cover. 'It's all right,' I told her. 'That's OK.' Still, I went home scared. It was time to have the talk.

I guess every adoptive parent fears the moment they will have to discuss adoption for the first time. I know I was terrified of telling my child. I was terrified I would say something irrevocably wrong, something that she would never get out of her thoughts. And I feared that when I told her I was not her birth mother, she would no longer love me with the strength she had. Actually, I would probably never have even gotten the word *adoption* out of my mouth were it not for Barney.

Yes, let no man speak against the big purple dinosaur, for it is to him that I owe this debt.

One day when Lu was about two, she was watching Barney (and, hence, so was I) when suddenly adoption was mentioned. It appeared that one of the little girls on the show was supposed to be adopted.

I seized the moment, and in a falsely cheerful voice, strangled with avoidance, I managed, 'Oh, LuLu. She's adopted. You're adopted, too.' LuLu nodded disinterestedly.

But the dreaded word was out of my mouth, and for a while I used it if people questioned us on the street. 'Yes,' I would say offhandedly, 'Lu is adopted from China.' And I repeated it until I felt that we were both accustomed to hearing it.

Once I had said it aloud, I no longer strangled on it, and it lost its bite. But saying 'adopted' and explaining its meaning to a small child are two vastly different things.

I had read several books on the subject. One was a hellish text of grim accounts of sadness and suicidal feelings from adoptees. But another, called *Talking with Young Children about Adoption*, was really helpful, and from it I got three pieces of important advice: 1) keep it simple – don't overexplain; 2) children can't really understand adoption if they don't understand birth; and 3) even very young children know more about their situation than you think they do.

The night of the Thanksgiving dinner, when we were lying in bed, I said to her, 'LuLu, I want to explain something to you. I want to explain why I am not Chinese.' She focused on me intently.

'I am not Chinese,' I went on, 'because I did not give birth to you. But I am as much your mother as any mother in your class, and you are my daughter. We just don't look alike, that's all.'

She seemed relieved to hear this.

'Do you want to hear the story of how I adopted you?' I asked.

She nodded yes fervently.

So for the first time I went into it. The parts she liked best and asked for over and over were the part about the adoption ministry deciding she was the perfect baby for me and sending me her picture, and the part about how Xion Yan, the woman who had facilitated the adoption in China, had called and asked, 'Would you like to meet your baby?' and how she had bowed and smiled when we met. The birth part of our story, if you will.

It gave her instant relief to have talked with me, and the next day when she came home from school, she sat down and asked me this exact question: 'Excuse me, Mother,' she said with odd formality, 'I wonder if you could tell me – why don't I speak Chinese?'

It had never occurred to me that she might wonder about that. It was a darn good question from her end. She looked Chinese. Why didn't she speak Chinese? Perhaps all this time she had been thinking that she was dumb in some way.

I replied that she did not speak Chinese because neither Neke nor I speak Chinese and so we did not speak Chinese at home but since we live in an English-speaking country, she is very lucky that she speaks such good English. This seemed to comfort her.

It brought her a lot of comfort, too, to hear about how her dear friends Sasha and LiLi and Emily and Gianna were there at her adoption, along with our friends, their parents.

In the next several weeks, she asked to hear the story every night over and over. I told it and made it warmer and more loving – and every time I did, I got more scared. I could not seem to bring myself to mention her birth parents.

Finally, one night in bed, I knew I had to do it. She asked for the story, and before I began I said, 'LuLu, I want to add something to the story.' Her ears went up, listening.

'The story really begins,' I said, 'with a nice Chinese couple. And they gave birth to you in Wuhu. You can call them parents if you want to. I call them your first parents. They wanted to keep you, but they couldn't, so –'

'Why?' Her little voice rang out strong and clear, all trace of toddler gone. This was evidently what she had been waiting to find out about but could not herself articulate. 'Why couldn't they?'

I swallowed. I was so afraid I would say something wrong. So I stuck to the truth.

'We don't know,' I told her. 'Perhaps they were too poor or the government wouldn't let them or something happened to them. We don't know. But I'm sure they wanted to. Because they took you to the Wuhu Children's Institute and told them to find the best mother for you, and the adoption ministry sent me your picture' – I pointed to it where I had it up in my bedroom – 'and when I saw it I thought, That's my baby, and I went and got you.'

I held my breath and looked at her. I couldn't tell what she was thinking, how this information had struck her.

'LuLu,' I whispered, because in some ways I'm a modest person, a humorist who's scared of feeling, and I had to go right down deep inside myself to be sure she knew the truth of how I felt. 'The best day of my life was the day I adopted you. I am so happy to be your mother.'

And tears exploded down my face. Immediately I panicked. I was terrified that she would think I was sad about it. She was only three, after all. 'I'm crying 'cause I'm h-happy, sweetie,' I stammered. 'Honest, this happens to grown-ups. There's so much happiness in my heart that it spills out of my eyes.'

I grabbed her and hugged her and prayed that she could feel the truth in what I was saying. I held her close and said softly, 'I love you so much.'

She hugged me close. 'I love you, Mama,' she whispered back.

About a week later, on a Sunday morning, she was sitting with me and Neke. He did not live with us but came and stayed on weekends. She looked suddenly very sad. I asked her what was wrong, and she said, 'My parents left me. They went away and left me with my grandparents.' I looked over at Neke. We were both stunned. 'Oh, Mom,' she suddenly said, 'I don't want to be adopted again.'

I put my arms around her. I was so torn up with emotion, I could hardly speak. 'You won't have to be adopted again, my darling. We will never leave you. Don't worry. Please don't worry.'

Now began a six-month period in which she seemed to be working out what she had learned. She became noticeably calmer right away. From the time she had learned to walk, she'd had long periods when she couldn't stop running or moving. In my ignorance, I had thought her high activity the result of having been swaddled for the first six months of her life – she, who was so athletic. And maybe, in part, it was. But as she worked on the problem of her identity, it became clear that part of her drive to move was pure anxiety, confusion about herself and her whereabouts that produced in her a desire to run. Because the more she understood about her origins, the more tranquil she became.

I immediately added the 'first parents,' as I called them, to the adoption story she wanted to hear each night. But I could not as yet bring myself to tell her that they had left her on the street near a police station. I couldn't figure out how to soften that. Perhaps this was in part because of something my friend Eshel, Sasha's mother, once brought to my attention.

Eshel called one day and said that her husband had brought home a book of photographs of China in the twentieth century. She'd been flipping through it and had seen a shot of a bunch of people standing on line, and on the pavement near them, wrapped in rags, lay an abandoned baby girl.

'It is incredible to see it,' she said, the sadness in her gentle voice, 'but there it is. Just incredible.'

For a long time I searched for that book, and then one day at a friend's, by accident, I found it. And it was incredible. A young woman in line is looking down at the little ragged wrapped bundle curiously, as if to say, What's that thing?

My daughter's first days were that stark, that real, a little ragged wrapped-up bundle placed on a street near the Qing Yi Jiang canal police substation. And having seen that photo of the reality, I could not pretend well enough that that was perfectly OK, so I couldn't tell her.

Although watching LuLu struggle to understand was almost unbearably moving to me, at the same time I was relieved to see that she was trying to make sense of it. In *Talking with Young Children about Adoption*, Mary Watkins warned that children must mourn their losses and that among the signs of mourning is a profound grief at not having been in the adoptive mother's stomach. This surprised me, that little children would think about that. But it happened exactly as the book said it would.

'OK,' LuLu would say to me, 'pretend you are getting your new adopted baby.' And we would reenact the 'birth' scene of the adoption.

That led to 'Pretend someone's in your tummy,' then to

'Pretend I'm in your tummy.' Then she wanted me to give birth to her, and I would pretend to, and she would lie on her back between my legs with her head on my stomach and wiggle out and cry. Then I would pretend to suckle her at my breast for a bit.

'I feel like I gave birth to you,' I would tell her as we played.

'I wish I was borned from you,' she would murmur from time to time.

Then we entered a period where she was the one who gave birth. I bought her a baby doll so she could have a new adopted baby of her own, and although LuLu was ordinarily completely uninterested in dolls, she played with it instantly, giving birth to it and employing it in our reenactments.

Once she put the doll to bed and propped its little milk bottle on the pillow near its mouth, exactly as they did in Chinese orphanages. Another time she gave birth to the doll and said to me, 'You're the sister. Tell me to throw it away.' And I did reluctantly, and she threw it in the bathroom and slammed the door. Then there was the rhino game she and I acted over and over after seeing Babar and the Rhinos war on a Babar video. 'Rhinos are taking your baby. Cry!' she demanded of me.

She began to have nightmares. She dreamed she was having a birthday at school and she went to the bathroom to pee, and her mother left the school and went away.

She dreamed she was in a museum, and a baby with an outstretched arm and bloody nose grabbed her. 'She liked me,' she said.

And in between, moments of grief surfaced. 'I'll never see my Chinese parents,' she said sadly one afternoon. I took my reply from something my friend Sara had so wisely said to her Chinese daughter when she had voiced the same sadness.

'Look in the mirror and you'll see them. They are in you.' I took LuLu to the mirror.

'In my legs?' she asked.

'In your legs,' I replied.

Once on the subway, LuLu sat next to a Chinese woman and asked her, 'Are you my mother?'

'Why did you ask that?' I questioned her later.

'I want a Chinese mother,' she said angrily.

'You have one,' I told her. 'We don't know her, but you do have one.' And she smiled.

Then there was the final game, which she orchestrated with three stuffed pandas. One panda was the baby, one was the mother, and one was the adopting mother.

When she started this game, she made me the birth mother and she was the baby. She tried to give me money so that I could keep her. I tried to explain that poverty was not cured with one payment. Then, as the birth mother, I took the opportunity to try to explain in simple terms the reasons behind the Chinese government's one-child policy: China's population problems and its relative lack of arable land for food, and how because of this the government deemed that I was not allowed to keep her.

This was not exactly simple stuff, but I felt I owed it to the woman who might have been forced to give her up – I wanted to lay the groundwork in the hope that, someday, LuLu would understand.

For months we played with the pandas. Sometimes I was the birth mother, sometimes she was. Mostly she was the baby. We both gave her away and readopted her many times over.

Then one day she announced to me with finality, 'OK. I'm going to call you Mama instead of Emily.'

And that was that. Her work was, for the moment, over. She came out of it more self-assured. It seemed that she had resolved something to her satisfaction. We took up hands again as mother and daughter and went on with life. We continued sporadically to play birth and suckling, but we never played the panda game again.

KISSING IT BETTER

Carol Lefevre

It was in the newspaper, a story about a South American city where the authorities tidied up ahead of an international summit by shooting numbers of street children. I am not even sure now where I read it, but I was just emerging from the tunnel of a gruelling and unsuccessful IVF treatment and decided on the spot to abandon the next round in favour of trying to save at least one child who was already in the world. It was one of those swerving moments in life when everything changes. Between the decision and the deed lay daunting quantities of paperwork and permissions, intensive language classes, and visits from social workers. But so ferocious was my energy, that within a year I was on a plane to Chile. In my hand luggage I carried an enormous Spanish dictionary and, pressed between its pages, a list of orphanages. There had been little time to consider the practicalities before departing, but flying in low over the snow-covered peaks of the Andes I had a dreamlike sense of being engaged in a bizarre and dangerous mission, like a spy, or an Interpol agent. The switch to Spanish added to the unreality, but the strangeness of being understood was an unexpected thrill that kept me afloat as I settled into a hotel and made the first calls.

Within days I had slipped into a parallel universe where small children free-floated without mothers, where they were not bonded to carers, where they sank from sight in institutions, or bobbed along on the surface, surviving as best they could.

It was September 1985, hot and sticky, and the city of Santiago wore a brooding and dishevelled air. Back in March an earthquake measuring 7.8 on the Richter scale had hit Central Chile, collapsing buildings and ripping up the pavements, but the greatest signs of upheaval were political. Twelve years of General Pinochet's dictatorship had forged a volatile society where running street battles erupted suddenly and were resolved by force, with water cannon, with tear gas, and sometimes with bullets. Curfews and power cuts were common. Army jeeps rattled through the city's streets at all hours and on Sunday afternoons the Mothers of the Disappeared protested with placards.

In the mornings I rose early, sipped cup after cup of weak tea and fiddled anxiously with my hair and clothing as I waited for a reasonable hour to telephone or to make the next visit. Pregnant women can dress as they please, but it was nerve-wracking to think I might be judged unfit to mother because of unruly hair or unpolished shoes. My days were spent knocking on doors. Some orphanages were staffed by stern-faced nuns. The others were state-run institutions in the charge of harassed social workers, desolate buildings that I fancied leaked sadness into the surrounding streets.

Everywhere I was met with the same answer: yes, there were children, but none could be adopted. In a population without access to contraception, abortion, or social security, one social worker estimated there might be as many as ninety thousand children stuck in orphanages.

'No more than one per cent will ever be adopted,' she said. 'Some parents keep children in care as insurance, so that when they grow up they can come out and support them in their old age.'

Small faces clustered at windows to watch as I arrived and departed. Standing on the pavement with my list, listening to their voices echoing around the playgrounds hidden behind high

stone walls, it was a struggle not to feel discouraged. I was running out of doors to knock on when a contact turned up news of
a baby girl in a city a couple of hours away up the coast.

At first sight the port of Valparaiso was so beaten up by
protest and broken by earthquakes that it was a test of courage
just to step down from the bus. Stray dogs roamed the streets in
great numbers, they slept anywhere, as if dead, and the speed
and spin of the local Spanish made every conversation an ordeal.
The faded splendour of Valparaiso grew on me over time, but
back then my first thought was for the unknown child and my
second was to leave as fast as possible.

She was already eleven months old. Malnourished and with a
shaved head, she was in a children's hospital, a tiny ward filled
with light, its windows facing out over steep hillsides where the
earthquake had carved a trail of debris amongst ramshackle
wooden houses. She had no visitors nor any belongings and had
been in hospital about a week, sent there by the courts to be
patched up before being moved on to an orphanage where she
would pass her childhood. In the hope that she would make a
favourable impression on me, the nurses had drenched her in
baby cologne. Simond's Golden Lotion. The scent raises hairs on
the back of my neck today. But she had no need of perfume.
Weary and vulnerable, with bandaged feet sticking out beneath
the hem of a much-washed pink cotton dress, it only took one
look from her enormous eyes and I was smitten. And yet our first
meeting – conducted on hard chairs in the social worker's office –
was awkward. We were not alone and with curious eyes following every move, our first physical contact was restrained.

What she had been through in the eleven months before I
found her was a mystery I gave little thought to as I struggled to
steer her adoption through the Chilean courts. Of course I knew
she had suffered, there was the malnutrition to prove it. Less
obvious was the inner damage, the deprivation of affection
endured in the tough back streets where she had been born. The
real clues, if I had picked up on them, were her silence and the

shocking intensity of her gaze, the way she rocked herself to sleep, or reached for a bottle of milk with her feet: these were signs of her loneliness and despair. I later learned that babies of her age sit up, but she would topple and her legs could not support her weight, which showed she had spent most of her time on her back in a cot. But I was an inexperienced mother and these developmental hitches did not strike me as crucial. In my exuberance I believed that loving parents and a comfortable home would rescue her from all that had gone before.

The weeks were filled with uncertainty and frustration. There was the infuriating incomprehension of other people and later, the terror that some slip of mine, of the law, or fate, would prevent me from rescuing a child with whom I was already bonding at a profound level. As the legal process ground forward there were moments of doubt during which I entertained wild thoughts of staying in Chile, far from my home, just to be near her. And as the hours we spent together totted up, she seemed to know that I belonged to her, too, so that each time I had to leave her we were both upset.

I had bought her a teddy bear for company and she was clutching it on the morning I arrived bearing the court order that would release her from the children's home where she spent her final days in care. I was too impatient to wait while the matron called a taxi and insisted on leaving at once. There were padlocks and chains to be undone and then we were standing on the pavement in watery sunlight, just the two of us for the first time. I ran with her in my arms, ran as fast as I could over the uneven cobbles of the street. Her tiny arms were clamped around my neck and as I ran – hugging the breath out of her – I whispered that from that moment on she would have two parents and all the love that she deserved and more. This promise, delivered at a moment of transcendent happiness, remains the only solemn vow in my life that I know to be indestructible.

There followed a time of immense happiness as we watched her learn to smile and laugh, to gain the confidence to cry in the night because she knew someone would arrive with a cuddle. From not being able to sit up unaided she walked at fifteen months, tirelessly, up and down the hall in her new red shoes, her tiny hand tugging us along hour after hour. It was as though, having been captive for so long, she couldn't get enough of movement.

For a few years it was easy to believe that adoption made no difference, that if anything, it made our family special. Certainly we could not have loved her more if she had been our biological child, but gradually, as she moved out into the world, it became obvious that it did make a difference. It made *her* different, when what she wanted and needed was to be the same as other children. We tried to let her grow up knowing the truth so that it would never come as a shock. But it was when she came home from school in Year One and announced that she had argued with her teacher about coming from my tummy that I began to feel uneasy. Still tiny, she was already being forced to grapple with huge unwieldy facts of life that she could barely comprehend.

And so it went on through the years of biology lessons and times when children were asked to take along a birth photograph for some class project. Suddenly I realized how much we didn't know, simple truths that other parents and children took for granted, like her birth weight and the time of day she had been born. These details may seem unimportant against a background of deprivation, but they are the seeds of identity and every bit as vital as survival in their way.

Later there were episodes of bullying at school. Gradually it took a toll. We spoke about it less at home and it was around that time that I admitted to myself that if I could be granted a miracle it would be that somehow she would become my biological child. Not for my sake but for hers, for the security and comfort it would bring her.

Facts that children can absorb at seven or eight take on a different aspect at twelve and thirteen and when the first rejection came it was like an electric shock. We were shopping for shoes and there was a disagreement.

You're not even my *real* mother!

Once it was out I saw that it had been buried there for years, a landmine waiting for one of us to stumble. I was shaking as I unlocked the car and we sat for a while in silence. Finally I told her I had been dreading this moment, but here we were and somehow we had both survived.

We had kept in touch with other adoptive families and the news that filtered through of exaggerated teenage problems – drug and alcohol abuse, eating disorders, underachievement at school and violent behaviour at home – might have warned us. But we had brought up our daughter with full knowledge of her adoption and believed that we were home free. Somehow we failed to realize that just at the moment when her origins had become distant and fuzzy to us, our bright child was struggling to assemble an identity. From her point of view, the raw material was missing and the clues she had to work with amounted to nothing more than scraps.

A month before her sixteenth birthday, our daughter stepped off the school bus one afternoon, walked into the house and took to her bed sobbing. At first we thought it was a temporary upset, but when it continued through the weekend and into the following school week with no sign of abating, it began to look more serious. Friends and family didn't understand what was happening; we barely understood it ourselves.

'Why don't you make her go to school?' they said. But her determination not to return was absolute and in any case, she was in no fit state. It was the beginning of a dark time for us.

The atmosphere in the house changed overnight: it felt unsafe, as if some invisible malevolent spirit had taken up residence. This sense of danger was so acute that I could only sleep when my husband was awake to watch over her. It was winter and the nights were endless. During my sleepless vigils I began to wonder about her birth mother. We knew her name but not her age, nor the colour of her eyes or hair. Soon this unknown woman haunted me as she was haunting my daughter. In the early years I had acknowledged her with gratitude, but during those solitary nights my gratitude was transformed into fury. I totted up the damage our daughter had suffered as an infant, the disastrous lack of love and affection in the early months. I wept for hours on those nights and sometimes during the days, certain that if I had been the biological mother I would never have relinquished her. But all the weeping in the world could not help and what mattered was finding a way to foster a sense of wholeness in this much-loved child.

Our GP referred us to a psychiatrist, who turned up at the house in drenching rain one Friday evening when our daughter was playing loud music and smashing things in her bedroom. She refused to talk to him. Instead, we did the talking, unravelling the weeks of anguish and despair while he sat nodding attentively on the sofa. As a last resort, we proposed to take her on a visit to Chile and the psychiatrist agreed it might help.

The return to Chile was extraordinarily painful for all of us on many levels. At times it felt to me like being flayed alive and I cannot really imagine how it was for her. In Santiago, we checked into a hotel opposite the terraced gardens of Santa Lucia hill, where fifteen years earlier I had filled a lonely Sunday afternoon dodging the courting couples and families eating ice cream to reach the summit. Then I had gazed out across the city and wondered if some nook or cranny held a child in need of the love I was bursting to offer. And here I was again, this time stricken by the possibility that all the years of care had been for nothing.

People in crisis look for omens everywhere. There was a lipstick kiss on the wall of our hotel room, the perfect imprint of a small mouth on the blue plaster. The height of it, and the size, suggested a child and it seemed to me symbolic, a reminder that our daughter wished to draw a line underneath her childhood and was determined to reject us. With my head on the pillow the kiss was level with my face and I woke each morning to its small, mute, yearning goodbye.

It was a journey on which she expected to leave us and although this was not a realistic option, it was impossible not to feel her struggling to detach herself from fifteen years of loving. Our relationship was tested constantly and at times the tests were scary, like the moment in Santiago when she walked away into the crowd on a busy street.

The only account that I had read of an adopted child's return to their country of origin described it as emotional but rewarding. Reunions took place in a haze of goodwill, with the subsequent return home a foregone conclusion and almost painless. Our angst-filled hours in various hotel rooms could not have been more different, but perhaps we are the kind of people who take such things hard.

There were spears of gladioli standing in buckets outside the church on our last morning, brilliant green bayonets with blood red tips. I remember looking past the flowers to the worn face of a woman begging in the entrance, the rattling cup she held out and her cotton skirt hiding the stool she had brought to sit on: poor as she was she had come prepared while I had not and after three weeks in Chile it was impossible to tell what tests had been passed or failed, what peace of mind lost or won.

If there was a high point of the trip it was meeting up again with a woman who fostered needy children. At least two of the children I had met on my first visit were still living with her and she had news of others. It was at her house that a five-year-old girl climbed onto my lap and pointed to a picture in the guidebook I had opened on the table. The picture showed a man and woman walking with a child between them. She ran a stubby finger across the faces and her own face grew wistful.

'Una familia completa,' she said.

We met kids with cigarette burns and other deliberate injuries, the damaged offspring of prostitutes and alcoholics, including a nineteen-year-old who, as a small boy, had been beaten so badly for crying that he still refused to speak.

These were children who would not easily be kissed and made better.

It is the random element of the attachment that adopted children find unbearable. And yet the profound and loving relationships that sustain and shape our lives most often spring from random collisions. In my own case I have always believed that syn-chronicity was at work when I found my daughter and that no other outcome was ever a possibility for either of us. Yet I can see what she has lost. In our affluent society there is a widespread view of children adopted from poorer countries as having hit the jackpot. But whenever I observe a mother bouncing a small baby on her knee and note their mutual absorption and delight, I am reminded that our child missed out on the one thing that most of us take for granted. Children like her need mothers, but in a sense they will always have one too many, for the biological mother is likely to become a ghost that haunts them.

Seventeen years on from that first fateful meeting, my daugh-ter insists that she and I are close, closer than many teenage daughters and their biological mothers. And it is true. With her wicked sense of humour she can make me laugh more often and harder than anyone I know. And she knows how to make me cry. But that eleven-month gap remains a black hole in her life and therefore in mine. It has etched distinctive patterns into her. For an eighteen-year-old of considerable beauty she cannot allow herself to be frivolous even for a moment and what she hates per-haps most of all is surprises. Yet somehow we have battled through and after a gap year she returned to full-time education, with creditable results.

Of the families whose adoptions I have tracked through the teenage years, all have experienced severe disruptions to family life. But was it any worse than might be expected with a biolog-ical child? Most think it was, because adoption magnifies the intense emotions of those years and offers an excuse for acting out. Of our six families, one appears to have broken down irretrievably while the rest have shown the same resilience and determination others muster for biological children in crisis, convinced that failure is unthinkable and that even when they appear to hate us our children are still too precious to desert.

While I am the real mother in the sense that I have raised this child, my daughter's separation from her birth mother is a wrong that will never be put right. It saddens me, but I understand this sense she has that her life will never be complete. An ordinary birth is greeted with joy and once the baby is named, registered, and the birth certificate issued, there are no unknowns, no blind spots. Parent and child are certain of who they are. But adopted children have no clear linear narrative to support them and although adoptive families long to manufacture happy endings, the fact that we are doomed to fail is one of the unacknowledged tragedies of adoption. Curiously, my daughter has always said that she would like to adopt children.

I am not a huge fan of the poet Kahlil Gibran, but these lines from *The Prophet* seem to carry a special warning for adoptive parents.

> *Your children are not your children*
> *They are the sons and daughters of Life's longing for itself.*

There is no question that I would do it all again, but another time I would ask more questions, demand the kind of details that later might go some way towards satisfying the natural curiosity of a child. I would arm myself, too, for what might come once the soft and fuzzy toddler years were over. Now that I have had time to reflect, I believe, as I did not before, that adoption is a terrible thing. But the truth is that more often than not the alternative is more terrible.

For adoptive and biological families, good days arrive as well as bad and to the thousands of children and adoptive parents just starting their lives together, I wish only happiness. But I would urge them to bear in mind that the ride might grow rocky and that when it does the important thing is not to deny what the child has lost but acknowledge it. Above all, never underestimate the strength of the bond that has formed between parent and child in the growing years, because whatever the child may say or think when struggling with the question of identity, that bond is tough and it is a huge part of who they are.

Only love is truly thicker than blood.

A few months ago a friend gave me another of Gibran's quotes, a grain of wisdom and common sense that might help adopted children when it comes to weighing up relationships.

He who understands you is greater kin to you than your own brother. For even your own kindred may neither understand you nor know your true worth.

THE BEAR HUNT

Mark Wormald

Most of us are grateful for the veil of discretion that convention or necessity pulls over the known but actually unimaginable intimacy of our origins. We fit snugly into a tradition, a genre, that we need never trouble ourselves with invoking, let alone criticizing. Until, at some point, with luck in a relationship that feels right, we throw caution and prophylaxis to the winds or across the bedroom and trust to luck and brute biology to provide an unnameable beginning to another family story.

My wife Sarah and I had always wanted children, and had every right, we thought, to add our own family story to this one, and soon. We hoped to begin it in the master bedroom of a bed and breakfast in West Cork in September 1992, while the host family settled themselves down for the night in the garage they had converted into their tourist season quarters.

An acquaintance of ours once told us that her brother was called Royston, their parents' not-so-private tribute to the place of his conception. For now, it need be said only that, when we finally had the chance to name a son, Schull and Skibbereen did not seem obvious choices.

It is probably also right to skate over in a single sentence the growing recognition that we, Sarah and I, were not 'most of us', that we might in fact have to think of other ways than our own parents had of becoming the parents of the children that already were entering our heads at night as we slept, already causing us to ache from a pain, a condition, that both of us came to share, if in different forms, at the predictable moment every month.

In fact, the real beginning of our family's long gestation is easy enough to place. Though none of our boys are yet of an age to be able to stand these gory details, it began in the community wing of a primary school barely a mile from home in an East Anglian city not so far from Royston, some time in the winter of 1993. With six or seven other couples, we clutched cups of coffee, sat on adjacent plastic chairs, not, I think, holding hands, while two social workers got up to welcome us. They were called Susie and Kate. They wore black – they always wore black – and smiled a lot. They spoke briskly about the needs of children, observed that nowadays there were hardly any babies available for adoption, emphasized the qualities you needed to give a child a home, and then handed over to a woman who, through photographs and her own descriptions, introduced her two kids, whom she had adopted as 'a sibling group'. She was real, they were real – they even looked like her, I remember thinking – and, that odd label apart, we felt real excitement as we settled down for a preliminary chat with Susie after the mum had sat down. I tried not to feel interrogated as Susie asked us about ourselves, and Sarah took the list of telephone numbers she gave us and folded it and put it in her bag. But very soon, nodding at what we were telling her, Susie said: 'But have you come to terms with your infertility?' She meant, it turned out: 'Are you absolutely sure you will never be able to have children of your own?' And that meant, it also emerged: 'Unless you have undergone all the medical investigations and treatments available, and unless these have failed, and unless you can come back to us and explain all this calmly, without breaking down, we simply don't feel you will be able to give any of these children, who have very particular needs and who must feel that they are not second best in your home, what they deserve.'

And we could see that, though it hurt. So we went away, and kept a number of appointments in a number of medical establishments that do not, otherwise, form a part of this family story, and failed to achieve a pregnancy, and waited, and in time felt strong enough to make a phone call to one of the numbers we had been given that evening. And that, after a period of flirtation with waiting lists, which opened and closed and opened again, led to a return to that primary school community wing. There, with six or seven other couples, we Prepared to Care. We brainstormed, we discussed categories of abuse – emotional, physical, sexual – and categories of learning difficulty; we felt, and discussed, our reactions to each. Sarah, experienced in working with children with special needs, was terrified of putting ourselves out of reach of our future by being too fussy. I could not follow her. As far as possible from that bright classroom, the two of us talked and talked. We wanted, we decided, simply to be able to give and to receive love.

Rather less simply than its jaunty rhyme, preparing for caring also led us back onto ourselves. The course unfolded in parallel with our Home Study, which consisted of eight or nine evening meetings, most of them an hour and a half long, about a week apart, with the woman who answered that call, Jenny. During these sessions Sarah and I worked hard at touching each other supportively from the appropriate distance apart on our sitting room sofa while our dog slept behind Jenny's chair, and by a magnificent joint effort managed to keep any hint of despair and pleading out of our voices as we talked about our upbringing, our relationships, our desire to have a family, and our expectations of what we wanted from it. Jenny kept full notes, but gave nothing away; she was a tight-lipped reader, the toughest of practical critics. Then she wanted corroborating evidence. We turned to our oldest friends as a couple, who had married a year after us. They drove across the country for the purpose; Jenny interviewed them about our habits and our weaknesses while we took their two small children to the park. Sarah and I were also interviewed separately; it felt like an invitation to betray each other. But we did not, evidently; for though Jenny did not give much away, she did in time ask us to produce a family album – a family album! – of pictures, with friendly captions, which could be shown both to any social workers interested in us, and to any children the social workers matched with us, and most immediately to the panel of social workers, councillors and adoptive parents who would decide, in about a month's time we were told, whether we could be approved as parents. This in turn led to a morning in another bed and breakfast, in Vermont, and a transatlantic telephone call, and to a lot of weeping with relief and joy. This was early April 1996.

To be approved as parents, and yet not to be parents yet: what a reversal of conventional perspectives! As months passed and the good news faded and no telephone calls from Jenny came, we entered that stage of our family's gestation for which, except for couples who have had embryos put back into a strangely conscious womb, there can be no equivalent in a natural pregnancy.

There are of course other agonizing uncertainties, other choices, that face the majority, the five in six who conceive a family without having to conceptualize one: in the summer of 1994, when we were obeying Susie's breezy recommendation and proving our failure to conceive in our future children's best interests, one friend confessed tearfully to Sarah that she had fallen pregnant at the worst possible moment for her burgeoning career as an artist; another couple shared with us their dread at the imminent results of an amniocentesis on their second child. (We had chosen not to exchange these confidences at the time.)

Now, as we continued our utterly invisible wait, our imaginations betrayed us with the truths the social workers had prepared them for. Within a couple of weeks of that Vermont morning, Sarah pointed out an irony that seemed to redefine irony's reach, but which I guess is no news to the patient waiting for an organ donor. Somewhere, she said, if we are lucky, our children are already being neglected or worse. She is right. In the vast majority of cases of adoption in Britain today, that old phrase, 'giving a child up for adoption' is a brutal distortion. There is no rendering, only rending, no gift, only exhausted abandonment, in some cases after contesting the matter in court; there are conscious cruelties, involuntary failures, acts of forgetting the fact of that other small self that, on some bed or in some moment of true, thoughtless passion, a frightened hopeless couple brought into being and then did nothing or not enough either to extinguish or to nurture. There is pain on every side. Great pain. Serial self-absorption on one hand, trying one's best in a vacuum on the other. Social services strive to keep birth families together, in often hopeless optimism that patterns of behaviour can be reversed. Foster care seems like a last resort; adoption the highly unusual, rarely reached end of the road.

Our own pain went unexpectedly into spasm, an approved adoptive couple's first Braxton Hicks, when, after months, Jenny did call. How were we doing, she asked, neutrally. What did she expect? Stung into speech, we told her. By choosing to adopt a sibling group, we had thought – and we had been told – that we would speed up the making of our family, as well as make up for lost time by leapfrogging our way into the position of a ready-made family; sibling groups were in urgent need of placement. Yet we had so far heard nothing, while two other couples on our Prepare to Care course had recently been in breezy touch offering wisdom or what they called consolation and inviting us to come and see their new babies. We had declined. Stung back, Jenny replied. She had come across a boy, a baby, she said. He was fourteen months old, much younger than we had imagined possible. But . . . and here she embarked on a list of his problems and challenges, that led as we listened from deformity to blindness to learning difficulty to developmental delay to other special needs I have since made myself forget. Between them, they had, all too early in his life, induced his birth mother to give up, and give him up. Jenny paused, waiting for us to contradict the assumption she had no need to voice. She was probably right, but it hurt to have her play God. After she had left, we sat on that sofa in our sitting room breathless with despair.

And then she phoned again. She wanted to see us, just to keep in touch. We were ready for her this time. Ready with the pile of magazines from one of the support groups we had joined – it had always felt like another form of betrayal, subversive of the efforts of the black-suited ones. In fact, it is an indication of the scale of their task, and its difficulty. The magazines have titles like *Be My Parent*, and *Children Who Wait*; the passport-sized smiles and the bright, urgent prose of the profiles accompanying the pictures gathered from every social services department are designed, of course, to persuade a desperate readership to consider them again, and to forget that these are children whom couples like us had declined, over and over again. We were each other's last resort. We said, 'Look, here are children, here, from all over the country. We have begun telephoning round.' We did not say what we meant: we have lost faith in you.

And then she produced a photograph of two boys sitting on a brown velour sofa. We are outside our own history in a moment. One blond waif, one a bonny chub of a thing. Staring out. At us. Smiling, but a little bewildered. Wide-eyed. Pale. On the right, a toddler with attitude. What lies behind that grin, in those bright eyes? They are brothers, three hundred and sixty-four days apart. Their birthdays are in late April; that made them almost three and almost two. We can keep the picture.

This is March 1997. We are about to go on holiday. It will be our happiest in years.

As we watch, we also listen, gulping down details about the boys which make us think, make us feel, 'Yes: here they are. Here we are.' Later, there will be the F9 and other forms with names like low-powered racing cars to read, implications and prognoses to take in.

Later?

The trimesters of adoptive pregnancies are predictably uneven in length. Adjusting to their terms means learning to play the very long game and then, out of nowhere, becoming master of the putt on slippery greens. Months, if not years, of preparing to care typically yield within weeks, if not days, to a frenzy of introductory meetings that, depending on the age of the child, can last between a day and a week. At this point, not having dared to buy beds or install stair gates, all DIY-ing hell breaks loose. And then the child is with you, living with you, is your child, often no more than a fortnight after you first heard of him or her, or – our situation – them.

The later stages of our family's gestation did not quite fit even that schedule. We returned from Crete eager for news. But what at first looked like due process following its own routine slow motion soon became something else. We were helplessly aware of tactical arguments about whether to 'free the boys for adoption' or to aim instead for a 'placement with a view to adoption' (how oddly the language of liberation sits alongside that grudging insistence on the provisional, the procedural). Court wheels that had creaked then came off. Files went astray, and weeks passed; a guardian ad litem, appointed to ensure that the boys' best interests were protected, was taken ill, and needed to be replaced, thus rewinding the whole process. And weeks passed; then the judge went on holiday, for weeks. We could not meet the boys; the pain and anger we were now beginning to feel at not meeting them would be as nothing, we were told, to the confusion of meeting them only for the wheels to jam altogether and the boys to grow older and drift irrecoverably apart from the future we were already imagining for them. (They, of course, knew nothing about us.)

But we were allowed to meet the older boy's doctor, and to

learn from him the details of the urinary tract infections he had been suffering since in foster care, largely – and here, in a consulting room in a town within an hour's drive of home, he casually pulled out an X-ray and showed us the bladder and ureters of a toddler we had not seen learn to toddle – because his birth mother hadn't gone in for the usual *in utero* scans during her pregnancy. The problem could have been corrected, we are told. But it will be manageable. Will. He believes we will be, we are, this little boy's parents.

It is the beginning of September 1997. We are given assurances that there will be no more delays. We insist, with an assertiveness that frightens and confuses us, that there can be no more. Our own lives will not bear it. There is another delay. We begin to dread the phone ringing. The kitten we brought back from a hastily scheduled break in the Lake District, rescued from a death by drowning, one remarkable silver tabby from a helter-skelter litter that a farmer had no room or food for, goes missing. He is out all day and half the night. I trace his mewls, tiny and piteous in the dark, to the roof of a garage at the bottom of a garden at the far end of our street, and feel him at the end of my fingers, coax him back into my grasp. If we have this difficulty protecting a kitten, I wonder, why do we not give up on adoption now?

It is early October 1997, and we are sitting on that brown velour sofa in a town within an hour's drive of home, planning the following day. The two small boys are out, but the smiling foster mum's other children, one, at nine, in a nappy, and dribbling as he smiles, drift through the house. Jenny is with us, and Julia, the boys' social worker, whom we finally met the week before. She is Italian. 'You look so alike!' she had said then, and grinned, proud of her matchmaking. We want to be sure of that ourselves. Then the foster mother produces a letter, dated a week earlier. It is from our local hospital, where a specialist unknown to us has been in touch with the doctor we met. There has been an exploratory operation scheduled for a month's time. It will involve an overnight stay. This is all right, isn't it? It is all right. Anything is all right. Tomorrow afternoon's visit to the local social services community centre on an adjacent estate, where we will meet the birth mother, is all right. It will be harder for her, we are told, and agree. As we leave, Jenny confirms with the foster mother that she has our family album. Yes, she says. She'll show the boys tonight.

We pull up, the next morning, outside the same house, ready to meet the boys and to take them to the local park. We touch each other's hands. And then, even before the car doors are shut, the front door of the house is opening, and two small figures are hurtling, not toddling, towards us, and 'My Daddy! My Daddy!' Matthew is saying, even before we touch. And here is George, circling, holding back a little, but happy for Sarah to sweep him up; and here we are in the kitchen, George showing us his drawing, Matthew snuggling his stranger, their foster mother talking about vegetables and regular bath times and giving us, once more, directions to the park. Matthew still asks me about that half-hour at the park. We played football. It is a mythical, magical time for him. The edge of us: where 'we' began. And after lunch, when we have dropped the boys back at the house, we spend half an hour in the social services centre with a bewildered waif of a nineteen-year-old, who says she hopes we'll have other children, and tells us about her favourite soaps.

The introductions last a week. This is expected. So are the drives back and forth along the dual carriageway between the two towns, a tape of Silly Songs on an endless loop; it greets me when I come out of B&Q armed with the stair gates late one evening. George points at the B on our SAAB logo and says, '8'! They learn red and blue and white. We talk ourselves hoarse.

One afternoon is not scheduled. Following an early morning call from their foster mother, we spend it in hospital. Matthew has a urinary infection. The paediatrician, who is Egyptian, is impatient with us, and a little with him. He finds it difficult to produce a sample. 'Is he always like this?' she asks. George and Sarah play with the waiting-room toys. Eventually Matthew manages a squirt of yellow oil paint. He is in tears. But we buy him a carton of drink; we go to a local farm to watch the animals; we bath them both and, a safe distance from the hospital, he wees again, apple juice this time. Good boy!

The following Monday morning, we take delivery of a VW camper vanload of clothes (they are dressed as twins), plastic cars, two Postman Pats, and Matthew, and George. They sleep in beds we had bought on approval, and assembled shortly after I managed the stair gates. Are they ours? Are we there yet? How much longer? Hours into our first week at home together, these questions do not seem to matter. Years spent looking quietly across into other, parallel, richly inhabited, perfectly paced lives have simply vanished. The present, this present, is everything, and very loud, and very bright. We are all children, all looked after, all looking after each other.

5 November 1997. Sarah's birthday, her first as a mum. Here she is sitting up in bed, propped up by two pillows and two boys. She is reading her cards, which she knows she will always keep.

At recent bedtimes, having started with *Meg and Mog Go to the Moon*, we have all discovered *We're Going on a Bear Hunt*. I cannot imagine how recently it was written, or how I managed to pass my own childhood without it. *We're going on a bear hunt. We're going to catch a big one. What a beautiful day! We're not scared.* This seems right, and comforting. The response to each of the challenges the family of hunters face is also just right. A field of long wavy grass, a river, mud, a snowstorm, a forest, and finally a cave, where they encounter the bear itself; each challenge is an opportunity for exaggerated hand signals and wild theatrical tones as we encounter the world of prepositions, still a mystery to boys for whom everything, including conversation itself, seems new and in their face, and so in ours. *Uh-uh! Grass! Long wavy grass. We can't go over it. We can't go* under it. *Oh no, we've got to go through it. Swishy swashy! Swishy swashy! Swishy swashy!* And then a wild reprise of each – *Hoooo woooo, Squelch squerch* – as they hotfoot it back through the wilds of what looks like the Suffolk coast, and take refuge under the covers of the family bed as the bear presses its nostrils against the glass of the front door and then turns, terribly sad and lonely, back for his cave.

The rhythm of our life, the scope of each day's adventures, seems as crowded and as vivid and as chokingly happy as that birthday morning in our own bed. It has narrowed and deepened; we are conscious of being loud parents in the park, endlessly playing and replaying chasing games and rough and tumbles, discovering rituals of totemic importance in every playground, on every walk together, where they are always rushing ahead. Our life together seems to resemble the boys' language, which the lack of a listener and of experience has left delayed; bold markers mostly, a litter of nouns and names and the odd adjective, with lots of 'Nos', a limited repertoire performed with utter conviction, a desperate semaphore that will get us by until grammar comes along. Why doesn't everybody we meet, in the superstore or on the street, see how remarkable all this is? Why don't the teachers and assistants at the nursery that Matthew has just begun see this also? The candles we have on Sarah's cake that evening are the first she has had since she was a girl.

8 November 1997. A different sort of evening. Two hours ago Matthew came round from his exploratory operation, which one of the junior doctors, who turns out to have recognized me from college, tells us eagerly went very well; silicon had been inserted to strengthen, and narrow, the valves in his ureters, which would in turn prevent the reflux he had been suffering, and with this the infections. But Matthew, at three and a half, begs to differ. The general anaesthetic has left him wild and confused. His screams in the recovery room brought nurses out to find us in embarrassment and their own distress. They asked: 'Is he always like this?' Remarkably, Sarah and I, in shifts, have

managed to calm him. 'My Daddy,' I remember him saying, and 'No, no, *no!*' Now it is time for me to take George home to his first night alone in his new room; Sarah stays at the hospital with Matthew. It is a long hot wet night but, we realize, the first of the several nights that Matthew has spent in hospital for which he has been accompanied. At about eleven that night as she is stroking his hair, our menagerie grows again; she finds the family's first headlouse.

Our first Christmas we spend at home, alone as a family; to have done the usual, and decamped to Sarah's parents' or one of my brothers', would, we are advised, have confused the boys, felt like another placement, another move. As it is, everything is very happy – if we discount, as we must, the unannounced arrival of large cards from the boys' birth family. A covering letter from social services explains: 'We thought you wouldn't mind.' We did. We have already reached an agreement to maintain contact, via letter, with the birth mum each summer, at the end of the school year and a safe distance from the emotionally heightened festivals. We have also agreed to inherit, and adapt, the boys' 'life story books', in their first incarnation as lurid as the Walt Disney folders they came in, full only of pictures of brittle smiles taken one afternoon in September 1997 at the social services centre, which we have edited, turned into first person narrative that Matthew, and perhaps George, will want to look at as the years go by; George, so far – he is nine as I write – is reluctant to ask the kinds of questions that his big brother risks, but occasionally says, of a class-mate's mum with a particular, resonantly familiar first name who has given him a lift home, 'I was in her tummy', and otherwise prefers stories about his own heroics as a baby, 'before I came to you, Mum'. Though George has landed himself in trouble at school with these fantasies, confusing teachers who have, under the pressure of dealing daily with thirty little fabulists, shown a remarkable tendency to forget what we have told them, patiently, about the boys at the start of each school year, it never takes much to remind us that these stories are natural and necessary.

Don't get me wrong about Walt Disney and his heirs: Sarah and I feel pathetically grateful for the support that those legendary armies of writers provide us through the medium of those brightly coloured cartoon features we know by heart. But we have also seen for ourselves the risks involved in the pursuit of that good work, these heroic, homely portrayals of our role in catching and nurturing our little fallen heroes. Of all the millions of parents who have squeezed companionably onto kids' sofas watching Disney's take on Hercules, how many are prompted to think ruefully of evenings in primary school community wings by the moment when old Amphitrion comes across the infant Hercules on the road, a diabolical snake just throttled in his chubby fingers, and takes him up in his arms with ne'er a mention of a form F9? And think of the moment when teenage Hercules, confused by his own enormous powers (George, too, a great breaker of other children's toys, we decided 'didn't know his own strength'), hides those flashing teeth for once from 'Mum, Dad', and tells them he loves them and will never forget them but, hey, he just has to follow the call to heroism he has just had from his other old man, Zeus. How many parents scan as we do their wholly absorbed children for signs of doubt, confusion, even longing? And how many cheer as silently when, turning his back on Olympus for the love of his mortal, faithless Megara, Hercules steps down back into the modest embrace of his merely mortal parents? How many clutch newspaper or knitting needles or go and get a coffee when Superman lays his stricken father down in the yard of his Iowa farmstead and turns his face to the crystalline north? To those who have not seen these films from the particular seat we occupy, such anxieties will seem opaque, even pathetic. But they are real enough, believe me.

Yet it is always as well to check our own self-indulgent responses to such moments against the truer, simpler, always more reassuring screens of our boys' faces. It was, I think, our second Christmas when, never having read the novel, Sarah and I were lulled by the cheery Geena Davis and Hugh Laurie, the brightness of a mouse's check trousers, and by a special offer at Tesco's into buying Matthew the video of *Stuart Little*. It was in the late afternoon of a wonderful day, with his godmother here, too, that we all settled down to watch. And for a while all seemed well. Though we exchanged the odd glance, the very distance of all this from what we had been through – the fact of the Littles' older son, George; the breezily stern interview with the woman from the orphanage, after they had made their own, simple, bold decision that, yes, the issues involved in adopting a mouse were things they could handle; the fact, above all, that it was an *orphanage* – made it all wonderfully easy to cope with, for all of us. Until, that is, Mr Little answers a ring at the door to discover an apparently empty front step. As he finally brings into focus the brash tiny couple standing there, asking for Stuart, and then as Mr and Mrs Little concede, reasonably, nobly, that yes, there must have been a tragic misunderstanding, involving separation shortly after Stuart's birth, that of course in these circumstances Stuart must return with these strangers to the . . . the *real* family home, how can we not feel for Matthew and ourselves? There are tears in his eyes as he sits beside Loraine, and we are cursing our choice of film. 'All right, Matthew?' we risk; he nods. We know we can't ask more, mustn't ask more; to do so would be to ask for the reassurance to which we're not entitled, this being his story, not ours. But it turns out that it belongs to us all. The happy ending comes long before the terrific flight through the cat-infested darkness of Central Park and the reunion at the window of the family home. Back in their low-life dive, Stuart confronts this pair and elicits the confession that they'd been put up to it, were only masquerading as his parents. Matthew gets up, beams, comes over to where we are sitting, like porcelain, and hugs us both. He means: he can come back home!

But that is still a year away.

In the first days of the new year, 1998, Matthew, who seems to have recovered well from his operation, becomes increasingly tired and pale. Sarah takes him to our GP, who is reassuring, thinks she is worrying unnecessarily. Sarah rings the doctor who showed us Matthew's tubes those months before. Well, it could be a reaction, belatedly, to what has struck Jenny and Julia as a very successful move, he advises; but much more likely it is just a winter bug. Not to worry. The next day, as the January night comes racing in over the afternoon's dull sand, I get a phone call from Sarah. Matthew has fallen asleep again; though she could wake him, he looks strained, really odd; and his fingers are puffy. She is taking him to the GP; when I meet her there after a hastily arranged appointment with another doctor, she is white. That puffiness in the fingers had persuaded the doctor to take Matthew's blood pressure, just to reassure us. It is very high. Then we are up at the hospital again. In A&E, first, where a medical student asks the standard unanswerable questions from which nothing will deflect her – ('What was his birth weight?', 'Is there a family history of high blood pressure?') – then in a pae- diatric ward, where doctors and nurses scuttle and keep their faces averted. Sarah will stay with Matthew overnight; on my way out, with George, to collect their pyjamas from home, I bump into a colleague, whose ex has had a heart attack. She has, she explains bluffly, almost ironically, as if needing to justify her presence here, been bringing her son to see him. I sympathize with her, then wonder if this is appropriate; wonder at how rap- idly distances between loved ones open and close, like doors in a draughty house, like wounds.

I am woken at 3 a.m. Sarah is lucid, but needs to repeat her- self. They are on their way to Nottingham, by ambulance and police escort; Matthew's kidneys have failed, she says, and Nottingham is the best place for him. He is very ill; he is in danger. I wake George at seven, having first telephoned a bleary- mouthed duty officer at social services to keep them informed, as we think we must. We drive north.

The Paediatric Renal Unit at Nottingham City Hospital is our home for the following month, while brilliant, fascinated nephrol- ogists and radiographers and surgeons and nurses balance curiosity and care in diagnosing, stabilizing and then treating this rare little occurrence, a boy whom fundamental neglect and then hi-tech intervention have left struggling for life. It appears, from a body scan I arrived in time to hold Matthew steady for in his distress, that the silicon inserted to strengthen those valves has come loose and blocked the ureters completely; urine, having nowhere to go, has simply flooded his kidneys, which have failed. The solution, for the moment, is to drain both kidneys through his back, using rubber stents and nephrostomy bags. We give our consent for this, not sure, quite, whether it is our legal right to do so, though we have remembered the little card that gives us permission, before the adoption has been finalized, to make such decisions; and then wait, and wait, and wait, while George gets to know the trikes in the unit's playroom. At last, good news, in a recovery room that, this time, earns its name. Those huge plastic bags at the base of his back look like angel's wings the wrong way up; already they are filling with urine.

As days pass, and we become expert both in gauging creatinine levels and in the business of emptying and replacing the nephrostomy bags, so huge simply because they are adult bags (there being no need, in these days of *in utero* scans, for children's sizes), another routine develops utterly without reference to either of our old lives. Sarah and I take it in turns to spend nights beside Matthew's bed on the ward and in a tiny, glass-walled cubicle called a family room, where George tosses, turns and snuggles us into a fitful sleep, asking, every morning within seconds of waking, 'Where's Matthew?' A tap dance in the lift to make it go faster and the wait at the entry phone reunite us all; at every greeting and every parting, the boys hug each other, this one deeper bond underlying rather than undermining our own love, which is absolute and, mercifully, taken for absolute by everyone here. Doctors who ask their rote questions and receive our patient answers – 'We don't know his birth weight', 'There is no family history' – say, 'But George is your own, surely?' No, we answer – and yes. Yes, definitely. As we watch him tearing down those long corridors on the playroom trike, swerving to avoid the meal trains, and then – as weeks go by and Matthew regains his strength sufficiently to face the operation that will finally bring shapeliness to all his tubes, colour to his cheeks and strength to his fingers – performing all kinds of risky slaloms around big brother's wheelchair, nothing has ever been more definite than this.

By the time we return home we are old hands; and it is time to take care of a bit of paperwork. Spring is upon us; the boys will soon have been with us for six months, the point at which the law can catch up with us at last. One morning in early May we meet Jenny at the magistrate's court; two minutes later the judge, as we explain to the boys, gives us the piece of paper that makes us 'a family for ever'. They play with this phrase, like it, come to make it their own. We all feel its weight. We sit in a tearoom; Jenny, beaming, we guess, with relief, says: 'I'm not a religious person, but I do believe that this was meant to be.' A fortnight later, we seek another view. A good friend conducts a baptism for them both, deciding that, because we don't know whether Matthew has or has not been baptised, another, provisional baptism would not go amiss. As it turns out, nothing is more natural. The words of the concluding prayer need no amending to fit our case: 'Lord God our Father, maker of heaven and earth, we thank you that by your Holy Spirit these children have been born again into new life, adopted for your own, and received into the fellowship of your Church.'

August 2004. Now we are six. Matthew, of course, is now strictly ten, and we have, just this month, begun to notice that his body is changing, preparing itself in very good time for the long slouch through his teens. He can't go over them, he can't go under them; which means, knowing Matthew, that we will all have to go through them with him, pursued by bears at every turn. He has just told me that he no longer believes in the tooth fairy. And George is, equally inevitably, strictly nine; he is emerging from the worst of his asthma and eczema, and is Just William, Horrid Henry, and the sublime Thierry by turns. He knows more about the length of Legolas's arrows and Aragorn's swords than anyone but hobbits or the god of PS2 can stand. Watch us for a minute on a beach, on a sofa, in the park, and we have, it seems, become our future; we seem to be disappearing into normality. It is, of course, a normality that asks awkward, even unanswerable questions, but few of these, even the most philosophical back-seat-driver variety – 'Can ghosts poo?', 'Do trees go to heaven when they die?' – are made any wiser or less wise, any more or less answerable, by a knowledge of the boys' past, or even a knowledge that they had one. (Nor, I had better add, are thoughts of the afterlife, vegetable or scatological, crowding their heads too frequently; this was merely a wave that both wanted to ride.)

For all that, as our seventh Family Day looms, I repeat: now we are six. Our boys are still very young.

This is not, or not just, a euphemism for the immaturity that, as best friends on a perpetual sleep-over, the mildest boys might occasionally exhibit. (Ours are not the mildest boys.) Nor is it a way of saying that their early years have permanently limited our two, stunted their growth. To hear middle-class phrases, our own private registers and pet names and, we like to think, generally excellent manners coming from these mouths, and to find Matthew, who struggled so hard to climb onto the first branches of the Oxford Reading Tree, consuming all three volumes of *The Lord of the Rings* by the time he has reached double figures, causes by turns pleasure, pride and some slight guilt. I love them saying, during a sharp shower, 'It's chucking itself down'; I wince when I hear Matthew describe a tennis shot he has just fluffed as 'dismal'.

I mean, rather, that our boys have an energy, and a balancing inability to inhibit that energy, that often remind me of our first days and weeks together. For all the love that we give each other, they remain greedy for more, touchingly ready to express it with a directness that I never once encountered as a child myself among parents or peers. But the boys are also terrified – though we have been lucky in not yet seeing more than the occasional glimpse of this – terrified of the risk of losing love, or even the attention from others they mistake it for. Relationships still confuse them, in the playground, over the phone, anywhere in fact where people expect them to be nine or ten or even on the verge of something older and more daunting. But at home – in bed, where a check last thing at night can still find them curled asleep together; on the sofa, where they lie like spoons, sharing sweets and space with a freedom that few people, sometimes not even their parents, can emulate or tolerate; occasionally also at family parties, where either of them will, entirely unprompted, take a toddler gently under his wing – in all these hidden places, what we are seeing is selves who are more innocent than our images of normal development allow them to be. And the energy, and their youth, is infectious.

We have always found ourselves, as a family, at our most complete in periods of genuinely free time, free from the pressures and chronologies of the world beyond the garden gate; this remains one of the boys' gifts to us, our version of what, thinking of another kind of improvisation entirely, Larkin called 'the natural noise of good'.

We have no doubt at all that we face many years of continuing noise. How long it will endure in its mostly benign form is another question. Whenever we face our current version of the future, we confront a clutch of abstractions that will be familiar to every adoptive parent who reads the magazines that drop monthly through the letter box or attend 'support' meetings in spare church halls, and to many for whom these are all too bewildering realities. The Anger. Attachment Disorder. These may, almost certainly will, lie ahead. One of the fears I have in writing, about boys who are still discovering the limits of the private, intimate but not, we tell them, secret story of the way they came to be who and where they are, is that this piece itself will come to seem to them, when they are of an age to read it, like a violation of that privacy, or at any rate an unwarranted definition of something that is, for the moment, and for years to come, bound to go on changing. That is one reason why I have here changed their names; a transformation, of course, that we were never able to effect on any other page. It is also why the essay takes the piecemeal form that it does. This is work in progress. Best not to make predictions. Much safer, much more certain, for us young parents and for those young boys, to recover and prolong impressions of these early boisterous years for as long as we all can. Now we are six.

And suddenly we are also five. Here, dashing around the corner of the sofa clutching keys, is Ben, sixteen months old and discovering nouns. He grabs at anything he can reach in his growing world, and as he grabs he grins. He started this habit early. First to be grabbed were his amazed mum and dad, of course, who will never forget the delight and the tears that came with that delight when first we saw him, a tiny astronaut, on the twelve-week scan. Then, at twenty weeks, his two big brothers. Matthew hugged us and squealed, and said we were on our way to a football team. George had a different question. 'How will we adopt him into our family?' 'Just as we did you,' we replied.

And we have done our best to hold to that promise. The same swirl of water over the forehead amid the same circle of friends, the same words spoken by the same friend fitting the third arrival just as snugly as they did the first two. But what we did not foresee, in seeing Ben enter the world as well as our family, is how much his coming and these first extraordinary years and months would do, what it would release, for his older brothers. None of us remembers our own first months, of course; but Matthew and George have more particular reasons than they can yet express for their own fascination and delight at Ben's discovery of his fingers, that starfish startle at patterns of light over our shoulder. When, at nine months, he began to crawl, he was crawling across time and experience that they had lost; it must have been like having a floodlight turned on a wreck and finding that its bullion, long thought lost, was within reach of salvage. And we, too, benefited from its illumination. We had often invoked the fact of their missing years to explain, to justify to ourselves, why certain basic habits of body and mind that others of their age took entirely for granted seemed so slow to seed in the boys. Now developmental psychological theory yielded to plain sight. When Ben began to stand, and then, totteringly, to walk, a single finger propped against a trouser leg he knew would be there, and then, a week or so later, when he began to take his first unaided steps, more or less in time to Sarah's guiding presence, I saw more sharply and more painfully than ever before why it was that Matthew had himself managed this feat of walking beside us, stopped running impulsively ahead of us in a nervous trot along a crowded street, calmed down, only a year or so before, when he was eight. Neither of them had ever had that reliable, infinitely patient calf to cling to. Family meals are likewise nowadays accompanied by a wash of sound, Ben's own glossolalia echoed and amplified by his two brothers' encouraging, sympathetic, but ultimately self-delighting cadenzas of baby boom. They need this; we, therefore, need to let them indulge in it, whatever its consequences for our sanity. At bedtime, the boys proudly read their little brother stories, among them, already, *The Bear Hunt*.

And they are also laying down their own bonds of which, again, we grown-ups are only enablers, witnesses. Weeks into Ben's life, George reflected, another piece of back-seat wisdom: 'When Ben is ten I'll be eighteen. When Ben is twenty I'll be twenty-eight. When Ben is a hundred and twenty I'll be a hundred and twenty-eight.' But George, I ventured, as gently realistic as I could; none of us will live that long. Infinite weary patience. 'I *know*, Dad. But we're brothers. We'll be in Heaven together.'

Last summer we went on holiday in the far north-west of Scotland. Too far north, it seemed, for rain. Among the hundreds of pictures snap-happy Dad took is one which I especially love. Matthew and George have decided to collaborate on a major engineering project within feet of the sea's edge. The tide, they know, is coming in, and they work frantically fast, digging like cartoon bunnies. And then Ben, his nappy matching their swimming trunks, toddles over, forces his way in on the act. All three of them go to it, heads down, hands reaching into the pit as the water races in behind them and the sun blinds the lens.

THE MANDRAKE CRY OF A CHILD

Mirabel Osler

'Shrieks like mandrakes, torn out of the earth'
(*Romeo and Juliet*)

Grief is corrosive. Like a virus that works slowly, destroying and eating into human fabric, it leaves an automaton in place of a person. A bane, a scourge, it never diminishes. The people who say time is a great healer are liars: they haven't found out for themselves the duplicity of such a platitude.

My sister Cordelia was our first visitor when we moved to Thailand in 1959. My husband Michael had come to teach English in a teacher training college and our first three years were in Lopburi, a hundred miles north of Bangkok. Cordelia came for an exotic respite from four young children and the treadmill of daily chores. Our time together was precious, magic and altogether out of our usual context. As we disentangled our arms at Bangkok airport on her return home she wistfully remarked that never again would she have such a wonderful holiday. She died five weeks later from a botched operation.

The news of my sister's death reached us on the other side of the world – in northern Queensland, where Michael and our daughter Tamsin and I had gone to visit friends while the Thai schools were closed in the hot season and our son David was at school in England. The telegram was delivered to us at a sleazy hotel on the coast where we stayed overnight. We never reached our friends: in a state of numb misery I knew without doubt there was only one place I must be – with Cordelia's family. We turned round and headed for England.

The death of my sister – four years older, my mentor and comforter – was impossible to assimilate. I was haunted by thoughts of her bones buried in the cold earth of a country churchyard, her skull looking skywards with sockets full of soil. Knuckles, nails, spine – a collection of bones – arms that had comforted me more times than I could remember and hands that had led me across the road on the way to school. The year following her death I was felled by a deep depression, a mood I had never experienced before. I discovered that depression is absence of emotion. Sterile – apathetic to everything – it left nothing palpitating. How could I have ever cared about *anything*? For the rest of my life I never experienced anything so eclipsing as grief – not even physical pain.

Although time doesn't heal, the momentum of living can give one a shove. And the seeds of regeneration are not always the obvious ones.

Two years after Cordelia died we became caught up in the complexities of adopting a child.

The reasons why people adopt are varied and complex. With us it seemed to grow from something instinctive, non-intellectual. Bereavement had something to do with it, but there were other more elusive motivations that evolved organically. We were living in a small town, the only foreigners. In the market, besides the colourful piles of comestibles, were throngs of people seeking cures, magic amulets, soothsayers or exorcists. Among them were men obsessed with virility buying powders, charms or snakes pickled in alcohol, and young women obsessed by acquiring a pale skin buying the white powder they smeared on their faces every evening when they returned from the paddy.

And there were the children with bronze hair.

The first time I saw them – roasting *kluey khai* (a kind of small banana) over charcoal – I assumed their mothers dyed their hair until a Thai friend put me right. Bleached hair was a sign of malnutrition. Later we were to see the same aberration among children in the vast agricultural regions or in the distant hills further north.

Emerging from depression sharpened my awareness of the country in which we were living – a longing to explore the bosky distance beyond the rice plains became irresistible. We would hire an empty rice barge drawn by a tug on the end of a rope, to float along rivers like arteries that penetrated the landmass surrounding us. Here we discovered a world of water people living in places inaccessible by road. We stopped at temples, were welcomed by the monks, talked to the farmers, bought provisions from wayside hamlets, ate in simple food stalls and each night unrolled mats to sleep on the floor of the barge. Wherever we stopped we met curiosity, friendliness and generosity. A generosity that occasionally included being offered a baby to take home with us.

Was this the way we were unconsciously coerced? I cannot remember if there was ever a moment when we said, 'That's what we'll do.' Rather, in the way some of the best things that happen are when you aren't searching but are just receptive and living in the moment, somehow the decision merely evolved. All I know is there was a day when we happened to be in Bangkok, that we consciously made time to visit a home for children.

Children abandoned, orphaned, disabled, unacceptable filled institutions. They had distended bellies and hands that surreptitiously curled round fingers of each visitor who crossed their threshold. The majority were not actually available for adoption. Parents could not be traced, or they refused permission, were temporarily ill, in prison or promised to return but never did.

We visited places where babies were for sale; where two toddlers shared one cot; homes for prostitutes' babies; nurseries housing babies left on clinic benches; institutions for older children abandoned in a fallow waste forever waiting to be claimed. We heard the mandrake cry of a baby – a torn root drawn the length of the ward – and the sound of a child relentlessly banging its head against the wall; we saw again and again the deformity of malnutrition; pleading fingers reaching through the bars.

'You want baby?' Smiling, 'No problem! Which one you want?' The question, direct, simple, was too raw to answer. Lurching through malodorous orphanages we geared ourselves up each time to face the ordeal of moving among children with an affected indifference that belied our inner turmoil.

Our search became a recurring nightmare; we were groping and everything felt warm.

The system appeared straightforward. It worked like this. Thais who needed a child to bring up as a kind of servant and handy helper about the place could take a child without any formalities. The method was not as heartless as it sounds. We saw this at first hand. A family living next door to us had a young girl from an orphanage whom they used for carrying their shopping and to run errands, who went to school, came to our house to play with Tamsin and, most crucially, had a place she called 'home'. Conditioned by our way of looking at things it may sound cavalier, but in fact it was a workable alternative to leaving a child to moulder away in no man's land.

For foreigners the system was altogether different. We needed pieces of paper; official permission; a passport, and a legal adoption that would allow us to take the child out of the country. But every question we asked floated like dandelion seed into the air and landed nowhere. We had entered a world full of anguish and nebulous answers, a twilight zone of sophistry and heartbreak. There was no recognizable logic, no prescribed system, just smiles and unanswered questions.

One day having visited countless institutions where we received the usual amorphous answers, we were told of two possible babies for adoption – except, as usual, hard facts were elusive. No one knew whether the parents were alive, could be traced, were in prison, in an asylum, or had promised to return. A young girl showing us round, twittering helpfully by our side, pointed to them among a roomful of others as she explained that the 'high person' was not there that day but, 'You come back . . . You take. Mother not want baby.' And then added the dreaded phrase: 'No problem!', which invariably foreboded the opposite.

Amidst the sour smell of urine, rubber sheeting, damp bedding and humid concrete I wrote the names of two children on the inside of my diary (still there forty years later). In one almighty stroke, by a random gesture, by a hair's breadth, we were about to change a child's life. And our own.

There was nothing more we could do that day. We returned home. It would be a while before we could return to Bangkok. Having no telephone, there was no way of making an appointment – anyway, that sort of thing was moonshine, appointments were fantasies. Not until weeks later did we again drive the slow road to Bangkok on the chance of finding the 'high person' on the premises. But she wasn't there. We stayed overnight with friends and, because the orphanage was on the north side of the city, on our way home we tried again. We were lucky. Serene, smiling, without an inkling of how portentous the occasion was, nor how casually we had decided to deviate off the main road, the head of the orphanage led us into her office. I showed her the two Thai names in my diary. One had already gone, she told us, but that one, pointing to the name on the page, was here. She led us into the nursery. There were children whose days were spent in boredom and lassitude, deprived of identity, language or love. Yet once an adult made any move towards them, paused to speak or held out a hand, response was immediate. Their desire for attention was pitiable.

Sureen was no different. Her smile was instantaneous. 'You can have this one if you like,' the matron said momentarily picking her up. But I wasn't going to hold the child – at least not until I was sure I need never put her down. I couldn't bear to see the look on her face as the matron replaced her on the floor. No one wanted her, it seemed, because her father was a prince. The reasoning, so a Thai friend explained later, would be a loss of face for a royal baby to be discovered in an orphanage; no Thai family would take a child to bring up as a servant with such majestic lineage.

In the past royal consorts were so numerous that titles spread like veins throughout the dynasties making it necessary in the following five generations for each prince or princess to lose a grade. This meant that great, great grandchildren born to a consort with the title of queen finished up as mister or miss. The grandfather of the child on offer to us, as a descendent of King Chulalongkorn, had the title *Momchao*; her father *Momrachawong* and his daughter, being one notch down, *Momluang*. Any children she had would inherit a humble label, *nai Ayutthaya*. Inevitably, nowadays, as monarchs no longer have several consorts the system is on the decline. (There's a satisfactory sequel to this. Many years later, in 1979 Sureen's first job after leaving the London School of Contemporary Dance was to take the part of one of her ancestors as a 'minor wife' to Yul Brynner in *The King and I* with Virginia McKenna.)

Back in her office, sitting on chairs with overstuffed embroidered cushions covered with plastic that stuck to our backs, we faced the principal. Behind her stood a glass-fronted cabinet with an unopened tin of Johnson's Baby Powder and a collection of toys (given by kindly charity ladies) that were never distributed. 'You see, the staff would take the toys back home unless we kept the cupboard locked,' she said, giggling behind her hand and then added disarmingly, 'Why not take the child now, today?'

Stunned, deflected from our assumption that certain formalities should be adhered to before actually taking a child, Michael said, 'Give us time to think! This isn't how we planned it . . .

Goodness! We haven't even a bed for her!' I simply said, 'Yes. Of course we'll take her.'

How naively innocent of us, seduced by the gentle charm and good humour of the Thais into doing something momentous which in other circumstances would have followed bureaucratic procedure. The Westerners' idea of doing business depended on form filling; for Thais it was simple, in this case a matter of expediency. Their universal mantra 'no problem' fooled us. Later we found out how misled we'd been. There were no notes, no registration, no birth certificate or health records. No one even asked us for our name and address.

Sureen was handed to me naked. The garment she was wearing was needed for another child. (How strange she feels, like a peeled stick. What am I doing with this small creature lying across my shoulder whose contours, weight and smell are alien?) She had bones deformed by malnutrition, a runny nose, a black front tooth and a scarred forehead – from a fall or abuse? and was unable to speak, although it turned out later she was over two years old. As we left the matron smiled, assuring us that if we changed our minds we could always bring her back.

We were incredulous. Were we talking about a human being or a commodity? We already knew she was with us for keeps, there was no question. You don't compromise over a child. How many times since – long after that day – have I looked at Sureen with a sense of awe at the fortuitous moment when, almost casually, we carried her back with us. But I haven't forgotten all the shadowy children – the ones we didn't take home.

Unsure of her age, her health, not knowing whether she was deaf or dumb, we bought her some clothes and then went straight to a missionary hospital in Bangkok to consult an American paediatrician. Sometimes missionaries with their zeal and dedication are infallible oracles when it comes to *scientific* answers. This kindly doctor took the screaming child, went over her from top to toe and handed her back with wise advice.

'I'd say she's more than two years old but less than three.

Look, she still has her Mongolian mark.' And she pointed to what appeared to be a bruise at the base of her spine. 'Asian babies have it for their first year or two. The black birthmark is a relic of the capacity of the skin to produce red blood cells in the womb. Post-partum this capacity fades but in newborn Asiatics the evidence remains.' Her smile was reassuring. 'She's neither deaf nor dumb; her squint will cure itself; the scars will heal and with care and nourishment her bones will straighten. Worm her immediately – she's sure to have a tapeworm, they all do – and if you intend taking her from the country you'll have to get a birth certificate for her. Good luck and God bless you.'

Thus Sureen entered our family. When I think of the arbitrary way we found her I can only believe in some strange way we had been moving towards each other long before she was put into my arms. Pathetic, unloved, communicating by tears not words for no one in the home had time to talk to her, she responded with immediate enthusiasm to everything on offer. Food, of course, but also love, bathing, childish rhymes, lullabies and toys of her own. She accepted it all as though she had never known any other life. But bedtime was a contest. She had never slept in a bed, just lain on a mat among other bodies. For weeks the only way I could get her to sleep was to lie on the floor, my arms enfolding her as a cat lies with her kittens. In a tropical climate the floor is the coolest place to lie but without supporting children surrounding her she rolled in her sleep until by morning I had to extricate her from under the chest of drawers.

In our small town the servants soon spread it about that the *ferangs* had brought back a child from Bangkok. Tongdee (the name means 'good gold' – hardly an apt name for a girl who slept with some of our bachelor visitors with an open-hearted sense of hospitality) came from the north-east to work for us at the age of seventeen. She was beloved by both the children and she stayed with us until we left the country seven years later. Slim and pliant as a willow she collapsed to the floor like crumpled paper whenever she was overcome by laughter, her long hair falling forward in a glossy mass across her face. Her response to the arrival of Sureen was one of amused astonishment. Not everyone was so uncritical. There was an underlying prejudice in Thai society about skin colour – a fact that disconcerted us when we first came across this discrimination among schoolgirls who always chose the lighter skinned pupils for leading ceremonies. (Tamsin in a way suffered from this bias by having her arms touched and stroked by adults and children alike as though her pallor was somehow transferable, and by sheer osmosis overnight they would become white as forced asparagus.)

'Why such a black one?' demanded the governor's wife with disarming frankness, a woman who was always asking me to order cream from England to whiten her skin. The colonel's wife remarked gloomily, 'She won't be able to eat your kind of food, of course.' Little did she know that our 'kind of food' was Thai and every course which appeared at the table was greeted by arms outstretched and wails of desperation from Sureen fearful that unless she was quick enough she would miss out on what was on offer. It took weeks before she felt sure that there would be more food tomorrow.

And yet in spite of her insecure origins Sureen has grown up to be the most generous person I have ever known. She's irrepressible. Any excuse – birthdays, Christmas, minor celebrations – and she arrives loaded with presents. She finds it impossible to meet her nieces without bringing them a collection of pretty clothes. Lasting psychological damage may occur in the first twelve months of a child's life and there was certainly deprivation in hers – yet despite her agitation at mealtimes, it's Sureen whose arms are now outstretched in the act of giving.

Of course, I had moments of panic. How could I not? Questions kept me awake night after night. Our son, David, being much older, already had his own identity, but what about Tamsin, now a four-year-old who suddenly had a ready-made

sister? She might well feel usurped. I worried about this particularly as Sureen from the start was a volatile child. Whenever she
erupted, her demands rang through the household with a reso-
nance that pulverized us all. (In fact she might have been my
mother's natural grandchild, their temperaments were so similar.)
Tamsin, a quiet child, found offers of hugs and teddies repudi-
ated: while the tantrum lasted Sureen was impossible to placate;
nothing could deflect her outburst until she decided for herself it
was time to stop. The following calm was a form of benediction.

I was also aware that we were taking a child away from where
her appearance was unremarkable. We were cutting her link
with centuries of delicate proprieties, obliqueness, the serenity of
Buddhism. Instead we would coarsen her gestures, impose our
history, language, education. And yet seeing her asleep I was
appeased knowing that long before labels or nationality she was
just a child. Why anticipate complications?

Quite fortuitously, Sureen's bonding with the family was in a
motor car. It was the rainy season of August 1961. David was
with us for the holidays and long before we'd known about
Sureen we'd promised him a journey north. As we drove through
teak forests David amused the girls by acting the fool whenever
it seemed their spirits were wilting, keeping them happily curled
up on the back seat, reluctant even to be winkled out whenever
we stopped.

Sureen learned to speak Thai and English simultaneously. It is
enviably easy to learn a language at that age and if at times her
words slid about overlapping one with the other, it was an
endearing confusion. Sureen and Tamsin became bilingual com-
panions intermeshed so closely I doubt if they thought about
their dissimilar origins.

Sureen in every way except legally was now ours. But there lay
the agony: we were due to go to England on leave in April but as
there was no formula at that time for foreigners to adopt a citi-
zen we waded into a morass of red tape. Every solution slipped
out of our grasp the moment we were told which office, which

bit of paper, whose signature would be needed first. We learned again the Siamese art of getting nowhere while sipping coloured water in numerous offices including women's hospitals, in one of which we did finally trace Sureen's birth certificate.

'That is the easy part,' said Khun Prawanee, an intelligent lawyer whom we used to negotiate the adoption. 'But nothing can be done unless by hook or by crook you have the father's signature on the adoption forms.' The father! Good God! Who and how? And where is he? For all we knew the man we were seeking might be surfing on Bondi Beach.

'Of course . . . you understand . . . there are easier methods. You know . . . hanky-panky . . . a little monkey business.' She looked at us across her desk, inscrutable, dead earnest. 'It's a piece of cake if you pay someone to sign in his place.' She saw our reaction. 'Oh yes, it is often done! You must hold out a carrot to certain people in offices and so forth and so on.' But we wanted everything to be legal. We were dealing with a child, not authenticating a shady deal and we lived in dread of failing and having to return Sureen to institutional limbo.

Without officialdom's stamp on every piece of paper it would be futile to go to the British Embassy in Bangkok to apply for a passport for her. Anyone who has tried to penetrate bureaucratic entanglements abroad will understand how happiness depends on martinets of the worst kind; the ones who pick their teeth while talking to you; wear dark glasses; flashy watches; and keep a row of miniature bottles of Cointreau, Grand Marnier, and Scotch whisky among Dunlop tyre ashtrays and Carlsberg beer mats on their desk. We felt as though we were being held up, not so much by red tape, but by the pointless leads we pursued leading to oblivion. Unable to think of anything else I felt witless, out of control. I woke every morning distraught.

At last, through some random encounter we were given a newspaper photograph of Sureen's father and the name of the town where he was living. Khun Prawanee was cool, unfazed; she reminded us, 'He is an important man – what you call "a bigwig". We must now use someone suitable in the town to find out his address. He must be approached with kid gloves.'

I couldn't speak. The love of clichés sprinkled through the language of those who had learned English through old-fashioned phrase books usually delighted me, but not now with Sureen's future 'hanging on a thread'. Nothing would ever be funny again while apprehension, perplexity and frustration bordering on despair, had taken over.

'I shall make inquiries. I can pull the wires, you will see. No problem! Meanwhile you must get a certificate to prove that the child's parents were legally married.' (Otherwise we would only have needed the mother's signature but why hadn't she told us before? So much time wasted.) We got up to go. As we made the *wai* gesture to each other she smiled. 'Leave it in my hands; I shall leave no stone unturned.'

Michael and I were despondent, chafing at the invisible obstacles forever delaying our progress. Yet miraculously – months later – it happened. Our lawyer 'gave us the nod' to board an overnight train for the distant town where Sureen's father was living.

At that time Thai trains were magnificent things: polished bottle green or black with brass fittings; punctual; fired by wood they panted patiently at every station while a man continuously swept the floor from one end of the train to the other. (Footprints on a lavatory seat were puzzling until we realized that squatting was the natural position for defecation.)

At every station we leaned out to buy food from children running the length of the platforms. Grinning, they scrambled and shoved offering us black coffee in evaporated milk tins hanging on pieces of raffia. Pieces of cooked chicken coated with curry paste, chunks of pineapple threaded on twine, coconuts with drinking straws implanted through their shells and woven trays loaded with whatever fruit was in season were thrust towards us by smiling, pleading faces. This was to be the final journey. It had to be. I was slowly being destroyed by legal uncertainties. All the hours spent in municipal offices facing closed doors must lead us to this final dénouement when we would confront Sureen's father with the fate of his child.

Through a convoluted sequence of contacts a message was relayed to us next morning that he went to the barber at the same time every day. At eight the following morning we were parked in a tree-lined street out of sight of the barber's, waiting to confront and persuade him; if that failed we were prepared to kidnap him. Although we had reached the point of no return, Prawanee reminded us he must be handled with delicacy. 'Face' was everything and his had to be preserved.

As he emerged from the barber's we recognized him instantly from the newspaper cutting. He was good-looking and taller than most Thais. We didn't hesitate. We walked up to him, introduced ourselves, explained what we wanted, and as deferentially as possible press-ganged him into our car. Touching a stranger would have been disrespectful but I do remember how we stood either side of him. We didn't frogmarch him exactly but we kind of hustled a bit without causing him embarrassment in the street. Anyway once in the car we depended on him to direct us to the *nai Ampur*'s office.

It was done! With unaffected grace and fatalism the man was ours. Two hours in the district office was all that was needed to fix what had been eluding us for months.

During those two hours our quarry made no attempt to escape, or plead other appointments or take evasive action. Instead it was he who courteously explained to the officer what we had come about. Official stamps on duplicated forms were needed; carbon paper between pages; signatures galore; the conversion of our parents' dates of birth to Siamese years all written in elegant script across pages in a book the size of a paving stone.

I thought of the child, the unloved infant ignorant of this momentous meeting, and I could have wept. While clerks padded barefoot to and fro bringing us glasses of pink water, the conversation between our hostage and us covered every subject but the one in hand. We spoke of their revered Queen Sirikit, discussed Thai silk, the temples of Bangkok, teak forests, elephants, orchids, the climate and whether being foreigners we could eat Thai food. Never once did the man refer to his child, ask where she was, show any interest in us, her future, or why we were living in the country. His manners were impeccable, his reticence diplomatic.

Somewhere in a small town there is an official book recording legal contracts authenticating an event that took place in what was for me the most consummate building in the world.

The first thing to be done now that we had the authentication of Sureen's adoption in our hands was to get her a Thai passport. The bureaucratic palaver for this was nothing compared to what had gone before and although we could have put her on one of our passports it seemed imperative that we gave her the option to reclaim her nationality in later years should she want to.

We were in England for two months before returning for a further four years in the northern capital Chiang Mai. In London on 23 June 1962 we went through the British adoption procedure. The distinguished Chairman of the Juvenile Courts, Baroness Wootton of Abinger, reputed to be outrageous and fierce at times, was intrigued to preside over a trans-racial adoption. She was charming, encouraging and the sight of a three-year-old Siamese blundering among two languages endeared Sureen to everyone in the court. She now had dual nationality. Some day in the future the choice could be hers.

Why don't more couples striving for a child adopt? Often it appears to be egotism, they need to reproduce their own flesh, a child not of their making might have 'God knows what inherited traits'. I remember the German woman – when we'd left Thailand to live in Greece – who asked me: 'But can you love an adopted child in the same way?' Then looking at seven-year-old Sureen she added: 'And anyway who will marry her?'

Some may classify adoption as second best, a compromise, but a child – whether flesh of my flesh or born through a process of documentation – is unique. Each is different in its responses, pleasures, problems and empathy. And if you cannot trace characteristics in an adopted child nor can you always with natural prodigy. How often do parents say of their child when they aren't the paragon they assumed they'd hatched: 'I can't imagine from where he/she has inherited that'?

And those critics who protested to us that we were removing Sureen from her culture have obviously never been in homes stacked with unloved children. If they had they might stop to ask themselves: '*What* culture?' Festering for years in an institution until puberty sends them one way or another is hardly likely to implant in a child a deep feeling for her civilization, which is why the current neurosis over trans-racial adoption misses the point.

The death of my sister brought us to an orphanage almost half a century ago. Through convoluted chance encounters we found a child who has enriched our lives and those of others who know and love her. Relationships within a family are often fragile, but neither Michael nor I ever questioned our decision to follow up those two names in my diary.

Sureen has two sons. One was born with the Mongolian mark at the base of his spine authenticating his origin like 'Brighton' through a stick of rock. When Sureen was taken into hospital with a sudden rare illness a few years ago, when the boys were still babies, an extreme unconscious protectiveness came to the surface in me. Anguish is overwhelming when your child is seriously ill, but a forsaken, unclaimed child produces an almost irrational defensiveness: instinctive and retaliatory. Ignorant of heredity, the threads of her illness were untraceable. Fear haunted my sleep.

Now more than two years later, she is better. Although she will be forever dependent on drugs, blood tests and X-rays, her buoyancy has returned but she broke my heart the day she remarked, almost casually, that she knew she wouldn't live long enough to see her grandchildren.

Sureen's skin, hair and eyes label her, yes. But those are superficial traits. In every other way she is Anglo-Saxon. She was a child lifted out of a no man's land and had the light fallen differently, she would have landed elsewhere. Conversely her sister Tamsin feels un-rooted. Growing up in different countries has left her in a strange way uncommitted, but not Sureen. Her total identification with England was exemplified in London once when I happened to comment on the number of foreigners who stopped to ask me the way somewhere. She said, 'How odd, Mummy, no one ever asks me.' 'Look in the mirror, Sureen, to see why they don't.'

She'd forgotten – a long, long time ago she had forgotten.

HAPPENSTANCE

Daniel Menaker

In the late eighties, the writer Harold Brodkey used to visit my office when I was an editor at the *New Yorker* to expound upon the subject of adoption. He knew that my wife and I had adopted a son, and it seemed that as he Harold had been adopted as a young child, and had dramatized that childhood, its psychology and emotions, in many dazzling short stories, he decided out of his usual patronizing noblesse oblige but also out of genuine friendliness to donate to me what he thought about the subject in more abstract, almost pedagogical terms. 'There can't be any greater love than the love of an adoptive parent for an adopted child,' he said on several occasions, as if to reassure himself as well as to instruct me about how I felt. 'You see, a biological parent is an absolute parent,' he said. 'Biological parents have to love their children, even if they don't like them. It is necessary love. On the other hand, adoptive parents have made a choice to love their children. They don't have to love them. It's contingent. It's not necessary, it's not tautological. It's an act of faith and will, not an act of nature. They almost always *do* love their children, but, mind you, they don't have to in the same way that biological parents do. This makes it in an important way a stronger kind of love.'

In one of his stories, Harold's young fictional *semblable*, Wiley, who is, I don't know, three or four, is being held up in the air by his adoptive father and appears to perceive the contingency of the man's love – strong, even passionate though it may be – and appears to realize, or at least intuit, a need to please the man beyond an unadopted child's eagerness to please, to feel some slight fear that the love could be taken away in a way that a biological parent's love for his or her child cannot ever be taken away. The sentences in that story are astonishingly beautiful and energetic, and I will tell you this about Brodkey – he could be a disdainful person, but that disdain, with which he could drip even on the mildest of social occasions, allowed him to write sentences like that, sentences that hold ordinary earthbound sentences in contempt, that defy metaphorical gravity – that, in other words, hold themselves aloft – and that manage to convey the immediacy and nuanced complexity of thought. What he couldn't escape – what no one can escape – in writing or in conversation or in art in general or in walking down the street, for that matter, is the human brain's evident need to narrativize, to turn our experiences into story. This ability of the evolved human cerebral cortex served our ancestors well on the savannah, no doubt – helped them return to where the gazelles had gamboled meatily the year before, enabled them to convey to their offspring the accumulated knowledge of the past and anticipate the future – and it continues to serve us in much the same (if a vastly more complex) way today. But as culture and art and literature came into being, as part of the establishment of geographically fixed societies, the human storytelling imperative has gained a layer of perceived utility that it probably lacked at the very start: it is our tool for trying to find shape and meaning in events inside and outside our lives – lives that now allow a lucky few of us the luxury of wondering about their shape and meaning. In this regard (unlike the situation with gazelles, or what the best time for planting the beans probably is), the storytelling we are bound to do is always something of a fiction –

however aesthetically pleasing and even psychologically helpful it may be. I mean, look at Brodkey's Parenthood Distinction. Adoptive parental love is contingent and therefore in some way greater than the love of biological parents, because that is not an emotional choice but a *requirement*. This formulation makes sense, in a way, I suppose, but it is also *just* a formulation, like the ordinary sentences Brodkey himself tried to rise above – a story woven out of and then superimposed upon, and willfully ignoring, the deep and universal happenstance of human existence (to say nothing of ignoring the multitudes of biological parents who demonstrably do *not* love their children). It implicitly posits that biological children are the inevitable children of their parents, while adoptive children arrive out of chance and randomness. But contingency operates mightily in biological families as well, of course. Your mother's headache before the time of your conception would have obviated you. Someone else would have been reading this, or, more likely, not, but instead repairing ailerons for Boeing in Seattle. Had your father not paused to catch his breath after running for and missing the 6:37, he wouldn't have met your mother, who herself wouldn't have missed the same train if she hadn't paused to have a brief conversation with a new man in her office who would have asked her out and ultimately married her and fathered the aileron repairperson if she hadn't met your father on the train platform as the fateful 6:37 pulled out.

The idea of contingency always plays an important role in any consideration of adoption but to my way of thinking, not to Brodkey's way of thinking, and seldom directly. Adoption virtually *commands* comment and discomfort and narrative and Brodkeyesque theorizing, precisely because it raises the vast and frightening issue of contingency so unignorably. Often, concerns about this issue, when they come up in any conversation, remain private and internal – on the surface out of 'niceness,' courtesy and manners, but deeper down out of anxiety. When it becomes natural to mention that your children are adopted, I believe that the usual (unspoken) response is, 'Something went wrong,' and awkwardness ensues. On the surface of others' thoughts, the something that they think may have gone wrong has to do with your reproductive life or an unwanted conception by the biological parents. But, below that, I think, and more frighteningly, swims a universal anxiety about how and why each one of us came to occupy our existences.

That is, people don't really want to think about the luck or lack of it that fetched *them* up with *their* particular set of parents. They emotionally need the *story* of the fetching up to be or at least seem inevitable. They yearn to see what *is* as somehow the story of what was *meant* – by God or fate or karma – *to be*. It appears to me that adoptive families provide comfort and reassurance to the biologically familied, and the illusion that they have a more 'natural' and necessary story, even though their presence wherever they're present is just as whacky, improbable, and arbitrary as that of the adopters and adoptees. It also tells them that no matter how foul their childhoods may have been, they at least did not suffer the apparent rejection of having been 'given up,' even though being given up might have benefited them enormously. The fantasy of there being perfect parents somewhere afflicts the adopted and the biological in almost equal measure, I'd bet – though it springs from different – opposite – emotional sources. (I loved my [biological] father, for example, but I believe I would almost certainly have done better psychologically with a less insecure one. I'm not complaining – truly I'm not. I was lucky in many, many ways. But still, there's the fact of it. Or the fantasy of it, maybe.) But the stories we make out of our own pasts and those of others and of historical events and facts are all essentially bogus. We can make the stories because what happened happened and we know enough about what happened to find some kind of pattern in it. But different people find different patterns. See if your psychoanalyst agrees with the view of your childhood with which you first walk into his or her office. Read opposing scholarly papers about the causes of the Renaissance. Then read a third that says that as the term is commonly understood, there *was* no Renaissance.

At Random House, we'll soon be publishing a book called *Black Swans*, by the stock trader, philosopher and mathematician Nassim Nicholas Taleb, which generally exposes and explains the falsity of this concept of an inevitable narrative in complex events in the past, events that were when they occurred the historical equivalent of black swans: exceptional, unique, unpredictable. Nassim will tell you, among many other wild and wonderful things, 'Historians are frauds.' One night, after a few drinks at a bar with a friend who is an historian – a much respected and widely admired one – I ventured out onto what I thought was this socially thin ice, with a few questions about historical interpretations in general. After a few minutes, I said, 'We have this author who says that, well, um, historians are basically –'

'Frauds!' my historian friend interrupted with an exactly correct guess. 'Of course we're all frauds. We know what occurred. We can structure it and show why it had to happen in any number of ways that fit the facts.'

Furnishing rule-proving, comfort-lending narrative exceptions as adoptive parents or adoptive children – that is, flying into a conversation or social setting as black swans – can make you feel bad. When we set out from Cape Cod in the summer of 1983 to fetch our excellent son, my wife and I had to change our plans for the vacation we were on and had to explain, to a few people, why we had to. One was a marvelously strange and irascible old writer who owned the house up on a bluff behind the one we were renting. To our news she responded, nervously, 'Oh, well, I'm sure it will all work out. A couple down in the village adopted a Korean child a few years ago, and she seems to be all right. She *is* a little short and boxy-looking, but I'm sure she'll turn out well.' When I brought my son into the *New Yorker*'s offices not long afterward, we ran into the then editor, William

Shawn, in the hallway – a man famous for his conversational awkwardness (which he used to great political advantage in the form of professional evasiveness). Shawn took our son's little fingers in his hand as if they were food he wasn't sure he wanted to try and said, with great surprise, 'Why, he's perfect!,' as if dramatically relieved not to have to deal with two heads or green skin. A young cousin of my wife's, obviously anxious but also obviously fascinated in a tabloid sort of way to meet our son said to me, after seeing him, 'But, I mean, is he really your son? Is he, you know, *yours?*' Sometimes – more often than one might think – it goes the other way, I'm happy to say, and *we* get to be in the community. On our flight back from Arizona, where we adopted our daughter three years after our un-green, one-headed son, a stewardess (leave me alone – I'm old enough to use that term if I want to) paused to adore the little girl my wife was holding. The woman was very attractive and seemed happy and easy with herself – confident enough to say to my wife, 'Well, congratulations, and my, don't *you* look terrific, too.' My wife said, 'Well, we've just adopted her.' And the stewardess said, 'How wonderful! Congratulations again! I was adopted, too.' Happily, this enthusiastic remark was not lost on our three-year-old boy, nor was it lost on him that in Phoenix we had stayed in a close to luxurious resort hotel. He didn't know or care about the dreary, heavy rain that fell in Atlanta when he came into our lives – all he knew about adoption at this point, really, was that it involved a warm whirlpool tub, cornucopic buffet breakfasts, and a fascinating, differently private-partsed baby.

As far as I'm concerned, my children need to know only as much about adoption and their own adoptive circumstances as they want to know. Our family has by tacit agreement tended to steer clear of the adoption 'culture.' At the beginning of our son's life with us, my wife and I met with a group of adoptive parents to discuss issues and problems and satisfactions – a self-made group of black swans who by getting together had turned themselves white. These meetings were worthwhile. But the rush and pressure of ordinary life overtook us, adoption in and of itself never became exclusively a cause or a curse or a blessing or a permanent community, and like most people we've just gotten on with our lives. (This is to say nothing against those who for whatever reason champion or question or debate adoption and its various modern forms and explore, investigate or celebrate its controversies and its psychological effects and its politics. This getting-on-with-it attitude characterizes at least two famous adoption stories that don't make much of adoption as a topic – the second of which provided my son and me with a wonderful and natural chance to see nobility in the arrangement. The first is a real cliché of adoption lore – the Old Testament tale of Pharoah's daughter finding Moses in the bulrushes and taking him in and making him part of the family without a whole lot being made of it and without being turned into any part of the story that so biblically followed – the stone tablets and locusts and threatened first-born infantcides. (I think Freud makes some-thing of Moses's adoptedness, but, then, getting into that would get us into the subject of what to make of Freud.) The other is that great American story *The Last of the Mohicans*, written by James Fenimore Cooper, and, for the purposes of this essay more pertinently, made into a movie in 1992 directed by Michael Mann, starring Daniel Day-Lewis – a movie that my son and I saw, and greatly enjoyed, together, when he was nine. Daniel Day-Lewis plays Natty Bumppo, aka Long Rifle, the orphaned child of settlers adopted by Chingachgook, father of Uncas and, after Uncas's death, the eponymous Last of the Mohicans Natty Bumppo has become a man who regards and repeatedly calls Chingachgook his father and Uncas his brother, and loves and is loved by them without reservation, seemingly without Brodkey's Contingency. Like Moses, Natty goes on to thrive, irrespective of this dramatically 'different' parental provenance – he is a crack shot, an unexampled wilderness scout, a hero, a primal and dashing lover for the daughter of the British general. I don't think my son and I ever talked about it directly, but I know for an emotional fact that this familial *given* of a de-facto adoption – the result of a disrupted infancy – and the story's message about playing the childhood cards that one is dealt and getting on with the hand of life made a profound impression on both of us. Long Rifle considered himself to be and simply *was* in almost every important way the son of the old Indian and thus the brother of his other son. But there was also, I now realize, a just-as-important ultimate genetic honesty in the story: son and brother though he may have been, Long Rifle could not be the last of the Mohicans.

That my family is and always will be 'different' has given me a similarly different and at least from my point of view inestimably valuable perspective on human life, life stories, contingency, the stories we tell ourselves about ourselves. There are things that we can and should try to control, both in our children's lives and in our own lives as citizens of our societies and of the world. But I've come to recognize more and more that chance will – far more often than many of us wish to understand – have its way with us. Happenstance can have joyous or tragic results (all the way from stumbling upon buried treasure to my brother's death from a hospital infection after routine knee surgery to the vast horrors of fate played out today, as in every era, on the world's stage), but it *is* just happenstance – being individually or collectively in the wrong place at the wrong time or the right place at the right time – and not punishment for some great sin or reward for some great virtue or in general just the ending for some kind of retroactively clear story. (It has taken thirty-five years for me finally to stop blaming myself for my brother's death, longer to realize that vain as I am about them, I'm not really the author of whatever skills I have.) The experience of adoption has given me a growing serenity about good luck and bad, achievements and reversals, defects and talents, child-raising triumphs and disappointments, political effectiveness and limitations, what can be known and what can't, and it has made me more content with the lottery that is to a large extent everyone's life. And while I am determined that this serenity will not preclude any active efforts I can mount to help myself and my family and my friends and my profession and the world around me, I am also determined to enjoy it as what I hope and self-flatteringly believe it to be – wisdom. Wisdom of the specific kind that understands that there is a very great deal indeed that it will never understand and, more important, that cherishes and fears and stands in awe of the ocean of improbabilities and imponderabilities out of which we all swim ashore here.

Don't get me wrong. I like a story as much as the next person, and while it can't do nearly everything people try to make it do, the telling of stories can in fact in many instances and many ways prepare us for things that will happen in the future. That is what really good fiction (and all other art) does, besides wrapping us up in itself and taking us out of ourselves – it dramatizes and thus explains different interpretations of peoples' feelings and motives and behavior. That is part of why a good book can literally change the way you look at the world and help you live in it. In a way, fiction is honest history – not the reverse. And this is why people write fiction as well as read it – to try to usefully and entertainingly shape and find meaning in their own lives and the lives they observe around them. In my own life and the life of my family, I am not so detached and wise as not to want to know more about my kids' biological parents – for practical reasons (medical histories) but also because I am just plain curious and like everyone else irrationally believe, on one persistent level, that I will understand a whole lot more if I know a little more. But I am relaxed enough about the whole matter to realize that this is at its core my kids' business, not mine. My life and their lives will be by logical necessity complete no matter what, and at the same time, and just as necessarily incomplete. My father, the son of radical Russian immigrants, did not know any of his grandparents' first or last names.

Contributors

Meg Bortin is an editor at the *International Herald Tribune* in Paris. The letter included here is excerpted from a longer version.

Sarah Cameron worked in publishing and is now a literary agent. She lives in London with her husband and son.

Dan Chaon's most recent book is a novel, *You Remind Me of Me* (John Murray, 2005). He is also the author of two collections of short stories, including *Among the Missing*, a 2001 National Book Award finalist. He lives in Cleveland, Ohio, and teaches at Oberlin College.

Dominic Collier has worked as an insurance salesman, pornographer, dot.com foot soldier, production manager, account director, CIO and software salesman. He currently edits a website campaigning for an end to conflict, poverty and injustice; and is also writing several books about God, computers and being human. He was mis/educated in Hong Kong and Derbyshire before attending Oxford University, where he read English. Dominic is married with four children and lives in London.

Bernard Cornwell was born in London in 1944. He read theology at London University, then worked as a teacher and in television. In

1979, he moved to America and began writing his series of books about nineteenth-century-hero Richard Sharpe. He has written twenty Sharpe adventures; a series about the American Civil War; the Starbuck novels; a trilogy about King Arthur; the Warlord Chronicles; and the Hundred Years War set Grail quest series. The first title in his new series of novels, *The Last Kingdom*, was published in 2004. Bernard Cornwell lives in Cape Cod.

Robert Dessaix is an Australian writer, broadcaster and translator, best known for his autobiography *A Mother's Disgrace*, the novels *Night Letters* and *Corfu*, and, most recently, the memoir *Twilight of Love: Travels with Turgenev*. He lives in Hobart, Tasmania.

Matthew Engel is a journalist and editor who lives with his family in Herefordshire. He worked for the *Guardian* for nearly twenty-five years, covering everything from cricket and tiddlywinks to war, revolution and politics, and currently writes for the *Financial Times*. He is also editor of *Wisden Cricketers' Almanack*.

Paula Fox is the author of many children's books and six novels for adults, including *Desperate Characters*, which was made into a film starring Shirley MacLaine, and a memoir entitled *Borrowed Finery*, from which the extracts in this anthology were taken. She lives in Brooklyn, New York.

A. M. Homes is the author of the novels *Jack, In a Country of Mothers, The End of Alice* and *Music for Torching*, two collections of short stories, *The Safety of Objects* and *Things You Should Know*, as well as the travel memoir *Los Angeles: People, Places and the Castle on the Hill*. 'Witness Protection' will form part of a full-length memoir to be published by Granta Books in 2007. She lives in New York City.

Tama Janowitz is the bestselling author of *Slaves of New York* and six other works of fiction including *A Certain Age* and

Peyton Amberg. Her non-fiction is collected into *Area Code 212*. She has received two National Endowment for the Arts Awards. Her work has been published in the *New Yorker*, *Paris Review* and the *New York Times Magazine*, among others.

Lynn Lauber's writing has appeared in the *New York Times* and other publications. Her books *White Girls*, *21 Sugar Street* and *Listen to Me* have all been published by W. W. Norton.

Carol Lefevre grew up in the Australian outback, and has worked as a singer with a Sydney rock band, worked for television news in New Zealand, written for glossy lifestyle magazines, worked as a paintress in a pottery and as a backing singer with a Pink Floyd tribute band. Her short stories have been broadcast on Australian radio and in 2002 she was awarded a mentorship by the Australian Society of Authors. She lives between the Isle of Man and Adelaide, south Australia, with her husband, daughter and tiny grandson. She is currently at work on a novel.

Daniel Menaker was born in New York City. He worked at the *New Yorker Magazine* for twenty-five years as an editor, before becoming a book editor. He is now Executive Editor-in-Chief of the Random House Publishing Group. The author of two books of short stories, a novel, and reporting, humour and essays for many magazines and newspapers, he lives in New York with his wife and two children.

Hannah wa Muigai (a pseudonym) now lives in Nairobi, Kenya, and is the mother of a six-year-old boy. She has a degree in statistics and computer science, and is looking forward to pursuing a creative MBA degree.

Priscilla T. Nagle is a writer/musician who lives in the Northern Arizona outback with her husband, Frank. Her oldest son having reunited with her when he was thirty-six, she rejoices in the lives of all her children and their families. She works to increase public awareness of the beauty in the fact that we're all on this earth together, that all life is connected.

Sandra Newman is the author of the novel *The Only Good Thing Anyone Has Ever Done* (Chatto & Windus). Her short fiction has been published in *Harper's*, *Conjunctions* and *Chain*; and her non-fiction in the *Observer* and *Mail on Sunday* in Great Britain. She is currently working on a second novel, *Cake*, due out in 2005.

Mirabel Osler was born in London, had an unconventional childhood and went to a co-educational boarding school during the war. With her husband she has travelled a great deal from the fifties onwards, has three children and only started to write after the age of sixty. She is the author of *A Gentle Plea for Chaos*, *The Secret Gardens of France*, *In the Eye of the Garden*, *A Breath from Elsewhere* and on her quest for the traditional food of France, *The Elusive Truffle* (originally called *A Spoon with Every Course*). She has contributed to magazines here, in France and in America and gives talks on the making of two gardens, adoption and on French chefs, restaurants and markets. She lives in Ludlow, Shropshire.

Emily Prager is the author of much praised novels, stories and essay collections, including *A Visit from the Footbinder*, *In the Missionary Position* and *Roger Fishbite*, and an account of adopting her Chinese daughter, *Wuhu Diary*, from which the extract in this anthology was taken. She has written for many publications, including the *Guardian*, *Daily Telegraph* and *New York Times*, and is a winner of the Online News Award for her journalism. She lives in New York.

Jonathan Rendall's first book, *This Bloody Mary Is the Last Thing I Own*, about boxing, won the Somerset Maugham award. His second, *Twelve Grand: The Gambler as Hero*, was made into the Channel 4 series *The Gambler*. His book about adoption, *Garden Hopping*, from which 'Oedipus Descending' is extracted, will be published by Canongate next year. He lives and works in Suffolk.

Martin Rowson's work appears regularly in the *Guardian*, *The Times*, the *Mirror*, the *Independent on Sunday*, the *Scotsman* and *Tribune*. In 2001 he was created London's first Cartoonist Laureate by Ken Livingstone, and is also Chairman of the British Cartoonists' Association and a vice-president of the Zoological Society of London. He has won several major awards for his work in cartooning and lives in London with his wife and their two children.

Lise Saffran is a graduate of the Iowa Writers' Workshop, where she was an Iowa Arts Fellow. A recent fellow at the MacDowell Colony, her short fiction has appeared in literary magazines and she has just completed work on her first novel.

Jeanette Winterson is the author of eight novels: *Oranges Are Not the Only Fruit*, (from which the extract in this anthology is taken), *The Passion*, *Sexing the Cherry*, *Written on the Body*, *Art and Lies*, *Gut Symmetries*, *The PowerBook* and *Lighthousekeeping*. She has also written a volume of stories, *The World and Other Places*, a collection of essays, *Art Objects*, and a children's book, *The King of Capri*. A new novella, *Weight*, will be published by Canongate in September 2005.

Mark Wormald is a Fellow in English at Pembroke College, Cambridge. He writes on nineteenth- and twentieth-century fiction and poetry, and is a regular contributor to the *TLS*. He is currently working on a book called *Watermarks: The Element of Consciousness in British and American Writing, 1690–2000*. He won an Eric Gregory Award for poetry in 1995.

Acknowledgements and Copyright